AESTHETICS AND REVOLUTION

AESTHETICS AND REVOLUTION

NICARAGUAN POETRY
1979–1990

GREG DAWES

UNIVERSITY OF MINNESOTA PRESS

MINNEAPOLIS

LONDON

Ernesto Cardenal, selections from *Vuelos de Victoria,* reprinted by permission of Ernesto Cardenal; Pablo Antonio Cuadra, "Agosto: Apólogo con elefante," "Ars Poética," "Enero," "Mayo: Oratorio de los 4 héroes," "Septiembre: El tiburón," and "El tío invierno," reprinted here by permission of Libro Libre; Carlos Martínez Rivas, "El paraíso recobrado," previously published by Editorial Nueva Nicaragua in Martínez Rivas, *La insurrección solitaria,* reprinted by permission of Carlos Martínez Rivas; Leonel Rugama, selections from *La tierra es un satélite de la luna,* reprinted by permission of Editorial Nueva Nicaragua.

Every effort has been made to obtain permission to reproduce copyright material in this book. The publishers ask copyright holders to contact them if permission has not been sought or if proper acknowledgment has not been made.

Published by the University of Minnesota Press
2037 University Avenue Southeast, Minneapolis, MN 55414
Printed in the United States of America on acid-free paper

Library of Congress Cataloging-in-Publication Data

Dawes, Greg.
   Aesthetics and revolution : Nicaraguan poetry, 1979–1990 /
Greg Dawes.
      p.   cm.
   Revision of thesis (Ph.D.).
   Includes bibliographical references and index.
   ISBN 0-8166-2146-2 (alk. paper)
   1. Revolutionary poetry, Nicaraguan—History and criticism. 2.
Nicaraguan poetry—20th century—History and criticism. 3.
Nicaragua—History—Revolution, 1979—Literature and the
revolution. 4. Social conflict in literature. 5. Aesthetics, Nicaraguan. I. Title.
PQ7512.D38 1993
861—dc20   92–16577
                                                                CIP

CONTENTS

PREFACE

The present study both stems from and reacts to my doctoral dissertation, "Contemporary Nicaraguan Poetry: Aesthetic Commitment in an Age of Postmodernism."[1] Originally I had argued that Nicaraguan poetry — in a developing quasi-socialist country — could be seen as vehicle for resisting U.S. imperialism and that Nicaragua presented an alternative "socialist" system to the Eastern Bloc countries and what I considered to be more authoritarian forms of socialism. Thus, in the political, economic, and aesthetic arenas, Nicaragua embodied, for me, a more flexible arrangement that had experimented with a mixed economy and with political pluralism and had resisted all temptations to "totalize" or to become too centralized. From a literary perspective, then, my dissertation was designed to identify the main aesthetic currents in Nicaragua from 1979 to 1989 and to demonstrate in practice not only that a more pluralist revolutionary approach could be carried out historically, but also that such a development was beneficial because it was very much in line with a gradual transition to democratic socialism.

When the Sandinistas were defeated at the hands of UNO (Unión de la Oposición Nacional, the National Opposition Union) and Violeta Chamorro in February 1990, it became clear that the Nicaraguan pluralist model had reached its theoretical and practical limits. I then began to reconsider the whole paradigm from another, more accurate perspective in a rethinking of a classical Marxist position. Seen from this vantage point, the presumption of the "unfixity of social class," "antitotalizing" efforts, the fruits of "pluralism," and the like all underwent a critical reading in which I began to see the Nicaraguan revolution as the inversion of my original interpretation. Nicaragua did, indeed, stand for a new type of "socialist" system or "third path" — which was, in so many ways, the incarnation of the ideals of the New Left and of certain Left postmodernists — and it was the adoption of a mixed economy and an assortment of political programs that led to an intensification of political and class conflicts and, finally, to the demise of the Sandinista government. The sociohistorical circumstances did not correspond to the Sandinistas' ideological interpretation of them. Like many leftists in and out of Nicaragua, I had initially glossed over much of the internal strife that was plaguing the FSLN (Frente Sandinista de Liberación Nacional, the Sandinista

National Liberation Front) from at least 1979 until their electoral defeat in 1990 and had seen these differences as the final proof that Nicaragua was able to maintain a pluralist (and, by analogy, "democratic") political system. By the time I left Nicaragua in late December 1988, the promise of the revolution and of its gradual road to socialism was reaching a critical stage where the Sandinistas either needed to implement workers' control of the means of production—once and for all—or would suffer electoral defeat at the hands of a political opposition.

To a large degree, the same was true of my evaluation of aesthetic production in revolutionary Nicaragua. Rather than envisioning class struggle between different ideological forces in this Central American nation, I tended to want to chronicle this historical process as part of an ongoing negotiation among revolutionary forces when, in fact, it *was* a class struggle. As this analysis documents, it appears that the FSLN cadres who came to power were originally part of the insurrectionalist tendency (the *terceristas*) within the party, and it was their political and economic strategies that ultimately led to the internal collapse of the Sandinistas. (For a brief history of the divisions within the FSLN see chapter 1.) After 1985 particularly, as the United States refused to stop harassing Nicaragua through the contras, the economic embargo, and political pressure, there was a noticeable shift in the government's treatment of working-class sectors and the bourgeoisie. Similar changes took place in the aesthetic sphere. By 1988, the government had essentially abandoned the national plan of democratizing culture, and bourgeois forces began to take charge of aesthetic affairs under the directorship of Rosario Murillo and the ASTC (La Asociación Sandinista de Trabajadores Culturales, the Sandinista Association of Cultural Workers).

What the reader will find in this new study of Nicaraguan poetry is a more classical Marxist account of class consciousnesss and class conflict without the bracketing of reality, class, or gender. It is an interpretation of Nicaraguan culture and politics that runs counter both to postmodernist idealism and to certain Left forms of postmodernism. An example of this latter tendency is to be found in John Beverley and Marc Zimmerman's highly important contribution to Central American cultural studies, *Literature and Politics in the Central American Revolutions*.[2] Here I am merely going to raise certain questions regarding the concept of ideology as it is developed in Louis Althusser's thought.

In *Literature and Politics*, Zimmerman and Beverley make an upfront, forceful, and compelling argument in favor of an Althusserian ideological analysis that propels their study forward and is aided by the adoption of Gramsci's concept of the "National Popular." This theory provides the authors with a foundation for elucidating a discussion on aesthetic commitment in the Central American context and for explaining why literature carries so much weight in Latin America. Briefly stated, poetry, for both Zimmerman and

Beverley, accrues a significant and unique value in the Central American region because it can function as a symbolic arena that gathers together—from the optic of Althusserianism—an assortment of feelings, images, and myths.[3] Poetry thus serves as a symbolic catalyst in forming national identity in revolutionary circumstances in Guatemala, El Salvador, and Nicaragua—all of which combine nationalism and socialism in their ideology.

Leaving aside the theoretical aspects for the time being, as a historical tract on literary and revolutionary vanguards in Central America, *Literature and Politics* succeeds in providing detailed accounts of the intersection of Roque Dalton's revolutionary commitment and his poetry, the fusion of liberation theology with the Nicarguan revolution, and the role of the *testimonio* as a transitional, narrational mode. Indeed, this work is unequaled in its treatment of historical, political, and literary formations in Central America. Beverley, of course, has been one of the most astute analysts of the *testimonio*, and this latest version (chapter 7) is an expansion of the work he has done in the past.[4]

It is to both Zimmerman's and Beverley's credit that in this most recent analysis, the *testimonio* (documentary or testimonial literature) is defined as a "transitional literary form" that, as the authors put it, "does not seem particularly well adapted to be the primary narrative form of an elaborated post-revolutionary society, perhaps because its dynamics depend precisely on the conditions of social and cultural inequality and direct oppression that fuel the revolutionary impulse in the first place" (207). While Central American testimonial literature emerges from conscious revolutionary activity, it is completely enmeshed in this praxis. Hence, as Georg Lukács argues in his analysis of Willi Bredel's novels, while working-class narrative production should be lauded as a great step foward, it strikes me that the *testimonio* can *potentially*— as in the case of Bredel's work—lead to a less complex development of the revolutionary situation.[5] There is, then, as Beverley and Zimmerman intimate, a problem with testimonials that respond to urgent or spontaneous political circumstances without having analyzed sociopolitical matters thoroughly, because they sacrifice too much in their representation of reality.

Another chapter that is unique to *Literature and Politics*—in the material it deals with—is Zimmerman and Beverley's interpretation of cultural practices during the Nicaraguan revolution. To a great extent, our versions of the aesthetic (and political) events that took place from as early as 1985 to the 1990 election corroborate each other. However, since the book was published shortly after the February debacle, it appears that the authors did not have time to evaluate the political and aesthetic effects that the collapse of the Ministry of Culture and the rise of Rosario Murillo and the professionalists could have on cultural production. In their study there is—understandably— a hesitancy to critique the model that they have seen as exemplary of a type of resistance to postmodernism in this hemisphere. This apparent weakness is due, in my estimation, to the theoretical framework itself, which I would like to turn to now.

One of the principal weaknesses of Althusserian theory is the concept of ideology. As long as ideology in general is specified in terms that have no reference to or place for the struggle between labor and capital, then it will be what Adolfo Sánchez Vázquez has called "theoretical ideology" and will cease to operate dialectially with material reality. Ideology will always appear as secondary, superimposed in fundamental, timeless struggles between sexes and generations, or strictly divorced from actual, material struggles. For Althusser, as Terry Lovell has perceptively noted, the

> empiricist fallacy lies in the belief that knowledge is "inscribed" in the world, and can therefore be extracted from the world through a process of abstraction from the experiences of a subject. To avoid this fallacy he produces, as we have seen, a theory of knowledge which eliminates experience altogether from the practice of knowledge construction, relegating it to the inferior realm of ideology. Experience becomes the product of ideological practice, rather than of social reality. It cannot therefore provide any guide to social reality.[6]

What we observe in Althusser, then, is a break with the Lukácsian notion of "reflection" in favor of the production of "ideological effects" within a given text. In the process, the French thinker resorts to formalist methods because the very material forces that generate such "ideological effects" are put aside. Following Althusser's mapping of ideology, history itself interacts rather mechanically and not dialectically with ideology because the latter is ostensibly "prescientific." When this gap between ideology and production takes place, then the Althusserian model relinquishes its materialist grounding in exchange for an "autonomous," free-floating ideological apparatus that is, according to Althusser, "ahistorical" and related directly to Freud's notion that the "unconscious is eternal."[7]

The danger implicit in this departure from materialism is borne out in subsequent analyses of a historical, political, economic, and aesthetic nature. Following Althusser, Beverley and Zimmerman in their work allege that ideologies have

> multiple power functions (of distinction, domination, subordination) that are not reducible to or intelligible in terms of class or group interests alone, although they are the sites in which class or group struggle occurs. Similarly, they are not always circumscribed by modes of production or concrete social formations; they can cut across modes of production and social formations, as in the case of religious ideologies. In particular, ideologies

are not reducible to politics or political programs or isms, because their nature is unconscious rather than explicit; their effect is to produce in the
subject a sense of things as natural, self-evident, a matter of common sense.
Political practices — say of parties, organized groups, or movements —
represent specific articulations on the terrain of ideology. (2)

In keeping with Althusserianism, this notion of ideology is rooted in the unconscious, that is, specifically in the "mirror stage" of development as elaborated by Jacques Lacan.[8] Althusser draws upon this Lacanian study in order
to formulate his theory of ideology, which returns to this stage when the individual cannot distinguish himself or herself from the social. This domain,
then, is located outside of rational apprehension. Lacan writes that it

> situates the agency of the ego, before its social determination, in a fictional
> direction, which will always remain irreducible for the individual alone, or
> rather, which will only rejoin the coming-into-being (*le devenir*) of the sub-
> ject asymptomatically. (2)

It is this "method of symbolic reduction" that will serve as the basis for
Althusser's theory of ideologies. The problem with such a philosophical position is that it is not anchored in actual, real-life processes, but rather is a theoretical model constructed — so to speak — "above" this material life. Consequently, in this method of analyzing ideological forces, one loses a grasp of
the conflictive nature of ideology (and, hence, of material life) because, according to Althusser, ideology is somehow beyond such a realm since it is
actually in the isolated "mirror stage."

One of the main difficulties with the internal logic of Zimmerman and
Beverley's Althusserianism is that the symbolic and the political are almost
seen as two separate entities. By alleging that literature in the Latin American
context — it is different, they maintain, in so-called First World countries — is
the symbolic site where ideological production and revolutionary consciousness take place, Beverley and Zimmerman endeavor to make the link between the ideological and the political more visible. Real historical events
must somehow find a place in Althusserian ideological criticism or — as both
Beverley and Zimmerman surely would admit — the approach will lose its
grounding. While this connection is made at certain moments in *Literature and
Politics*, seen as a whole, their work fails to break convincingly with this dualism. An immediate case in point is apparent in the beginning of the first chapter when they declare that

> the "work" of ideology consists in constituting (Althusser: interpellating)
> human subjects as such, with coherent gender, ethnic, class, or national

identities appropriate to their place in a possible social order. Ideologies provide human beings with a structure of experience that enables them to recognize themselves in the world, to see the world as in some way created *for* them, to feel they have a place and identity in it. (2)

In this post-Marxist definition—in contrast to Marx's rendering of ideology as inversion—ideology acts as a social catalyst that allows one to grasp one's life in the social order in a more reasonable way. But at the same time, ideology seems to operate independently of human beings: Beverley and Zimmerman state that ideology enables human beings "to see the world as in some way created *for* them." By whom? Cannot human beings identify the material world as part of themselves that they can create and change? This gulf between human beings and the production of ideology is also clear when the authors argue against the Marxist notion of "false consciousness":

The traditional problematic of ideology in the social sciences, founded in both its positivist and Marxist variants on the epistemological question of distinguishing "true" from "false" forms of consciousness, had been displaced in contemporary cultural studies by the recognition suggested in psychoanalytic theory that truth *for* the subject is something distinct from the truth *of* the subject, given that it entails an act of identification between the self and something external to it. (4)

But why focus *only* on the *distinction* between the self and what is external to it? Why not concentrate on the *dialectic* between subject and history? Furthermore, why should we believe that what rules in aesthetic experience is this marginalized, individual *jouissance* in contrast to "external reality"? Does this theory not fall into the same false consciousness as Freudian psychoanalysis in its privileging of subjective sensations over reality?[9] Ideology, it would seem, is asked to bridge the gap between the individual and the society because the integration of the two does not come about in analyzing them.

In sum, Beverley and Zimmerman's exhaustive historical analysis largely contradicts the theoretical position that they have chosen to assume—Althusserianism. In a rare set of events, the authors' pluralism is so elastic as to incorporate formalist views of art asserting that the aesthetic is autonomous, or independent of ideology. According to Zimmerman and Beverley, the politicization of aesthetics is contingent upon delimited historical, political, economic, and geographical factors. In other words, once the authors have rejected the "reflection" theory—and separated ideology from the social relations of production—they come upon the familiar terrain of philosophical idealism. For Beverley and Zimmerman it is not that politics is part of the intrinsic and extrinsic character of ideology, but that political determinations of ideology correspond to *a segment* of ideological production. By implication we assume that there are some "ideological effects" that are not political. In addition, as I have noted, the materialist analysis of culture is further diluted when the authors inform us that ideological production is rooted in the unconscious (2–5). Once this is acknowledged, Beverley and Zimmerman's theoretical foundation begins to crack.

In order to close the gap that they have created between ideology and politics, Beverley and Zimmerman then turn to an Althusserian solution to this dilemma: "We rejoin here the point that revolutionary political consciousness does not derive directly or spontaneously from exploitative economic relations, that it must be in some sense produced" (8). Thus, as I have suggested, literature serves as that desperately needed link between ideology and politics that aids in the "development of subject identity." In essence, then, literature (and specifically poetry in their study) is a semiautonomous territory for the production of political consciousness in Central America, but it is somehow divorced from the actual social relations of production itself. According to this logic, it is the production of a certain type of literature — "political" poetry, for instance — that enables subjects to reflect on "private experiences of authenticity and alienation to the awareness of collective situations of social exploitation, injustice, and national underdevelopment" (9). But the weakness in such an argument — in addition to the separation set up between individual and social experience — resides more fundamentally in the privileging of the unconscious in aesthetics. For if we agree that the driving force of ideology is the unconscious, then what power do revolutionaries have to change it, much less to interpet it? If there are no scientific methods to follow, then how do we prove that this or that thesis is actually valid? Must aesthetics be consigned to philosophical relativism, or can it be perceived as a mode of abstracting reality?

All this theoretical footwork pushes Beverley and Zimmerman's study into a corner on more than one occasion. One such moment is in their analysis of literary production in revolutionary Nicaragua. Before turning to this section, I would note that another problem with this discussion of Central American literature and revolutions is that Beverley and Zimmerman fervently adhere to postmodernist interpretations of the "unfixity" of social class (i.e., pluralism) and of Ernesto Laclau and Chantal Mouffe's notion of "radical democracy." The idealism in the writings of Althusser and Laclau and Mouffe will come back to haunt *Literature and Politics* when the analysis extends beyond the theoretical to the practical realm. For example, in their study of Nicaraguan poetry during the revolutionary period, Beverley and Zimmerman give a very accurate account of the aesthetic and political debate of 1985, yet the authors overlook the fact that the deficiency in the Nicaraguan political, economic, and cultural system *was* the vulnerability of pluralism. Thus, they assess the situation as follows:

> Though the debate had repercussions inside the Frente, the Sandinista leadership was reluctant to take a firm stand one way or another on cultural policy, for fear of making the mistake of the Cubans in the late 1960s of favoring one cultural "line" over others. But this commendable commitment to pluralism also meant that cultural policy was made ad hoc, without any real budgetary priorities or control. (103)

Since their post–Althusserian approach automatically excludes a more organic and materialist understanding of the consequences of the economic and political situation — because ideology is supposed to be relatively independent from these spheres — Beverley and Zimmerman do not interpret this aesthetic crisis on a more global scale as the crisis of this type of "third path" to socialism. Since representation, for Althusser, does not transcend the aesthetic realm, they fail to acknowledge that the crisis in aesthetic agency is also a crisis in economic and political agency, that is, they fail to note that pluralist economic, political, and aesthetic institutions are affected by their internal limitations and by imperialism.

This weakness in their analysis is largely a result of the fact that they do not truly take a critical distance with respect to this "third path." Their own study advocates an aesthetic and political pluralism that does not effectively distinguish itself from liberal pluralism. Even late in chapter 4, Beverley and Zimmerman continue to hold this position vis-à-vis political and artistic representation: "We are far from thinking that cultural forms have an essential class location or connotation, as our discussion in the previous chapter of the ideological mutations of vanguardism suggests" (110). Here the fateful error of Althusserianism is fleshed out. When aesthetic agencies are separated from the social relations of production, then history itself will have a way of turning any such idealist study on its head. In the postscript to this chapter, Beverley and Zimmerman run into precisely this dilemma:

> The perspective we adopted in our presentation of this chapter — that the revolutionary process was irreversible, despite problems and setbacks — clearly has been problematized. It may be that the revolution will go forward; on the other hand, we may well be witnessing the first stage of a more long-lasting restoration. We had hypothesized in chapters 1 and 2 that one of the key roles of literature in the revolutionary process in Central America generally was to constitute a discursive space in which the possibilities of alliance between popular sectors and a basically middle- and

upper-class revolutionary vanguard could be pragmatically negotiated around a shared sense of the national-popular. (111)

Here their postmodernist theory meets the limits of its interpretative abilities because history itself has proven that this multiclass alliance, the concept of nationalism, and the experimental nature of a mixed economic system were not able to sustain themselves. As Carlos Vilas has demonstrated, it was the Sandinistas' transformation from a vanguard predominantly supported by the working class and the campesinos to a party that catered to the interests of entrepreneurs in the last years of the revolution that lost the elections of 1990.[10] Similarly, in the cultural realm, the Frente abandoned its cultural democratization project not only because of financial problems, but also because there was a shift in ideological positions within party cadres, who now suggested that culture follow more professional guidelines. As a result, those who favored professionally developed artists clashed with those who defended the democratization program. Thus, the content of this debate—which I discuss extensively in *Aesthetics and Revolution*—boiled down to differences in political, economic, and aesthetic form among the revolutionary forces.

By critiquing *Literature and Politics* I do not want to underestimate the very important sociohistorical contributions that Zimmerman and Beverley make to Central American cultural studies. It is an in-depth look at revolutionary movements in the region as well as a provocative new attempt to explain the role that poetry has played in social change. The Althusserian theoretical framework, however, suffers from certain idealist tendencies that undermine the analyses contained therein. In brief, as the reader will see, it differs philosophically from the materialist analysis of aesthetics that I conduct in *Aesthetics and Revolution*.

I would like to sketch here a concise version of the theoretical postulates that, I hope, are clearly presented in this book. The root of the argument put forward in these pages is found in the social relations of production. Since the proletariat is the social class that most absorbs the impact of the labor process and feels the intensity of class struggle more acutely than any other—since it alone creates value—it follows that it has more empirical or objective contact with the driving force of production and that the proletariat is conceivably conscious of this relation.[11] In *Capital* Marx states that the conflictive or antagonistic relation between workers and capitalists increases in intensity because the workers sell their labor and create value in the form of a commodity (which congeals their labor). Capitalists, on the other hand, collect the surplus value that is produced as the workers create value beyond what is invested in the means of production. This surplus value, according

to Marx, becomes the pool into which the capitalists dip in order either to
reinvest in productive means or to amass wealth for their own benefit.

I argue that the centrality of the working class allows it to perceive the
class struggle more clearly than any other other social class. In this regard I
am following Lukács:

> The proletariat, however, does not face this ideological barrier. Its social
> being allows it (and thus also proletarian revolutionary writers) to tran-
> scend this barrier and clearly see the class relationships, the development of
> the class struggle, that lies behind the fetishized forms of capitalist society.
> Clarity about these connections and their laws of development also means
> clarity as to the role of the subjective factor in this development: both the
> determination of this subjective factor by the objective economic and
> historical development, and the active function of this subjective factor in
> the transformation of objective conditions.[12]

As Nancy Hartsock's and Catherine A. MacKinnon's work has proven,
an analogous argument can be constructed for the notion of gender.[13] When
we get to the root of gender formation, however, we find, as Hartsock maintains, a deeper understanding of historical materialism than that explored and
developed by Marx and Engels. For if the working class is central to the
means of production, women, through the sexual division of labor, are central to the means of reproduction. Thus, this angle on the perpetuation of
capitalism must be taken into consideration if we are to comprehend how
capitalism establishes patriarchal institutions and how women are exploited
in it. Women, then, are potentially exposed to double exploitation in capitalism if they are working class. Traditionally, however, women from various
classes sell their labor power in the domestic environment. From a societal
point of view, women go through the physical laboring process of giving
birth and, consequently, allow the society to survive. But they also create
less-tangible goods that are involved in household production (housework).
These life-sustaining activities are an integral part of the investigation I carry
out.

These economic relations unfold into the political and aesthetic realms as
well. In contrast to Zimmerman and Beverley's *Literature and Politics*, I contend that literature should be seen as intraclass accounts of the class struggle.
If the working class and its political allies — those sectors that make up the
vanguard — are potentially able to detect the ebb and flow of capitalism in
ways that other social classes are not, then it follows that their literary depictions of reality will reveal more of the complexity and inner workings of the
system. Following Marx and Engels in *The German Ideology*, I suggest that,
as an inversion of real historical process, ideology emerges as a distortion or

misrepresentation of actual life processes. It is not that thinking or consciousness is diametrically opposed—in a dualist fashion—to material life, but rather that, as Marx and Engels argued, consciousness never ceases to engage itself with life.[14] Ideology, then, refracts a clear, palpable cognition of reality when it is assumed that consciousness cannot somehow survive without the assistance of life. It is at this juncture that classical Marxist theory of ideology breaks with Althusserianism.

This work may also differ from Zimmerman and Beverley's because it calls for a more scientific analysis of the role of the working class in the political economy. In this approach, agency does not limit itself to the political alone; rather, it is located at the intersection of politics, economics, and aesthetics. In each of these spheres, according to Lenin's *What is to be done?*, the proletariat acts decisively in spearheading the vanguard, which is composed of a revolutionary political party that aims at seizing the means of production as well as the political apparatus. In aesthetics this means that the vanguard would appropriate the aesthetic "means of reproduction" and begin to represent itself.

This process initially bore fruit in Nicaragua: there is evidence to suggest that by democratizing culture some Sandinistas were committed to a "proletarian culture." My thesis is that the vanguardist role of the Frente must be described and critiqued in both the political and the aesthetic realms. We must begin to examine exactly how the FSLN attempted to function as a vanguard and whether it was effective in leading the class struggle. In the Leninist tradition, as Marta Harnecker has poignantly shown,

> the question of the vanguard is, at this level, none other than the problem of the leadership of the class struggle from the revolutionary perspective, that is, from the perspective of the sole class capable of struggling for a radical transformation of society that will resolve the contradictions inherent in capitalism and that will serve simultaneously as an objective support for the building of a new socialist society.[15]

As I argued earlier, and will maintain throughout this study, it appears in retrospect that the Sandinistas tried somewhat successfully to fulfill this role until 1985. After this date, these problems were compounded by the United States' placing an economic embargo on Nicaragua and refusing to withdraw its financial assistance to the contras as well as by the conservative turn in FSLN political and economic policies. Richard Stahler-Sholk's research in this regard indicates that the Sandinistas were unable to sustain a mixed economy with a multiclass composition.[16] My own investigation led to similar conclusions, not only in the economic and political realms, but also primarily in the cultural arena.

The collapse of this semisocialist state means that socialists in Latin America should perhaps not be so hasty in discarding the Cuban revolution as yet another example of "totalitarian" socialism. I believe a more cogent response to Cuba is to recognize that it was not just insular factors that contributed to the political system created on the island, but mainly outside historical pressures. In comparing the Nicaraguan and the Cuban situations, one historical lesson is that less class tension on the inside means less of a chance that outside forces can destabilize the socialist regime. This, however, leads us to the principal economic and political objectives of a socialist—or maybe more appropriately, a communist—system: workers' control. In spite of all that the Cuban revolution has accomplished while being subjected to economic and military harassment by the United States, the truth is that the workers continue to depend on a wage system and do not fully own the means of production; the state does. Could the abolition of the wage system and self-determination (communism) be history's next step?

On the Methodological Scope

Some words on the limitations of my study are in order. In writing this work I intended to cover only the main aesthetic tendencies in Nicaragua during the revolution, and consequently I did not analyze several poets who have played significant roles in the development of the revolutionary arts. Most of these political and artistic actors figure in the broader framework of this historical analysis, but their works per se are not examined. This is so because in most cases I saw some sort of overlap with one of the poets whose work I did study, and where it was possible I made references to these similarities.

The most well known of those whose works are not included here is Rosario Murillo, wife of former president Daniel Ortega, head of ASTC (the Sandinista Association of Cultural Workers), and the author of three books of poetry. While I do take account of her position in the aesthetic debates in Nicaragua as head of the ASTC, I do not analyze her poetic works. If my objective had been to carry out an even more detailed historical and literary analysis, I would have opted for covering Murillo's as well as Belli's poetry. I see clear formal and thematic affinities between these two poets. If the reader is looking for a broad historical analysis of Nicaraguan poetry, I recommend Beverley and Zimmerman's *Literature and Politics*.

Another major gap in my book is that I do not include any poetry from Nicaragua's Atlantic coast. This is at least partly because of the language differences. Another reason is that, as far as I am aware, there are no full-length poetical works available in print, but only collections of individual poems. I do feel that including them would have strengthened rather than diminished my thesis.

Several poets who belong to *vanguardismo*, the generation of 1940, the so-called Betrayed Generation, and the Ventana and Gradas groups appear tangentially as participants in these literary periods but not in an in-depth study. Including them would have provided greater detail and expanded the impact of my thesis.

Most of this manuscript was completed in early 1990 and substantially revamped in the fall of that year when I completed the first version, Ernesto Cardenal's last major book of poetry, *Cántico cósmico* (1989), had just been published. (The first printed edition came off the presses in November 1989.) At that stage, I decided to devote my time to rewriting the manuscript, thinking that a reading of *Cántico cósmico* would set back completion of my study, which explains the omission of this work in chapter 3. Any future revision of *Aesthetics and Revolution* will most assuredly incorporate a literary and theoretical evaluation of *Cántico*'s impact on Cardenal's oeuvre.

Finally, I should forewarn the reader that in *Aesthetics and Revolution* I assume some familiarity with the historical, political, and economic affairs of the Nicaraguan revolution as well as with literary theory. This is not intended to be a primer in aesthetics and revolution nor in Nicaraguan poetry, but rather a theoretical and sociohistorical intervention on aesthetics, revolution, and Marxism.

ACKNOWLEDGMENTS

The initial helpful readings of this manuscript were done by Tony Geist and Francisco Lopes at the University of Washington. I would also especially like to thank Cynthia Steele, who helped me through earlier versions of this book. I benefited greatly from her energetic and complete critique of both formal and thematic matters. My colleague and friend at North Carolina State University, Larysa Mykyta, did a very insightful reading of the Preface, chapter 1, and chapter 5. To Neil Larsen I am particularly indebted because he was almost single-handedly responsible for my reassessment of the nexus of Nicaraguan poetry, postmodernism, and Marxism. Our constant communication on these matters has been an inspiration to me all the way along. Thanks to the readings of Marc Zimmerman and Roger Zapata, I was able to improve on the breadth of the manuscript by filling some gaps. I thank Biodun Iginla for his many helpful comments and suggestions to me throughout this project. For innovative ideas that reached beyond technical concerns, I am very grateful to my copy editor, Lynn Marasco. The original spark for the study was set off in the fall of 1988, when I met and gained much knowledge about Nicaraguan culture from Jorge Eduardo Arellano, Francisco Arellano, Daisy Zamora, Ernesto Cardenal, Gioconda Belli, Ana Ilce Gómez, and others. I hope that in some way I have returned the favor. Finally, I would like to dedicate this book to my constant companion and dialogic partner, my wife, Françoise Sinet.

CHAPTER 1
SANDINISMO AND POSTMODERNISM

My intention in writing this book is to outline the dialectical relationship between revolutionary Nicaragua and this age of postmodernism. At first glance this may appear to be an incongruous association, unless one maintains that postmodernist theory is also a political practice and that this "praxis" can be seen in Nicaragua — which was often hailed as a new "socialist" alternative to the more "recalcitrant" socialist models to which we were accustomed. Unlike the Mexican, the Soviet, and the Cuban revolutions, Nicaragua's experiment was to be more "open," more "pluralist" than those of its predecessors. In fact, it was considered innovative precisely because it adopted a mixed economy and garden-variety political ideologies.[1] These were seen as alternatives to the bureacratization of socialist economies and to the extreme centralization of political power in the hands of a central committee and not in the domain of workers' soviets. Finally, a broad nationalist revolutionary movement appeared to be preferable to that historic agent of classical Marxist thought: the proletariat. In sum, what needed to be abandoned — as certain "Left" postmodernists continue to remind us — was the working class as a sole revolutionary agent, the state as the bearer of power, the intransigent character of the socialist economy, and the party as a "totalizing" and "homogenizing" force in social change.[2] That the Left would have to reconsider its political tactics after May 1968 was understandable given that — twenty years hence — those "social revolutions" had been enveloped and later coopted by an increasingly international capitalist order. In hindsight one could argue that Nicaragua appealed to the New Left (or the "postmodernist Left") as a socialist quasi utopia that — understandably — presented a more plausible and conceivable socialist alternative to Stalinism.

In aesthetics too there was a return to earlier utopian fantasies — the avant-garde as a revolutionary body — in spite of the fact that since the 1960s at least, the bourgeoisie had effectively appropriated its "revolutionary" character and turned it into an innovative commodity on the market. In its most recent manifestation, French poststructuralist theory considered the "multiplicity of meaning" "revolutionary" because it confronted the "homogeneity" of discourse in multinational capitalism. The "new" avant-garde in this age of postmodernism, however, cannot help but follow in the footsteps of the original avant-garde. Rather than destabilizing art as institution — through Marcel Duchamp's experiments, say, and Walter Benjamin's "shock value" — formal experimentation today seems to testify to the individual value of avant-garde art. One thinks today, for example, of Severo Sarduy's esoteric novels, in which the formal exploration of the "wealth of the sign" creates a broken plot that refuses any sort of centralization to the point that the content falls apart. With rare exceptions, it is only the literary specialist who will bother to disentangle his stylistic web. Ideologically, then, avant-gardist creation cannot help but call attention to itself, and this self-critical attitude ultimately reflects back on the producer and not on the audience. Thus, by taking up this vocation, artists artificially isolate themselves from the social body rather than affirming their links with the community.

To be sure, realist literature is not able to fully overcome the influence of its precursor: nineteenth-century literature. Yet it is equally true that, more often than not, it communicates a vision of a particular sociohistorical context in an unobtrusive way and that a large audience reads realist works. Hence, in the formal aspects alone there lies a social commitment that we do not encounter in modernist or avant-gardist work. But, in considering the content, we can observe a great disparity in the manner in which the "producer" recognizes and then empowers the narrative with this radical political dimension.

My thesis is that in order to do a materialist analysis of literary production, one ought to focus on the heterogeneous working class — which carries society on its back and should, consequently, control the artistic means of production. Art, which has for centuries been under the sway of noble or bourgeois power, should first serve those who create value. Since, as Marx's work exhaustively demonstrated, the working class is historically central to economic production and can appropriate a determining position in political representation, it follows that the force of the working class in creating an image of itself — in aesthetics — can be at least as strong in socialism. In art, the absolutely pivotal status of the proletariat is legitimized by its deeper knowledge of objective reality because it lives out the contradictions in capitalism in a way that no other class does and, consequently, can potentially communicate that complexity more vividly. So there is a sociohistorical reasoning attached to this privileging of working-class consciousness even in that domain in bourgeois production that is supposed to be assigned to the traditional intelligentsia. Rather than being an instrument of exploitation of the proletariat, aesthetics — as a means of production of values — becomes the mouthpiece of revolutionary agents.

What I have attempted to do in *Aesthetics and Revolution* is to map out the main poetic tendencies during the revolutionary years in Nicaragua.[3] The product of such an investigation is a series of struggles between different ways of perceiving (and acting upon) class and gender values. Initially, the camps can be divided rather neatly between the avant-garde (Pablo Antonio Cuadra, Gioconda Belli, and Ana Ilce Gómez) and the realists (Ernesto Cardenal, Daisy Zamora, and the workshop poets). But there are sharp ideological differences on a horizontal level—for example, between the socialism of Belli and the liberalism of Cuadra. On a vertical level the poets' work itself consists of contradictions between—let us say—Gómez's conservative Catholic upbringing and her feminism, or Ernesto Cardenal's latent machismo and his Christian Marxism. These thematic nodes cut across aesthetic boundaries into the realm of politics, from which they are never separated. It is in this sense that these poetic works record the political battles that took place in Nicaragua between 1979 and 1990 and that continue to play themselves out today.

As I have indicated, many literary critics, historians, theologians, and political scientists wanted to find a "Left" utopia in Nicaragua that corresponded in many ways with the contemporary beliefs of the postmodernists. In the process, they abandoned some fundamental (classical) Marxist instruments that were so effective in analyzing the dynamic movement of history. I take up these tools as I analyze political and aesthetic forces in revolutionary Nicaragua. Given the trends in literary theory in the past twenty years—in this age of postmodernism—it is evident that critics continue to distance themselves from a historical materialist and Marxist conception of the world. In so doing, as I will contend later in this chapter, they deal, almost without exception, with "pure ideology" or "pure theory" and, concurrently, discount the economic and political roots of history.

The Limits of Postmodernist Idealism and Politics

Postmodernism is based on the concept of undecidability and is centered on the Derridean concept of *différance* and not on the dialectic. Taken to an extreme, one is left with a series of slippages until—for reasons that are not necessarily rational—one simply acts spontaneously in favor of this or that ethical stance or one does not act at all. As Peter Dews has noted:

> Rather, the disruption of identity and the recovery of identity are simply two moments of the same process [i.e., there is a dialectical relation between the construction and deconstruction of identity]. We cannot speak of a final adequation of intention and expression, but only of a perpetual interplay of adequation and inadequation. The movement which Derrida attributes to the "play of the differance" itself, is rather the movement in which—in an incessantly repeated gesture, since the gap can never be

finally closed—the speaking subject attempts to render explicit what is implicit, and in so doing continually surprises itself.[4]

To found a political theory on such a philosophy—as Chantal Mouffe and Ernesto Laclau do—is even more problematic since it only compounds the fissures in deconstruction. For undecidability can lead to a passive political practice that underlines mutual understanding and liberal pluralism. To maintain otherwise would be to adopt a radically different political practice, one that would examine and act upon economic and political inequalities in a more global way.

Given the historical tradition of socialist regimes—particularly the artificial heritage in Eastern Europe—it is not entirely surprising to see the poststructuralists moving in such a cautious way. Against the authoritarian tradition of political institutions in socialist regimes to date, the postmodernists posit a tenuousness, a noncommittal stance. Yet by assuming such a political position, their argument can easily collapse into indifference, or, in the best of cases, into an idealism that does not fully absorb the errors of Hegelianism.

If the epistemological foundation of postmodernist political theory does not rest on a solid base, it risks throwing the whole theory off. The practical result of this procedure is borne out in the case of Laclau and Mouffe's *Hegemony and Socialist Strategy*, in which the historical and real notions of social class and class struggle are dismantled and then reassembled until they are finally abandoned:

> What is now in crisis is a whole conception of socialism which rests upon the ontological centrality of the working class, upon the role of the Revolution, with a capital 'r,' as the founding moment in the transition from one type of society to another, and upon the illusory prospect of a perfectly unitary and homogeneous collective will that will render pointless the moment of politics. The plural and multifarious character of contemporary social struggles has finally dissolved the last foundation for that political imaginary.[5]

For Laclau and Mouffe, in other words, the working class is no longer the central agent of revolutionary change, and revolution is not a scientifically expected outcome of exploitation. These postmodernists maintain that a new, plural agency has arisen in the "third world" to replace the inadequacy of the proletariat:

> It is the original forms of overdetermination assumed by social struggles in the Third World, with the construction of political identities having little to do with strict class boundaries; it is the rise of fascism, which would bru-

tally dispel the illusion of the necessary character of certain class articulations; it is the new forms of struggle in the advanced capitalist countries, where during the last few decades we have witnessed the constant emergence of new forms of political subjectivity cutting across the categories of the social and economic structure. (Laclau and Mouffe 13)

There can be little doubt that new forms of political subjectivity emerged in the 1960s in Latin America, the United States, and Europe (the women's movement, the civil rights movement, the student movements, etc.). But it is equally true that these social movements were not seriously and consciously engaged in revolution; that is, they were not ideologically committed to changing the capitalist system. To be sure, minor sectors of these social groups were dedicated to such a cause (the Black Panthers, the *foquistas* in Latin America, the African National Congress in South Africa, etc.), but at that historical moment they were not able to gain enough ground to establish a broader revolutionary movement. Concerning Laclau and Mouffe's contention that class is giving way to less identifiable revolutionary agents, the question that must be asked is this: are these postmodern forms of political subjectivity necessarily *revolutionary*, or do they seek to incorporate themselves more fully into the mainstream of a liberal state and a capitalist system? In other words, can they not easily become *petit bourgeois* social movements that intend to demand reforms *within the capitalist system?* If so, where does that leave Laclau and Mouffe's thesis?

In Europe (especially May 1968 in France) and the United States these diverse forces were quickly assimilated into the mainstream of bourgeois culture precisely because this was their main focus. If there had been a widespread interest in overthrowing the system and not working within it, and if these struggles had been accompanied by a parallel uprising among workers, the results would have been radically different. Instead of becoming institutions within bourgeois society (such as the NAACP in the United States and the MLF [Movement for the Liberation of Women] in France) they would now be revolutionary organs.

Latin America was most heavily marked, of course, by the Cuban revolution in 1959 and by the continued guerrilla struggles (*foquismo*) in Argentina, Uruguay, Bolivia, Peru, Nicaragua, and so forth. In many ways, this contrasting development in these countries indicated that the "sixties revolution" in Latin America was grounded in working-class struggles as well, and did not circulate solely in the universities. There were a number of reasons why these movements were not successful. First, the United States had begun to invest heavily in Latin America and had launched the Alliance for Progress, the Peace Corps, and other ideological weapons in order to combat the strength of the guerrilla groups. Second, according to Adolfo Sánchez

Vásquez many of the Marxist historical roots in Latin America were implanted with the ideas of the Second International and, thus, were characteristically more reformist, evolutionist, and idealist than those of the First International.[6] While a workers' revolution was perhaps more palpable in certain Latin American countries, workers' interests were betrayed by this reformism. Beginning in Brazil in 1964, the military in several South American countries and the U.S. State Department instigated neofascist military dictatorships that for all practical purposes eliminated civil society and guaranteed the reign of multinationals in Brazil, Argentina, Chile, and Uruguay. The military was able to conquer state power in these countries thanks to the support of "moderate" political forces that were frightened by the proposition of a radical systemic transformation.[7]

In tracing a very brief history of the differing roles of social movements in the postmodernist period, I am responding to Laclau and Mouffe's privileging of these sectors of the population. By affirming the centrality of the social movements in the "democratic process," they seem to want to displace the working class from this historical role and to contend that the nature of "democratic" struggles has fundamentally changed in the twentieth century. It appears that Laclau and Mouffe are describing *political alliances*, that is, movements with revolutionary potential if they align themselves with the working class in order to militarily challenge the hegemonic class. But as Laclau and Mouffe test their theory of social movements and pacific solutions to class conflicts—in opposition to classical Marxism's ontological belief in the proletariat and revolution—they disregard the role of the military in Latin America. It is the military, with the help of the State Department, that is able to swing the most weight in negotiations and to pit several moderate or centrist parties against left-wing parties. As James Petras has convincingly argued, the

proceso de negociación y el calendario electoral se convierten en armas políticas empleadas por los militares para mantener a la oposición dentro de los límites políticos aceptables. Las acciones militantes de las masas son condenadas por 'poner en peligro la transición democrática', y los militares pueden así alistar a los sectores civiles negociadores en la tarea de disciplinar a la oposición ingobernable.[8]

[negotiation process and the electoral calendar become political weapons employed by the military in order to keep the opposition within politically acceptable limits. Militant actions by the masses are condemned for "endangering the transition to democracy," and the military can consequently enlist the support of civilian sectors that cooperate in the task of disciplining the ungovernable opposition.]

Broad political coalitions of social groups are self-defeating unless they are able to act on the sociopolitical reality in a radical way and not be mesmerized by the dreams of liberalism or by the "peaceful road" to socialism. Placing too much confidence in the goodwill of the middle class and in democratic pluralism are tactical errors that were fatefully committed by the Allende government in Chile and the Manley government in Jamaica[9] and that serve as practical political lessons that verify the fact that capital will not idly sit by as socialist candidates are elected. Furthermore, there is a deeper question of whether it is even possible for socialists to govern in a capitalist society without contradicting their own principles — witness the hypocrisy of the Spanish Socialist Workers' Party (PSOE) and the French Socialist Party (PSF).

Laclau and Mouffe's thesis on pluralism and social movements derives from a certain tendency within postmodernism that alleges that social reproduction has become the primary motor of the imperialist economies, while production — as we knew it before the postmodernist stage of capital — is being carried out abroad.[10] Once this is acknowledged by Jean-François Lyotard and Toni Negri — united in this regard, but quite different ideologically in other respects — they contend that the shape of the labor force is changing in "developed" countries. There is validity in this economic and political analysis, for it is true that the composition of the labor force has been altered considerably during this postmodernist period. But it is also true that the "old" types of production are still present; now, however, the great majority of this kind of labor is being done in developing countries.[11] In essence, imperialism — which Lenin called the "highest stage of capitalism" — is still in full force, and in fact, international capital has created a larger gap between the major industrial powers and the developing countries. Imperialism has taken hold of the globe and unified it at the expense of labor, and particularly against the will of workers in the so-called peripheral countries.

Returning now to the initial question of revolutionary agency, it appears that Laclau and Mouffe have not sufficiently analyzed this economic period, or they would not be so willing to herald the coming of new revolutionary agencies and the advent of an age of information. They are certainly not alone on the "Left" when they take such a political stance. Andrew Ross opens *Universal Abandon?* by claiming that it is "clear that we can no longer envisage a grand tug-of-war between Capital and Labor (the old 'war of manoeuvre' in which a gain on one side is necessarily a loss on the other)."[12] But *where* has there been a decline in the class struggle? *How* can this be proven economically and politically? It appears that the globalization of capital has been so effective that "leftists" are not able to detect it! As Neil Larsen has poignantly noted, in the examples of Laclau and Mouffe and Ross, we are expected to base our arguments concerning postmodernism on irrational premises or to take a leap of faith:

> The fact that the "third path" calls itself "radical democracy", draping itself in the "ethics" if not the epistemology of Enlightenment, the fact that it outwardly resists the "fixity" of any one privileged subject, makes it, in a sense, the more perfect "radical" argument for a capitalist politics of pure irrationalist spontaneity. And we know who wins on the battlefield of the spontaneous.[13]

Indeed, the past thirty years of historical struggles have clearly taught us that the constitution of social movements has changed, but that has not lessened the conflict between labor and capital. The redemocratization process in Latin America does not indicate that there have been fundamental economic and political developments in Brazil, Argentina, Uruguay, and Chile—much less in El Salvador, Guatemala, and Peru. To cite one example, we might turn briefly to Chile. As recently as October 18, 1990, not one military officer had been prosecuted for the atrocities committed during the years of the Pinochet dictatorship.[14] While the military is no longer terrorizing the populace in its genocidal manner of yesteryear, it remains intact as the most powerful anti-democratic sector in the society. With history working against these grandiose visions of "radical democracy" and the social movements that are their foundation, it is doubtful that the proletariat will simply disappear from the production lines and, thus, from the focal point of the means of production.

Postmodernist Idealism and Aesthetics

> But this realism of the "anything goes" is in fact that of money; in the absence of aesthetic criteria, it remains possible and useful to assess the value of works of art according to the profits they yield. Such realism accommodates all tendencies, just as capital accommodates all "needs," providing that the tendencies and needs have purchasing power.
>
> Jean-François Lyotard, *The Postmodern Condition*

Lyotard's lucid argument denouncing the collaboration between realist art and the capitalist market is curious because he does not find this same weakness in modernism and the avant-garde. The relation he describes between capital and the ideologies of realism can be applied in a somewhat similar manner to the modernists. There are, of course, differences and difficulties in outlining this relation between these literary media and capital. On the one hand, realism reaches a larger audience and can be produced by a broad range of people. It can mediate the movement of capital and the intensity of the class struggle. On the other hand, as Lyotard points out, it is common to associate a work of art with its use value so that aesthetic value becomes virtually indistinguishable from the activity of the market. But is this not true of the avant-garde as well? What makes modernism even less appealing is its esoteric character, which limits the number of consumers and producers of literature. As Lyotard notes, however, one could argue that modernism is the epitome of experimentation, and it is problematic to hold that this "freedom of expression" should be repressed or restricted in any fundamental way. At the same time, this affirmation is followed by a negative remark regarding the writer and the community, and it turns out that Lyotard seems more concerned with the individual freedom of exercising that right than with the well-being of the community:

> But in the diverse invitations to suspend artistic experimentation, there is an identical call for order, a desire for unity, for identity, for security, or popularity (in the sense of *Öffentlichkeit*, of "finding a public"). Artists and writers must be brought back into the bosom of the community, or at least, if the latter is considered to be ill, they must be assigned the task of healing it. (73)

The implication here is that writers can very well choose whether or not they wish to be part of the community. Here the mythical individual artist bursts forth in Lyotard's writing and magically denies what he or she is: a social being. As in the case of Michel Foucault particularly, I detect the shadows of a binary opposition between a ubiquitous totality (read: any type of socialism that is directly connected with realism) and the "heroic" entreprenuer (read: free market capitalism, which is linked with modernism). It seems that readers have no choice: they can choose one of the two extremes, or such a choice could become "undecidable" (Derrida).

Rather than confronting the legitimacy of realism with his analytical tools in hand, Lyotard paradoxically confirms Georg Lukács's claims about modernism:

> The ontological view governing the image of man in the work of leading modernist writers is the exact opposite of this. Man, for these writers, is by nature solitary, asocial, unable to enter into relationships with other human beings.[15]

Consequently, Lyotard undermines his own arguments in favor of modernism, first by not dealing with the cooptation of modernism, and second by resorting to a defense of liberal individualism to support his discussion in favor of formal experimentation.

Before returning to Lyotard, we need to consider the arguments of two of the most significant theorists of this period: Lukács and Theodor Adorno.

The ultimate issue in their aesthetic debates was and is whether the distortion of life under capitalism is more adequately represented by realism (because it makes this alienation evident in content) or by modernism (which internalizes these contradictions in the form). Lukács accused the modernists of operating in an ideal realm, under the illusion that individual exploration has no social repercussions. Rather than presenting a view of unified, conscious alternative to capitalism, they succumbed to the cult of the new:

> But self-knowledge and knowledge of the world cannot be mutually divorced. It is impossible for someone to overcome the decadent illusion in himself without a knowledge and experience of the deeper connections of life, without breaking through the brittle and encrusted surface that conceals these connections under capitalism, conceals the deeper and contradictory unity, this ossification being fixed ideologically by the ideology of the decadent epoch and mystified into something conclusive and final. The depth of the literary vision, of the realist approach to reality, is always passion—no matter how the writer might formulate his world outlook intellectually—the passion not to accept anything as naked, cut and dried, dead experience, but to resolve the human world into a living interrelationship between human beings.[16]

Modernism inverts the relation of subject and object, it denies human beings what Marx called their "species being." According to Lukács, the modernists, in attempting to represent the forms of alienation and oppression so prevalent in capitalism, undermine their own project by impeding the reader's recognition of this reality. Or maybe more to the point: the alienated modernist presents a disfigured, estranged form that invades content to the degree that both content and form put on a masquerade of reality that negates the fundamental social nature of human beings. Like the commodity—which as Marx keenly noted is composed of an abstract substance so that it appears one way but acts another (it seems to have value in and of itself, but that value is actually attributed to it by its relation to other commodities) the work of art in bourgeois society seems to be an autonomous entity when, in reality, it accrues value according to its relation to other works of art. This process is a result, as Neil Larsen eloquently argues in *Modernism and Hegemony*, of capital's invasion of every sphere of life:

> Modernism can emerge as the impulse to constitute a nonabstract locus of agency that at the same time escapes the collapse of representation—the modern formula for aesthetics—only insofar as the unfolding of the social abstraction is equally and progressively felt in all superstructural spheres. In order to be sensed as the final destruction of all qualitative identity—as the

real, social abstraction—capital must already have become the universal ground of sensation.[17]

The all-pervasiveness of capital can be expressed in the mediational form of the avant-garde. Despite Adorno's criticism of realism, his approbation of the avant-garde must be seen as provisional or tacit. For the German philosopher, the major limitation of Lukácsian aesthetics is that it assumes a homology between art and reality that—according to Adorno—"can only converge if art crystallizes out its own formal laws, not by passively accepting objects as they come."[18] Adorno maintains a dialectical interplay between the subject and the object, while Lukács erects a binary opposition between them. Adorno alleges that it is Hegelianism that interferes with Lukács's aesthetic theory and makes it a noncontradictory totality.

From the philosophical foundation—where irrationalism (modernism) and rationalism (realism) collide—to the conclusions, Adorno contends that Lukács fails to take dialectical movement into account and, thus, freezes these epistemologies ahistorically: "It was doubtless his book *The Destruction of Reason* which revealed most clearly the destruction of Lukács's own. In a highly undialectical manner, the officially licensed dialectician sweeps all the irrationalist strands of modern philosophy into the camp of reaction and Fascism" ("Reconciliation" 152). According to Adorno, from there Lukács lumps together the various tendencies within modernism by drawing this categorical division between irrationalism and rationalism and later dismissing modernist literature as "decadent" (i.e., the product of a period of capitalist decay). Against the argument put forth by the Hungarian thinker—that modernist innovation draws from a subjectivist and alienating perspective—Adorno claims that when this estrangement is taken to an extreme, it becomes its opposite: "the solitary consciousness potentially destroys and transcends itself by revealing itself in works of art as the hidden truth common to all men" ("Reconciliation" 166).

Let us sort out the charges leveled by Adorno against Lukács, and vice versa. The weakness in Adorno's aesthetics lies in his belief—which he shares with Marcuse—that *all* art is potentially liberating. By positing art as ontologically radical, Adorno attempts to move beyond the "oppressive" limits of socialist realism and beyond Sartre's famous theoretical argument about the committed artist in *What Is Literature?* Rather than locating commitment in authorial intention, as Sartre does, Adorno wants to transcend this notion until he adopts a philosophically relativist position: "Even in the most sublimated work of art there is a hidden 'it should be otherwise.' "[19] What the great German philosopher skirts altogether is the question of proletarian art and, I might add, a materialist analysis of aesthetics. For the only mention this receives is when he scornfully examines socialist realism, and once he is overcome with disillusionment regarding this experiment in the Soviet Union he abandons hope of a proletarian culture. Had he not jettisoned this conclusion, he might have critically assessed the possibilities of planning the means of production, distribution, and reception in a socialist society and reasoned that workers should take over these means. Neil Larsen has commented on Adorno's idealism in this regard:

> Within the enclosed space of late capitalism's "totalitarian" ideology, then, a modernist aesthetics filters out as the vestige of an autonomy whose nineteenth-century version was a concrete historical subject: a revolutionary proletariat. The place of this subject in Marx's discourse shows up in Adorno as the formal possibility of a modern art. That is why art, for Adorno, cannot simply be placed at the service of the proletariat; rather, art must redeem the historical failure of the proletariat by opening up a tiny negative and emancipatory fissure in a history without revolutionary agencies. (Modernism 11)

Thus, in the case of Adorno, the radical open-endedness of art glosses over class conflict and uneven development as they are manifested in aesthetic representation.

There is never any such vacillation in the case of Lukács: artists must commit themselves to representing the contradictions of capitalism (critical realism) and to offering a humane alternative to the degradation of human beings (socialist realism). Lukács's position, however, is not as clear as one might imagine. In fact, his attempt to establish internal aesthetic laws for the work of art provides the contemporary reader with a skeletal frame of a materialist analysis of literature, but it remains incomplete because Lukács does not indicate how these laws operate. At any rate, it is by following this analytical course that Lukács tries to move toward a more objective analysis of art.[20] This theoretical investigation differs from his earlier writings, in which he relies on subjectivism (relies on the subject) as the determining factor in artistic production:

> Partial revolts of this kind arise continuously and on a massive scale in the course of life itself, though it needs a great intellectual and moral power, particularly in conditions of general decay, for an individual genuinely to break through them and expose this semblance of human existence for what it is. ("Marx" 134)

He is, of course, referring to the writer who lives and works in a capitalist country and not to the conditions of artistic production under socialism. But Lukács's reliance on "moral power" only shows the revolutionary weakness of art under capitalism. Thus, either we could conclude that aesthetics has no major revolutionary role to play in the overthrow of capitalism, or we could end up recognizing the revolutionary agency of the political equivalent of reformism and overlook the fundamental, material contradictions between capital and labor. As I have pointed out, however, in Lukács's later writings this subjectivism begins to disappear and a more objective approach to culture arises as he contends that art is also governed by laws.

Let us now turn to the implications of Adorno's charges to the effect that Lukács sustains an undialectical opposition between irrationalism and rationalism, and that it is this epistemological decision that affects his view of ideology and of literature in particular. In fact, however, in "Marx and the Problem of Ideological Decay," Lukács approaches both irrationalism and rationalism in a dialectical manner:

> The ideologists of today deck out this irrationalism in the most seductive colours of a "primordial and profound truth". In actual fact, a continuous line runs through from the confined superstition of the peasant, via the skittles and card games of the philistine, through to the "meaningless refinements" of emotional life, whose rootlessness is lamented by Niels Lyhne. Rationalism is a feeble and shameful capitulation before the objective necessities of capitalist society. Irrationalism is a protest against it which is just as impotent, just as feeble, just as empty and thoughtless. ("Marx" 130)

In this reading, Lukács considers both irrationalism and rationalism — as separate systems of thought — to be equally susceptible to bourgeois life. He is referring particularly to an apologetic rationalism that defends capitalism to the hilt, and to an irrationalism that — knowingly or not — distorts the social nature of human beings. At first glance, then, what appears to be an analysis of exclusive antinomies turns out to be a dialectical understanding of the philosophical strands. Basing his aesthetic theory on this observation, Lukács regards modernism as the negation of traditional nineteenth-century realism and socialist realism as the negation of the negation.

By contrast, as Terry Eagleton has lucidly observed, for Adorno, the art work

> transcends the antagonisms of everyday life without promising to abolish them; it is therefore, perhaps, "the only remaining medium of truth in an age of incomprehensible terror and suffering". In it, the hidden irrationality of a rationalized society is brought to light; for art is a "rational" end in itself, whereas capitalism is irrationally so. Art has a kind of paratactic logicality about it, akin to those dream images which blend cogency and con-

tingency; and it might thus be said to represent an arational reason confronting an irrational rationality. If it acts as an implicit refutation of instrumentalized reason, it is no mere abstract negation of it; rather, it revokes the violence inflicted by such reason by emancipating rationality from its present empirical confinement, and so appears as the process by which rationality criticizes itself without being able to overcome itself.[21]

In many ways, Lukács's position does not seem that distant from Adorno's. Both appear to carry out a dialectical analysis of the relation between irrationalism and rationalism. They differ fundamentally in their conclusions, however. As I stated earlier, for Adorno art always negates the irrational rationalism of the capitalist system; it is always already a liberational medium. In contrast, Lukács sees the interpenetration of art and society in addition to — and this is his decisive break with Adorno — positing a qualitative leap in relation to capitalism. In other words, Lukács believes in a revolutionary agent and a revolutionary art that will be victorious in its struggle with capital, while Adorno leaves the question of agency open.

One of the main objections to Lukácsian aesthetic theory lies in what is perceived as his totalization of the class struggle and sexual politics. As Peter Dews has indicated, many of the antitotalizing postmodern philosophies are themselves guilty of totalizing, so that what we end up with is a series of molecular struggles without any objective beyond spontaneously destroying capitalism.[22] There are alternatives to what amounts to an anarchist political philosophy. It is worth quoting Terry Eagleton at length in his extension of Adornian aesthetics and subsequent critique of Lukácsianism:

> For Lukács, totality already exists in principle, but has yet to come into its own. Literary realism prefigures that fortunate day, recreating each phenomenon in the image of the essence it belies. For Adorno, things are quite the reverse: there is indeed, here and now, a total system which integrates everything relentlessly down, but to emancipate non-identity from its voracious maw would be to transform this miserable situation into some future historical "constellation", in which rational identity would be constituted by that hiatus within each particular which opens it to the unmasterable otherness of its fellows. Such a political order would be as far from some "totalitarian" regime as it would be from some random distribution of monads or flux of sheer difference; and in this sense there is the basis for a politics in the work of Adorno, as there is only dubiously in that of some of his theoretical successors. Adorno does not abandon the concept of totality but submits it to a materialistic mutation; and this is equivalent to transforming the traditional concept of the aesthetic, turning it against itself by redeeming as far as possible its proto-materialistic aspects from its totalizing idealism. (*Ideology* 356–57)

The conclusions at which Eagleton arrives are not, I think, as obvious as he seems to suggest. It is clear that Eagleton is interpreting Adorno's aesthetic theory politically and perhaps a little too willfully. In offering this explanation, the great English Marxist is wanting to invoke an aesthetic equivalent for "permanent revolution," a socialism that will avoid stagnation and bureaucratization in its very dialectical movement. But is it not also possible to read Adorno's theory as a dead end politically? In a sense, it exhibits many of the same problems that Peter Dews notes in Foucault, Lyotard, Derrida, and Lacan: if identity and nonidentity simply exchange hegemonic positions incessantly and can never be pinned down, then we do not come to even a temporary "leap" that makes identity hegemonic and nonidentity still part of the formula:

> One of the central ironies of post-structuralist thought, in other words, is that it fails to comprehend the internal relation between the subjective disintegration and the restoration of a featureless pre-subjective totality. For in order to comprehend this relation, rather than merely becoming caught up in it, it would be necessary to reflect on the dynamic of identifying reason from the standpoint of reconciliation—the interplay of identity and nonidentity. Instead, post-structuralism tends to oscillate between totalizing ontological postulates and a more or less explicit perspectivism. (*Logics* 231)

How does Adorno's theory avoid this entrapment? According to Dews, Adorno considers identity in its dialectical relation to nonidentity. This is, no doubt, Adorno's response to the concept of totality, but what does this tell us about revolution? Adorno does the "manual work" of interpenetrating identity and nonidentity without offering a clue as to what the qualitative leap will entail. Neil Larsen has maintained that, in the absence of a revolutionary subject and a material revolution, Adorno supplants this lack with modern art:

> Modern art thus retains at least an anticapitalist aspect (if not a revolutionary one) in its conscious "resistance" to the reification (instrumentalization) wrought by exchange. And where revolution has failed for the foreseeable future, modern art can measure what are at least real, if small, victories in the capacity of its works to "hibernate" through the long winter of counterrevolutionary ascendancy. *Capital* is read as much for its political abstraction as for its concrete analysis of capital itself. Its theoretical terms, transposed into a discourse of aesthetics, become the renarrativized players of a nineteenth-century drama whose protagonist and political setting have been purged but whose plot continues to be played out. (*Modernism* 11)

Postmodern Interpretations of Realism and Modernism

In continuing this discussion, I would like to examine briefly the questions of discursivity, information as a "mode of production," "low" and "high" art, and marginality. All of these topics are commonplace in postmodern theory today and should be subject to scrutiny, as they challenge some of the major tenets of Marxism.

Jean-François Lyotard is not, of course, the only contemporary theorist who narrativizes history, or who passes over the raw material of history in favor of historical discourses. Chantal Mouffe and Ernesto Laclau, in their haste to dispense with Hegelian totality, succumb to a fate similar to Hegel's at the hands of Marx: they need to be stood on their heads. Mouffe and Laclau would find a kindred thinker in Lyotard, for whom the ideational realm can somehow be divested of its materiality:

> A noteworthy result of the speculative apparatus is that all of the discourses of learning about every possible referent are taken up not from the point of view of their immediate truth-value, but in terms of the value they acquire by virtue of occupying a certain place in the itinerary of Spirit or Life—or, if preferred, a certain position in the Encyclopedia recounted by speculative discourse. That discourse cites them in the process of expounding for itself what it knows, that is, in the process of self-exposition. True knowledge, in this perspective, is always indirect knowledge; it is composed of reported statements that are incorporated into the metanarrative of a subject that guarantees their legitimacy. (*The Postmodern Condition* 35)

In order to analyze discourse, Lyotard must first surgically remove it from substantiation, or from referentiality as though reality were not already embedded in discourse, as though discourse did not already depend upon reality for its livelihood. By artificially isolating discourse in this way, Lyotard veers in the direction of subjectivism so that the dialectic between subject and object is tilted in favor of the subject. In his critique of *Discours, Figure,* Peter Dews perceptively identifies the idealism that we confront in *The Postmodern Condition*: "For what is omitted in the understanding of language as a closed system of signifiers doubled by a system of signifieds is any sense of the referential dimension of language" (*Logics* 114). Lyotard's theory is heavily influenced by the effects of J. L. Austin's speech act theory, which purports some sort of neutrality and autonomy for language. Thus, for example, further on in the discussion we learn that ideology—which we formerly assumed was a sociodiscursive construct—can be legitimately severed from discourse. It turns out that "if the discourse that was meant to legitimate it [science] seems to belong to a prescientific form of knowledge, like a 'vul-gar' narrative, it is demoted to the lowest rank, that of an ideology or instru-ment of power" (38). Instead of unearthing the real, historical foundation that occupies discourse, discourse for Lyotard, it would seem, determines reality. In this respect, Lyotard follows in the footsteps of Derrida. At the very best, Lyotard's political position leads to undecidability; at worst, it freezes dis-course in place as a sine qua non. The great master narratives, from which Lyotard remains detached, are the ones — in the words of Fredric Jameson — "that suggest that something beyond capitalism is possible, something radi-cally different; and they also 'legitimate' the praxis whereby political mili-tants seek to bring that radically different future social order into being. Yet both master-narratives of science have become peculiarly repugnant or em-barrassing to First World intellectuals today."[23]

Another issue that is deeply ingrained in postmodernist thought today is the contention that the new mode of production is information. Lyotard and Toni Negri have presented two cogent studies of this thesis. It is certainly true that there has been an increase in the number of laborers in the service sector in the most developed industrial countries and that this has affected the labor force as a whole. It appears, however, that the issue of imperialism (i.e., the exploitation of developing countries by developed nations) is skirted in such analyses and, with it, the dialectic itself. We need to cite Lyotard here, for he takes the step of outlining the importance of the production of knowl-edge in the world market, yet does not delve deeper into the matter and ex-amine how the superstructure interacts with the infrastructure:

> Knowledge in the form of an informational commodity indispensable to productive power is already, and will continue to be, a major — perhaps *the* major — stake in the worldwide competition for power. It is conceivable that the nation-states will one day fight for control of information, just as they battled in the past for control over territory, and afterwards for con-trol of access to and exploitation of raw materials and cheap labor. (5)

That the control of information about production will have even greater im-portance in developing societies and that it is a crucial development to ana-lyze explains why Lyotard's *The Postmodern Condition* has contributed signi-ficantly to sociology, politics, economics, and aesthetics. In this regard, however, Lyotard's reasoning is also incorrect because — as I noted before — he inverts the material and the ideal. Here this inversion is more subtly put: "It is conceivable that the nation-states will one day fight for control of infor-mation, just as they battled in the past for control over territory, and after-wards for control of access to and exploitation of raw materials and cheap labor" (5). By implication, the production of information will be *just as impor-*

*tant as—or more important than—*the material mode of production. Are we to assume then that this new mode of production will dictate terms to the material mode of production? Or (put in what is perhaps today considered to be an anachronistic way of thinking) will the superstructure wield more influence than the infrastructure? What evidence do we have that there is a dissipation of working-class forces in the world? Again, a reading of Lyotard runs up against the limitations of his idealism. For is he not discussing the economies of developed countries while discarding the role of developing nations and thus ignoring the movement of international capital? He would have to pass over the stage of imperialism and the international labor theory of value in order to arrive at such a conclusion.

Toni Negri presents a similar, yet more complex, elaboration of this theory in "Interpretation of the Class Situation Today." As in the case of Lyotard, however, the reader is left with one key feature of the dialectic while its dynamic opposite is apparently cast aside. In other words, Negri's analysis also seems to focus unduly on developed countries without taking into account production in developing nations. To overlook production in developing nations, Negri would have to sidestep, or disregard, Lenin's analysis of the imperialist stage of capitalism. Let us turn to Negri:

> What is the "form of value" of the "mode of production" which is called the "real subsumption"? It is a form in which there is an immediate translatability between the social forces of production and the relations of production themselves. In other words, the mode of production has become so flexible that it can be effectively confused with the movements of the productive forces, that is, with the movements of all the subjects who participate in production. It is the entirety of these relations which constitutes the form of value of the real subsumption. We can develop this concept affirming that this form of value is the very "communication" which develops among productive forces.
>
> If "communication" constitutes the fabric of production and the substance of the form of value, if capital has become therefore so permeable that it can filter every relation through the material thicknesses of production, if the laboring processes extend equally as far as the social extends, what then are the consequences that we can draw with respect to the law of value?[24]

There is little doubt that Negri is correct when he says that we should examine the role of "all the subjects which participate in production." But then we must identify *the central force of production.* While Negri tangentially recognizes this, he also contends that the "intellectual and scientific forces which have gradually become central in production, are nonetheless powers of labor" (6). What factors have tilted the balance in favor of the "intellectual and scientific forces"? Following this last assertion, Negri declares that the dominant mode of production in this third stage of capital is communication (7). As with Lyotard, among the questions we could ask would be: Where is this true geographically? Does this mean that international capitalism no longer depends on the material mode of production (or that the superstructure is more valorized)? We have no empirical grounding to believe that, as Negri contends later, "the composition of the proletariat is social, as is also the territory where it resides; it is completely abstract, immaterial, intellectual, from the point of view of the substance of labor; it is mobile and polyvalent from the point of view of its form."[25]

I would like to extend this discussion further by addressing an issue — so often heralded among certain postmodernists — that suggests that postmodern art succeeds in bridging the gap between so-called low art and high art. It seems to me that there is a correlation between this "new" mode of production and the "blurring" of the boundaries separating popular and elitist culture. The first question that comes to mind is this: what artistic examples do we have that deny the binary opposition between "low" and "high" art? (I deal specifically with the bourgeoisie's appropriation of popular culture in chapter 2.) It is difficult to consider this question without weighing its political implications because we may be reminded of several Latin American novels of the 1960s (the "Boom") and the way social movements during this period were coopted by the capitalist system.

Néstor García Canclini has maintained that in Latin America

> desde los 40 el cine y a partir de los 50 la TV revolvieron lo popular con fragmentos de lo culto, y fueron subordinando a ambos a la gramática de producción y a la lógica de circulación de las industrias culturales. La débil autonomía de las artes de élite y la incipiente reivindicación de las artes populares fueron sujetadas a estrategias populistas: usando los medios masivos, los nuevos interpeladores (Perón es el caso paradigmático) cumplen la operación de convertir "a las masas en pueblo y al pueblo en Nación". En parte por los movimientos políticos, en parte por la modernización comunicacional, la autonomía de una estética culta y el desarrollo autónomo de tradiciones populares quedan como empresas fallidas.[26]

> [since the 1940s, movies, and from the 1950s on, television mixed the popular with fragments of refined culture, and submitted both to a grammar of production and to a logic of circulation of the culture industries. The weak autonomy of the elitist arts and incipient right of popular art were subjected to populist strategies: using mass media, the new interpellators (Perón is the most paradigmatic case) to carry out the operation of converting "the masses into the people and the people into a nation." The autonomy of refined aesthetics and the autonomous development of popu-

lar traditions become failed missions partly because of the political movements and of the modernization of communications.]

It would seem logical to conclude that the hegemonic power—the bourgeoisie—appropriated popular forms and utilized them in its national project,
that is, the perpetuation of its reign. But García Canclini warns that it is no
longer possible to "vincular rígidamente las clases sociales con los estratos
culturales" (82) (rigidly tie social classes to cultural strata). On the one hand,
this conclusion is understandable since many sectors of the population are
not absolutely identifiable in the class struggle (the service workers, for example). On the other hand, we cannot dismiss the centrality of the struggle,
which continues to reside in the intense contradiction between labor and capital. Yet there are some postmodernists who would like to displace this whole
material conflict in favor of an ephemeral aesthetic project. For Baudrillard
—as for Lyotard—for example, modern art needs to "save" us from alienation
in capitalism; yet adhering to this aestheticopolitical ideology would still
confine us to capitalism and not allow us to create a new economic system
(socialism). Likewise, according to García Canclini, popular culture is often
a deterritorialized culture; it is part of the heterogeneous marginal social force
(92). And we can sense that there is no specific political alternative available
to hegemonic power in this ideological stance; rather, the "multiplicity of
heterogeneous forces" enacts itself within the demarcations of a complacent
liberalism or anarchism.

George Yúdice and Laura Kipnis have worked within the same general
domain of marginality and, I would argue, with somewhat similar results
ideologically.[27] In many ways, Yúdice's writings attempt to corroborate
Mouffe and Laclau's thesis about the displacement of class struggle to plural
forces in the aesthetic sphere.[28] Latin America consists of various cultures
that testify to the heterogeneity and complexity of race, class, and gender relations; this is by now well grounded in contemporary Latin American cultural studies. Consequently, there is also an uneven development of social
groups, which combine these elements in differing ways. For Yúdice, the
conflict between labor and capital, then, is met by a plural resistance that includes groups on the periphery of hegemonic power. And it is this heterogeneous body that is the new revolutionary subject at this stage of postmodernism:

> Today, it is declared, the "marginal" is no longer peripheral but central to
> all thought. Contemporary poststructuralist thought has apotheistically
> reclaimed "marginality" as a liberating force. By demonstrating that *the*
> "marginal" constitutes the condition of possibility of all social, scientific,
> and cultural entities, a new "ethics of marginality" has emerged that is

necessarily decentered and plural, and that constitutes the basis for a new, neo-Nietzschean "freedom" from moral injunctions.[29]

Considering that this new political subject is supposed to be much more flexible than a "totalitarian" praxis — such as Marxism — it is interesting to note that the vocabulary used to identify this new revolutionary agency appears to contradict itself. The reader expects supple or pliable nominations of such a "plural" and "decentered" group, yet runs into "fixed" language — to borrow one of Mouffe and Laclau's accusatory terms. Marginality is defined as "*the* condition of possibility of *all* social, scientific, and cultural entities" (emphasis in the original in the first instance and my emphasis in the second), which is "*necessarily* decentered and plural" (my emphasis). It is curious to confront such determinations of meaning in a theory that purports openness. In fact, these exclusive qualifiers (*the, all*, and *necessarily*) conflict with the very discursive context in which they appear, since they betray the apparent strength of this ostensibly antitotalitarian ideology. If this "post-Marxist" political theory anchors itself in such an absolutist way — while maintaining that it is not doing so — how is it less "dogmatic" than the classical Marxist theory of class struggle? More than this, if the New Left is so vehemently against any form of "totalization" as it proceeds to totalize, then does it not become a reactionary ideology that preys upon communism as much as the bourgeoisie does?

Yúdice, like Mouffe and Laclau, is aware of the dialectic while still being suspicious of it. On the one hand, they cannot discard the historical role of the conflict between labor and capital, and on the other, they declare that a number of different social groups confront the interests of capital:

> In countries of the Third World, imperialist exploitation and the predominance of brutal and centralized forms of domination tend from the beginning to endow the popular struggle with a centre, with a single and clearly defined enemy. Here the division of the political space into two fields is present from the outset, but the diversity of democratic struggles is more reduced. We shall use the term *popular subject position* to refer to the position that is constituted on the basis of dividing the political space into two antagonistic camps; and *democratic subject position* to refer to the locus of a clearly delimited antagonism which does not divide society in that way. (*Hegemony* 131)

There can be little doubt that the international proletariat is a heterogeneous body in itself — that it consists of men, women, children, blacks, mestizos, whites, and so forth — and that its labor consists of myriad forms of creating value. Consequently, the existing conflict between capital and labor can be observed in such a myopic way only if one considers Marxism to be a mechanistic or monolithic praxis. In order to uphold this view, one would have to dissect the dialectic from Marx's works, simplifying them to such a degree that they would no longer belong to Marx. In addition, one would have to conveniently ignore the historically antagonistic relationship between capital and labor; Mouffe and Laclau would rather avoid "a clearly delimited antagonism which does not divide society in that way."[30] What evidence do we have that would indicate a transcendence of this antagonism and would warrant a "rearticulation" of revolutionary agency?

The theory of marginality translates into a politicoaesthetic exaltation of "survival" that almost replaces revolutionary change (instead of class struggle we are left with a struggle for survival). Thus, Rigoberta Menchú's testimonial novel, *Me llamo Rigoberta Menchú y así me nació la conciencia* (I, Rigoberta Menchú), becomes for Yúdice "a testimonial of incorporation and embodiment made possible by the struggle for survival."[31] In this interpretation of Menchú's work, the revolutionary testimony loses much of its force. The role of liberation theology and its nexus with Marxism is analyzed in more detail in chapter 3, but I should comment in passing that Yúdice's selection of Enrique Dussel and not of the more explosive "materialist theology" of Gustavo Gutiérrez is also a significant indication of what has become "acceptable" in post-Marxism.[32] Indeed, in "Postmodernity and Transnational Capitalism in Latin America," Yúdice addresses the link between politics and aesthetics and the question of the redistribution of wealth, but, curiously, never mentions revolution. If the proletariat is part of these rising "new" social movements, one would never know it.

A similar consideration of marginality is developed in Laura Kipnis's "Feminism: The Political Conscience of Postmodernism?" In contrast to Yúdice, Kipnis seems to recognize the danger of social movements' being coopted.[33] Moreover, she critically analyzes the role of the subject in contemporary theory and the relation it might have with the crisis in modernity. What makes her study appealing is that Kipnis considers the crisis in modernism to be tied to the crisis of capital:

> Given that discourse is also productive, it is not hard to see this theoretical proliferation of the subject—its production as a site of attention, investigation, and speculation—as symptomatic of some kind of necessity. Its insistent visibility, which provides a certain bolstering of the category itself, provokes the question of what exactly it is that the subject needs bolstering against—its fragmentation in the chop shop of late capitalism, or perhaps a glimmer of self-knowledge that the necessary historical precondition for a critique of the subject is the loss of its legitimating function? What other political determinations can account for such excessive visibility of a category that operated precisely from a blindness to its own determinations, whose greatest desire was to turn itself into an effect of nature? (157)

Many of the theoretical speculations of the post-Marxists are not found in Kipnis's article. She refuses, for instance, to believe that aesthetics — whether it is the avant-garde, modernism, or realism — can lead to any substantial political and economic changes. In addition, when Kipnis examines French and American feminism, she recognizes that their politics have been displaced to the theoretical sphere. In that light, she poignantly asks:

> What would it mean to find these operations now in literary confinement, these procedures held to deconstruct binarisms, dismantle phallocentrism, and decenter subjects, *outside* writing, to suspend the current orthodoxy that reality and history are simply texts, while retaining the radical insights of feminist deconstruction? (160)

The deconstruction of phallocentrism should be one of the main objectives of a revolutionary movement; this is clear and indispensable. But it is at this moment that we should undertake a deeper dialectical assessment of the sociopolitical situation and acknowledge the limits of deconstruction: we cannot relentlessly oscillate between identity and nonidentity and expect to engage in praxis. If Kipnis were positing the construction of a self-critical and heterogeneous revolutionary body, her praxis would not differ substantially from classical Marxism. But for Kipnis revolutionary agency is incarnated in a similar type of marginal: the colonial subject. On the one hand, it is true that both sexism and racism appear in history before the genesis of social classes, but it is also true that equality can best be conquered when all three are considered the basis of a revolutionary movement that seeks to put an end to oppression. This will happen, however, when a conscious, heterogeneous revolutionary proletariat and its political alliances challenge and destroy the power of capital. Otherwise we will have failed to learn from the tragic lessons of micropolitics in the social movements of the 1960s.

My critique so far has focused on certain tenets of postmodernism that have broken away from classical Marxism and — as I have attempted to show — have consequently drifted into an ideological realm that is akin to social democracy because they have been unable to disprove the Marxian notions they criticize. Healthy questioning of classical Marxism revolves around its linchpin: the proletariat and class struggle. As I have sought to demonstrate, the "post-Marxists" suggest that the current political and economic climate calls for a reassessment of political strategy and a serious reevaluation of revolutionary agency, the notion of class struggle, and its momentary dialectical outcome: revolution.

The root of this tendency within postmodernist thought is to be located in the dialectical method itself. In its place we find Derrida's notion of "indeterminacy" or "undecidability," which, more often than not — as Peter

Dews convincingly argues — does not lead us to a new praxis, but rather seems merely to reproduce the ideology of the status quo. The result of this theoretical position, then, is a political project that never quite gets off the ground, or if it does, it protests vehemently within the domain of bourgeois thought itself. And the contours of this political position, if I may suggest some semblance of "fixity," can be mapped out as they relate to the French Communist Party (PCF) and, particularly, to a certain fear of Stalinism. One could hardly fault Foucault, Deleuze, Guattari, Cixous, and Lyotard for reacting against the rigidity of such a theoretical and political stance given the atrocities committed in its name. To be critical of this current within orthodox Marxism can only be seen as salutary. Nevertheless, its dogmatic method is met by an equally stern, antitotalizing system of thought that makes such a conscious attempt to swerve away from dogmatism that it falls victim to it. Any sense of "closure," of "fixity," of "determination" is to be opposed at any cost, for it invariably steers us toward totalitarianism. Consequently, it is not surprising that these activists of May 1968 have had a tremendous impact on literary theory, but they have not come up with a historically tested praxis. Their solution points toward freeing the individual from psychic and somatic repressions and relying — in the best of cases — on the spontaneous uprising of the "masses." In avoiding the destructiveness of Stalinism, they abandon the only catalyzing force — some sort of political vanguard — that has successfully carried out revolutionary activity. Rather than seeing the party as a self-critical, fluid apparatus, they totalize a perceived totality (all Marxism) and dismiss the notion of vanguard. It is indeed ironic, as Terry Eagleton accurately observed, that this turn in philosophy occurs at a moment when capital appears more omnipresent than ever before:

> The supposed discrediting of this idea [totality] is, historically speaking, deeply ironic. For it springs from just that recent political period about which it would be highly plausible to contend that the system which radicals oppose has never, for a long time, shown itself quite as *total* — where the capillary connections between economic crisis, national liberation struggle, the resurgence of protofascist ideologies, the tightening hold of the state, have never been quite as palpable. It is at just this historical moment, when it is clear that what we confront is indeed in some sense a 'total system', and is sometimes recognized as such by its own rulers, that elements of the political left begin to speak of plurality, multiplicity, schizoid circuits, microstrategies and the rest. (*Ideology* 381)

The capitalist system has never been as total, I might add, and the conflict between labor and capital perhaps never so acute, so brutally destructive. So it is now more than ever that the wool needs to be removed from our eyes so we can begin anew with an international revolutionary struggle against capital.

The Case of the Nicaraguan Revolution: Politics and Aesthetics

As I have mentioned, terms such as *pluralism, unfixity, différance,* and *totality* — commonly associated with Derrida in theory and Laclau and Mouffe in politics — have been frequently evoked when historians, political scientists, and literary theorists have turned their gaze toward Nicaragua. The changes carried out during the revolution seemed to embody the characteristics of a new, third path that would somehow lead us away from a "totalitarian" socialism.[34] In this work, I submit that there is a correlation between a certain type of postmodern theoretical language that has included a revival of the philosophy of Nietszche, Heidegger, and Spinoza — more often than not — at the expense of Marx and Lenin, and the "post-Marxist" revisions incarnated in the politicoaesthetic alterations that have taken place in Nicaragua since 1979. I argue in *Aesthetics and Revolution* that the Nicaraguan economic, political, and aesthetic spheres exhibited these characteristics, and it was precisely their adoption of this "third path" that led to the internal collapse of the Sandinistas. From without, there is little doubt that U.S. imperialism did its best, at least from 1984 to 1990, to undermine the Nicaraguan revolution in many ways, not the least of which were the funding of the contras, the National Endowment for Democracy's aid to UNO, the economic embargo, and the blockade.[35] I am focusing, in particular, on the dialectic between aesthetics (especially poetry) and politics, and I am suggesting that the closing of the Ministry of Culture was a result not just of external factors, but also of internal strife. In retrospect, it appears that this interior battle of aesthetic tendencies foreshadowed the fate of the Sandinistas themselves.

The Making of the FSLN

From the very beginning, there were three major ideological strands in the FSLN: the Guerra Popular Prolongada (GPP, the Prolonged People's War), the Insurrectionalists, and the Tendencia Proletaria (Proletarian Tendency). By 1975, the FSLN directorate was divided in the following manner: five supporters of GPP, four supporters of the insurrectionalists, and three who favored both.[36] By August 1978, however, as Donald Hodges has shown, five members of the directorate had been killed in battle and were summarily replaced so that the balance in the directorate shifted in favor of the Insurrectionalists. As early as 1977, then, the Insurrectionalists advocated pluralism, that is, as Sergio Ramírez noted, "an alliance with democratic sectors of the national bourgeoisie through a group that would provide political support for the Sandinista Front and that eventually might be included in a government backed by the FSLN" (Hodges 246). In Orlando Núñez and Roger Burbach's *Democracia y revolución en las Américas* (Democracy and revolution in the Americas) one finds a postrevolutionary manifesto that epitomizes this ideological stance: "Nosotros creemos que bajo el capitalismo estas formas de explotación han sido un factor fundamental para desarrollar una 'tercera fuerza social' que está compuesta por la clase media, la pequeña burguesía en general, los intelectuales, los cristianos revolucionarios y los movimientos sociales"[37] (We think that under capitalism these forms of exploitation have been a deciding factor in developing a "third social force" that is composed of the middle class, the petite bourgeoisie in general, intellectuals, Christian revolutionaries, and social movements). It is this third group that gains a majority of the leadership of the FSLN and calls for a spontaneous insurrection, and it is they who finally assume control of the revolutionary government. Class alliance is a natural historical gesture that makes revolution possible; without it there would probably be no revolt. Yet negotiating a political and economic agenda among heterogeneous forces potentially can betray the views of the more radical sector.[38] In other words, pluralism taken to an extreme can navigate in one of two directions: it can lead to liberalism or to anarchism.

In order to understand how class negotiations can misrepresent the interests of the working class immediately following a revolution, it may be instructive to compare, for instance, the ideological status and political tactics of the Sandinistas with the French Communards. In both cases, their struggles consisted of heterogeneous revolutionary bodies that took power via insurrection. The FSLN had sought to reach out to bourgeois sectors of the population and they had responded affirmatively at the time of the revolution (to defeat Somoza), but they sided with UNO during the 1990 election. Had the Sandinistas shown a face that was not their own—that is, did they remain loyal to the working class to the end? Or did they favor the interest of the bourgeoisie to such a degree that they were sapped of their revolutionary mission? Perhaps the FSLN was so anxious to return to a peace-time economy—to finally call an end to the war with the contras and return to normalcy politically and economically—that the radical undergirding of the party was suppressed in favor of reaching the alienated petit bourgeois and bourgeois sectors. Following this logic, then, one could argue that the party lost its strongest political support. Once this rupture between the party and the working class occurred, the latter may have swayed in its loyalty to the FSLN and the bourgeoisie saw in Violeta Chamorro a much more stable ally in the transition to a "market economy." Carlos Vilas clearly identifies this break in the political campaigning for the April 1990 elections:

Ortega's U.S. and Nicaraguan handlers did all they could to wipe out anything that would remind voters of his guerrilla past, of the war, and eventually of the revolution itself. He doffed his spectacles and olive green uniform, switching to jeans and cowboy boots—a youthful, debonair image,
known by all as the "Danny look." He took to demonstrating his Catholic
devoutness by attending mass and referring to "the Lord" in his speeches.
The Sandinista slogan was upbeat: Todo será mejor (Everything's Going to
Be Better); and their program claimed all the country's problems would be
solved through foreign assistance once the elections were won and the
Contras were demobilized.[39]

Of course, it did not help matters when, the day before the elections, the
White House declared that it would continue to observe the economic embargo if the Sandinistas won. The political scenario does begin to look like
the shifting of alliances and the dumping of the working class during the
Paris Commune in 1871. Lenin too observed this process: "Only the workers
remained loyal to the Commune to the end. The bourgeois republicans and
the petty-bourgeoisie soon broke away from it, the former afraid of the
revolutionary Socialist proletarian character of the movement, and the others
dropping out when they saw that it was doomed to inevitable defeat."[40] All
this sounds too familiar.

How far can we take this analogy between the Sandinistas and the Communards? Would it be accurate to say that, like the Communards, the FSLN
did not fully proceed with the "expropriation of the expropriators"? Nicaragua was certainly not a workers' and campesinos' state. And the Sandinistas
were proud of the fact that 60 percent of the economy was still in private
hands.[41] This may have been their gravest error: not to declare straightfor-
wardly that Nicaragua was socialist, that is, that it was a workers' and
peasants' state, and to proceed accordingly (i.e., to support the appropriation
of the means of production by the working class). Lenin said of the Paris
Commune that the "second error was the unnecessary magnanimity of the
proletariat: instead of annihilating its enemies, it endeavoured to exercise
moral influence on them" (18). As Ramírez indicates, the FSLN also felt it
needed to reach certain bourgeois sectors in order for the insurrection to suc-
ceed. Once the FSLN had extended its invitations to the liberals, social
democrats, and social Christians, it did in fact guarantee the triumph of the
revolution; but whose revolution would that be if the very constituent elements of the insurrectionalist tendency could not envision and work for a socialist society? (Hodges 253)

We can see results of this strategy today: the reign of pluralism in both the
political and the economic spheres led Nicaragua down the road to a nationalist, bourgeois revolution. One could perhaps argue that the strikes that we
witnessed in the summer of 1990 and this call for "ruling from below" are

indications that the Sandinistas have learned the tragic historical lesson that they should not have abandoned the working class and the campesinos. With regard to postmodernism, we could say that Laclau and Mouffe's political thesis has been met with resistance both from capital and from its own ideological limits. In other words, the openness of "radical democracy" has been startled with the overwhelming tenacity of the "logic" of capital. In light of the Latin American experience over the past two decades, Andrew Ross's contention that "we can no longer envisage a grand tug-of-war between Capital and Labor" can only be seen as patent idealism.[42] During these moments the "articulation of different subjects" and the alliance between the social movements in Nicaragua is torn asunder by the *historic* forces of imperialism in its *raw, material* form, as devastating as ever in its disregard for human life.

The Democratization of Art

If these internal political conflicts have been largely passed over by the Left, so too have the contradictions among different aesthetic factions in Nicaragua. Like most socialist countries (including the Soviet Union, Cuba, and China), postrevolutionary Nicaragua took on the project of socializing the modes of cultural production. Until 1988 this institutionalization of cultural democracy operated in a wide variety of art forms, including dance, music, art, poetry, and theater. The Ministry of Culture was formed shortly after the revolution, under the direction of the eminent poet Ernesto Cardenal. Artists and politicians alike agreed that culture should be accessible to all social classes and that the revolution should socialize the productive, distributive, and receptive organs within the society.[43] The key at this juncture, of course, was to devote particular attention to the development of working-class and campesino culture, not only to recognize its existence, but also to celebrate openly the value of its art. This was done with mixed results.

By 1985 critics were concerned about artistic freedom in the poetry workshops. They pointed specifically to Cardenal's seven poetic rules — designed to guide young poets — maintaining that the participants were urged to avoid metaphors and deal with the concrete events of everyday life. These opponents (Jorge Eduardo Arellano, Gioconda Belli, Juan Chow, Rosario Murillo, and others) felt that the ministry should have applied less stringent regulations in the workshops. But what clearly lay beneath the issue was a heated debate that pitted "high culture" against the democratization, or what some termed the "massification," of art. Or, to couch the debate in familiar terms: there was a conflict among the modernists, the avant-gardists, and the realists.

Throughout these debates Cardenal advocated universal access to the production and consumption of art in Nicaragua. Mayra Jiménez personally supervised the workshops and Julio Valle-Castillo was in charge of editing workshop poems that were submitted and published in *Poesía libre*, a quarterly journal. On the other hand, Rosario Murillo, then president of the ASTC (the Sandinista Association of Cultural Workers), the literary critic Jorge Eduardo Arellano, and others felt that there should be greater access to consuming and appreciating art, but not necessarily to creating it. At least on the surface, this argument implied that only the truly "gifted" could produce worthwhile poetry. In many ways it sounded as if more traditional and elitist aesthetic standards were being resurrected. However, judging from my personal interviews with several key participants in this debate, and from the October-November 1988 issue of *Envío*, it appears that the professionalists felt that the concept of popular poetry, while valid in itself, had failed in its attempt to build a democratic, grass-roots poetry movement.

Tomás Borge's seemingly neutral position on democratization may have been a little too cavalier and was typical of the general attitude toward aesthetic practice in Nicaragua. In essence, he advocated open pluralism: "Sólo es posible," he was quoted in *Envío* as saying, "la democracia cuando se cambien las formas de producción en la búsqueda de compartir con vocación de igualdad" (38) (Democracy is possible only when the forms of production are changed en route to sharing the goal of equality). Indeed, altering the means of production is paramount if a society intends to establish a socialist system. And similar changes in the cultural means of production would need to take place as well so that the working class and the campesinos — once deprived of cultural existence — would be allowed to produce, distribute, and receive art. But equality does not take an ontological course; it can go nowhere without political and economic channels, and if they have not been opened up — so that instead of depending on the good graces of the bourgeoisie for its cultural livelihood, the proletariat will determine the course of cultural affairs — then we will return to the mystification of the "free market." But the FSLN's ideological stance, perhaps because of its pluralist composition, does not stray too far from bourgeois nationalism. As Donald Hodges has noted, for Víctor Tirado, for example, the issue in Nicaragua was

> whether the people wanted dictatorship or democracy. The FSLN's objectives were democratic: overthrow of the tyrant; installation of a provisional government representative of *all social classes*; creation of a people's army in place of the elitist National Guard; formulation of an independent and nonaligned foreign policy; support for popular causes in Central American and the Caribbean. (191; my emphasis)

As I will contend, the weakness in this position lies in the plurality of social classes. To posit such an agenda immediately indicates that the working class and the campesinos who create all the value will be able to compete equitably with the bourgeoisie (on uneven ground). Likewise, the bourgeoisie will be supported by the Sandinistas and will be able—we assume by implication—to continue to amass its surplus value.

By contrast, Ernesto Cardenal's position on aesthetics and politics is more explicitly Marxist:

> Si esta revolución se hizo con la grande masa de los desposeídos, entonces el énfasis, la prioridad de nuestros esfuerzos son para ese 52% de analfabetos. La pintura primitivista, todos nos damos cuenta, es la pintura de los humildes, es la pintura que retrata el paisaje del país, de Nicaragua. Tiene así dos dimensiones: la democratización de las artes plásticas y, por otro lado, el aporte que este pueblo puede hacer a su propio país, porque el paisaje—según lo han dicho críticos autorizados—ha sido rescatado por los pintores primitivistas." (*Envío* 40–41)

> [If this revolution was carried out by the marginal masses, so the emphasis, the priority of our efforts are for that 52 percent of the illiterate. We all realize that "primitivist" painting is the painting of the disenfranchised, it is the painting that portrays the landscape of our country, of Nicaragua. Therefore it has two dimensions: the democratization of the plastic arts and, on the other hand, the support that the people can give to their own country, because the landscape—as reputable critics have said—has been rescued by the primitivist painters.]

Cardenal's concrete or exteriorist poetry—as I attempt to clarify in chapter 3—is grounded in a "materialist theology." Suffice it to say for now that his poetry is anchored in the oral tradition and that he employs photomontage techniques within the framework of a realist tradition. His personal commitment in his poetry cannot easily be disentangled from the energy he injected into the popular poetry workshops, and here his ideological position is quite clear: the political correlative of this aesthetic project is a socialist system governed by the proletariat.

The most challenging and revolutionary Sandinista aesthetic project was clearly the establishment of the popular poetry workshops. In an age of postmodernist art, it seemed to actually pose a threat to bourgeois notions of the aesthetic. For instance, the writing of the poetry was done in groups, and the poems were critiqued collectively and were not the product of the alienated subject in capitalism. Rather, recalling Marx's concept of human nature, the subject's "species being" was revived as art became a social act at the level of production. Furthermore, the participants tended to recount incidents that had taken place during the insurrection, and these personal memories were closely tied to the making—not to the shunning—of history. And, finally, these campesinos and workers were able to publish and read their poetry. Once the Ministry of Culture was closed, however, their poetic voices were silenced; their testimonies no longer appeared in *Poesía libre*.

By autumn 1988, the professionalists, or the pluralist tendency, had essentially supplanted the Ministry of Culture as the prime artistic force in Nicaragua. As for the Ministry of Culture, it was subsumed by the Ministry of Education, allegedly for economic reasons, though, as we have seen, tensions had built up between different political factions within the FSLN. Given the developments sponsored by the ASTC particularly in 1988 (when I was there), it appears that this coup d'état has encouraged professional artists of any type to participate in cultural events. There is now, however, no institution that openly has taken up the challenge of the democratization—much less now that UNO has taken hold of the political reins. Consequently, a shift has taken place: the ASTC tends to recognize and encourage those who already have artistic training and who have the leisure to continue with their vocation pretty much as they please. By implication, it is accurate to say that the working class is not fully engaging in cultural production, but the petite bourgeoisie or the bourgeoisie—artists like Pablo Antonio Cuadra, Rosario Murillo, Daisy Zamora, and Ernesto Cardenal—have continued to occupy center stage.

In *Aesthetics and Revolution* I seek out the major aesthetic tendencies that represent the revolution from their own particular class and gender formation. I then attempt to define the relationship between national and international culture by examining the mediation between Nicaraguan arts and this postmodern era and to assess these connections by analyzing thematic nodes at the intersection of sociohistorical, political, and cultural discourse, embedded as they are in the material conflict between these forces. On the whole, there is a very real sense in which the issue of aesthetic production undergoes a radical transformation in Nicaragua and the whole vertical alignment of artistic figures is disturbed. In the first years of the revolution, the petite bourgeoisie and the bourgeoisie were rudely awakened—as in the political and economic realms—by a new way of conceiving art and artists. By 1988, however, democratization had come to a halt, and the bourgeois political forces began to return to the old ways of thinking the aesthetic. The popular poetry workshops became vestiges of an idealist past that, sooner or later, had to reckon with the essentialism of bourgeois art.

The variety of aesthetic and ideological representations that emerge in this book can be variously summarized as falling within the domain of realism or avant-garde art. The former will suffer a heavy blow—as will the cause of the working class—and the latter will come out victorious. Thus, the initial revolutionary fervor begins to evaporate as the bourgeoisie and petite bourgeoisie try on new masks—now as revolutionaries, now as entrepreneurs. But it is always possible for the Sandinistas to submerge themselves in the real, material conflicts between classes once again in order to apply the lessons of history.

In light of these developments in Nicaragua, we would do well to recall a postmodern obsession of Laclau and Mouffe's discourse: the unfixity of social class. For it is quite apparent that if there is no *proletarian* revolution — in aesthetics, politics, or the economy — then the bourgeoisie would much prefer to look out for its own interests and, hence, would conveniently "forget" that it was after all the proletariat that made the revolution possible. Recent strikes in Nicaragua indicate, however, that the working class and the campesinos are not likely to allow the bourgeoisie to fall into a state of dormancy, much less with "history weighing like a nightmare on the brains of the living," as Marx remarked in *The Eighteenth Brumaire*.

CHAPTER 2
IDEOLOGICAL FLUCTUATIONS AND DESIRE IN THE POETRY OF PABLO ANTONIO CUADRA

There is little doubt that Violeta Chamorro's victory in the 1990 presidential elections in Nicaragua stunned political analysts who had predicted that the Sandinistas would surely win. One needed to have been in this Central American nation for some time to know that bourgeois sectors were brewing this coup as early as 1988. In fact, I would suggest that these changes were marked in a particular way in aesthetics. The collapse of the Ministry of Culture was emblematic of internal strife in both the economic and the ideological realms.

While it is true, as I indicated in chapter 1 that the ministry was closed because of lack of funding, the closing coincided with general unrest and disappointment in the popular poetry workshops. Within ASTC (Asociación Sandinista de Trabajadores Culturales, the Sandinista Association of Cultural Workers) itself, aesthetic factions sided with Ernesto Cardenal—the minister of culture—and with a professionalist tendency spearheaded by Rosario Murillo and Jorge Eduardo Arellano. An established and highly respected artist, Pablo Antonio Cuadra felt that art had been unnecessarily politicized during the revolution. Furthermore, his political beliefs, as I will argue in this chapter, tended to favor a vaguely defined democracy that generally falls in line with that espoused by Chamorro and the Christian Democrats. Concurrently, Cuadra attempted to blend popular with high culture. This unique kind of "populism" in both his poetry and his ideology could be seen as a nationalist vision that poses little opposition to the dictates of capitalism.

Cuadra's poetic identity is built upon his founding of the Nicaraguan *vanguardia*,[1] and in many ways his poetic corpus cannot be divorced from the sociohistorical conditions and consciousness of the 1930s and 1940s, both in his homeland and abroad. To analyze his poetry is to evaluate the relation between the Latin American and European avant-gardes and to consider the *vanguardia*'s dialectical association with the contemporary or "postmodernist" literary scene.[2] By examining this nexus, we should be able to appreciate more fully one of the most influential aesthetic theories in Nicaragua today.

Clearly, the Nicaraguan avant-garde is not a mere epiphenomenon of the European avant-garde; there are ideological peculiarities that separate the two, just as there are discrepancies and oddities that distinguish different movements within the European avant-garde from one another (the dadaists from the surrealists, the latter from the futurists, the anarchist from the Marxist wing, the proponents of formal fetishism — or "pure" art — from those who attempted to institute radical changes in both form and content, etc.). Yet, as we will see, the Nicaraguan *vanguardia* essentially differed from its European counterpart because the country — like most Latin American nations from the 1920s through the Second World War — was economically and politically on the periphery in relation to the United States and Europe. This status in what was becoming a rapidly growing international industrial economy left an indelible imprint on social imagination, that is, on Nicaraguans' perception of their country and the rest of the world.

The poetry written in Nicaragua at this historical juncture is marked with signs of industrialization, class antagonism, the decline of religion as a social force, the division between city and country, nationalism, and the racial and historical origins of the Nicaraguan people. What sets poetry in Latin America, and particularly in Nicaragua, apart from its European counterpart is its more overt reference to these issues. This poetry, however, was written from the perspective of a bourgeoisie that would feel the repercussions of decisions made abroad and that was attempting to wrest political and economic power away from foreign interests such as the United States. Thus, while we could say that Nicaraguan poetry emerged from the bourgeois class and its efforts at defining itself, and that major characteristics of the avant-garde were shared by Europeans and Latin Americans, the manner in which the sociohistorical and political circumstances of this modernization were interpreted differed greatly. Briefly stated, while Latin Americans leaned toward a nationalist reading of this period (as a moment in which modernization was to touch dependent nations as well), they could never conceive of this historical period as strictly Latin American.[3]

Fascism, Nationalism, and the Nicaraguan *Vanguardia*

> *National consciousness, instead of being the all-embracing crystallization of the innermost hopes of the whole people, instead of being the immediate and most obvious result of the mobilization of the people, will be in any case only an empty shell, a crude and fragile travesty of what it might have been. The faults that we find in it are quite sufficient explanation of the facility with which, when dealing with young and independent nations, the nation is passed over for the race, and the tribe is preferred to the state. These are the cracks in the edifice which show the process of retrogression, that is so harmful and prejudicial to national effort and national unity.*
>
> Frantz Fanon, *The Wretched of the Earth*

José Coronel Urtecho, a cofounder of the *vanguardia* between 1927 and 1932, has openly discussed the movement's political ideology and the way his own ideology has since changed. *Vanguardia* members Manolo Cuadra, Luis Alberto Cabrales, Pablo Antonio Cuadra, Joaquín Pasos, and Urtecho—all of them from bourgeois, liberal, anticlerical families—felt that Nicaragua needed to break with traditional oligarchical rule and engage actively in capitalist modernization. The most efficient means to this end, they reasoned, was to support strong rule and not to relinquish power to the masses, since, according to Urtecho, that would lead to chaos: "Pensábamos que nosotros necesitábamos un gobierno estable, salir de la lucha por el poder . . . que es lo que ha producido todas las guerras civiles que han sido el mal endémico de Nicaragua"[4] (We thought that we needed a stable government, to depart from the struggle for power . . . which is what has produced all the civil wars that have been the endemic sickness of Nicaragua). The movement was at a volatile stage and its participants were searching for an ideology that would challenge them intellectually and politically.

Formulating an ideology at this historical moment meant they had to choose between polarized extremes that were the product of the international class struggle: fascism and communism. The stock market crash of 1929 and the accompanying worldwide depression sent people scrambling for new solutions to these acute economic problems. In the Soviet Union the pursuit of industrialization in a nearly feudal society led to the creation of a bureaucratic state apparatus that began to distance itself from the original bolshevik socialist plans set forth after the 1917 revolution. In Germany, roaring inflation was a chief cause of an opposite—yet still exceedingly centralized—state apparatus: national socialism. It was the United States' strategic and economic interests, coupled with internal, nationalist armed opposition to those interests, that most affected political ideology. As U.S. military pressure mounted and the government continued to bolster the National Guard so that American troops would no longer be needed in Nicaragua, resentment to foreign intervention built up. The most popular manifestation of political disenchantment with this state of affairs crystallized, on the one hand, around Augusto César Sandino's peasant revolt and, on the other, around the military forces led by General José María Moncada that had decided to collaborate with the U.S. government. Even when Moncada won the United States-supervised 1928 election, the political situation only became more critical. From 1927 to 1933 Sandino obstinately and successfully fought government troops and U.S. Marines.[5] What certainly influenced political persuasions was the White House's refusal to grant self-determination to Nicaraguans. Once the United States had openly intervened in political and economic affairs and the bourgeoisie had determined that class collaboration was not a viable option, multiclass alliances could be consolidated.

The *vanguardistas*, of bourgeois extraction, were interested in promoting incipient nationalism—perhaps unconsciously supporting the values of their social class. During these times of economic duress, the bourgeoisie backed an authoritarian alternative to "chaos" (the label applied to any vital threat to the system). According to Urtecho, given the threat that Sandino posed as a representative of the popular peasant revolt, the bourgeoisie supported Anastacio Somoza: "La verdad es que a Somoza lo apoyó casi todo el mundo burgués" (94) (The truth is that most of the bourgeosie supported Somoza). This political swing to the right, saving the bourgeoisie's political and economic interests, took place in Spain, Italy, and Germany as well. The *vanguardia*'s political stance, however, wavered between a monarchist absolutism, based on Maurras's monarchist revival in France, and blatant fascism, especially akin to Francoism. Francisco de Asís Fernández maintains that the *vanguardia*'s resurrected offspring, the Betrayed Generation, which included Pablo Antonio Cuadra and José Coronel Urtecho, continued to support and promote reactionary politics as late as 1962.[6] It should be noted, however, that both these poets now openly distance themselves from their extremism of the 1920s and 1930s. They contend that these right-wing persuasions reflect a romantic oscillation of interests, of beliefs held momentarily during their youth. Cuadra claims that the motivation came from Urtecho: "He got us into a political venture that now seems absurd to me. I was never very sympathetic to the reactionary utopia that Coronel spoke to us about with a fantastic array of verbal and ideological pyrotechnics."[7]

Support for Sandino, on the other hand, seems incompatible with the political and aesthetic ideology that the *vanguardistas* espoused. Understandably, the bourgeoisie felt that the fight against U.S. intervention in Nicaragua would give them more economic, political, and cultural influence. Thus, it is not surprising that Sandino's popular, nationalist insurrection would work in the interests of the bourgeoisie, in spite of the ideological differences that separated both nationalist tendencies. In referring to the link between *sandinismo* and the *vanguardia*, Cuadra has commented:

Sentíamos un cambio universal que nos obligaba a verter nuestro canto— nuestro mensaje—en forma nueva; en una lengua poética que inconscientemente robábamos al futuro o quizás a los incandescentes y misteriosos custodios de la belleza. Por otra parte, y agravando esta necesidad inefable de creación, sentíamos el enorme vacío de una Nicaragua inexpresada, en los mismos momentos en que el sacudimiento nacionalista de Sandino conmovía nuestros iniciales, puros y ardientes amores patrios.[8]

[We felt a universal change that forced us to spill our song—our message—in a new way, in a poetic language that we were unconsciously stealing from the future or maybe from incandescent and mysterious custodians of beauty. On the other hand, and aggravating this ineffable need for creation, we felt an enormous emptiness of an unexpressed Nicaragua, in the moments in which Sandino's nationalist tremors moved our initially pure and burning patriotic love.]

This passage seems to suggest that the *vanguardia* was not particularly interested in Sandino's political platform, but rather in the geographic and demographic repercussions. During this period of intense industrialization in Europe and the United States, this aesthetic group thought that Nicaragua should also launch itself into "modernization." But as Cuadra's poetry makes clear, they simultaneously attempted to recover their historical and cultural heritage by exploring the countryside and the life of the campesino, the Mayan past, the mestizo legacy, and so on. In other words, in response to the globalization of capital, the *vanguardistas* turned to the issue of national identity. It is apparent that one of the projects that the *vanguardistas* held in common with *sandinismo* was nationalism. Sandino's ideology, however, was anchored in the plight of the campesinos and the oppressed and in anti-imperialism, and did not entertain any ideas of including the intelligentsia. Sergio Ramírez has said: "La visión de nación de Sandino, parte de su irreductible posición de ser parte de un pueblo oprimido y de realizar la guerra desde el pueblo, con un ejército 'de trabajadores y campesinos que aman a su país. Los intelectuales nos han traicionado y a causa de ello hemos tenido que empuñar las armas.' "[9] (Sandino's national vision begins with his irreducible position of being part of an oppressed people and of carrying out this people's war with an army "of workers and campesinos who love their country. The intellectuals have betrayed us and, consequently, we have had to take up arms"). Nonetheless, it appears that the *vanguardistas* continued to support the peasant uprising, as did other segments of the population. As Anastacio Somoza García began to concentrate enormous wealth in his own hands, encroaching upon bourgeois territory as he did so, the opposition began to increase. In fact, Cuadra was arrested in 1956 for having worked on the opposition's newspaper—then, as now, *La Prensa* (White 27). Thus, if the *vanguardia* did side with neofascist politics at the very beginning, they then veered in the direction of political democracy (in the Christian Democratic tradition) and worked with the FSLN to depose Somoza, as Cuadra has remarked:

We collaborated with the Revolution. We participated in it. We produced all the propaganda possible in the most subtle but constant way to favor the revolutionary movement's getting rid of Somoza. That means we were allies of the Frente Sandinista. We knew all the commanders of the Revolution. With some of them, such as Tomás Borge, I maintained clandestine relations. This was our Revolution, made possible by everyone. (White 27)

We can see, then, that Cuadra supported at least the nationalist tendency within the Sandinista revolution. In contrast to Cardenal, as a member of the bourgeoisie Cuadra supported the interests of his class and opposed, as I will demonstrate, the socialist direction of revolutionary Nicaragua. Examining his poetry, one finds that it is in this strong correlation between poetry and politics in Nicaragua that his class and political positions are articulated. Throughout his work there is an insistence that the arts can somehow be isolated from the political, the social, and the historical. The "autonomous" domain in which his poetry evolves consists of a more orthodox Roman Catholicism that places few barriers in the way of the desires of the bourgeoisie.

Poetic Authority in *Vanguardista* Poetry

> *Torres de Dios*
>
> Pablo Antonio Cuadra

As perhaps could be expected, poetry during the 1930s and 1940s could not help but absorb at least a reified representation of this historical and political moment. Pablo Antonio Cuadra describes this process by placing the poet at the forefront of ethical development in society. As we shall see, in Cuadra this messianic impulse clearly gives the poet a privileged place as spokesperson for the rest of society. This conceptualization appears to derive from Cuadra's ideological background, his strong Catholic upbringing in a bourgeois setting. Attending Jesuit schools as a child instilled in him an intellectual appetite that he still has not lost. But his mystical experiences are expressed hierarchically in poetry, where he finds in traditional Catholicism the eternal faith that he needs in order to make sense of his life. Unlike Cardenal, he feels that the imperfection of human beings, beginning with original sin, prevents them from creating the proverbial heaven on earth. For Cuadra the promised land is rather a symbol of paradise lost, where the soul encounters Christ once more. He attempts to go through mystical stages of faith in which the believer abandons his or her intellectual pursuits in favor of the everlasting love of Christ. Thus, in "Poetas de la torre: Memorias del movimiento 'vanguardia' " (Poets of the tower: Memories of the *vanguardia* movement), naming is something magical and hermetic, divine and prophetic. By extension, the poet is a prophet or spiritual leader who manages to interpret "esa evasión de lo indeciso, de lo caótico sobre el gran instrumento del espíritu: la Palabra"

(*Torres* 155–56) (that evasion of the indecisive, of the chaotic over the grand instrument of the spirit: the word). Poetry becomes a spiritual vehicle, a religious practice. What is illuminating about this poetic theory is its collusion with a neo-Hobbesian political absolutism. For, in spite of the *vanguardia's* ideological vacillation between left- and right-wing solutions to Nicaragua's economic underdevelopment, a single mythic (and authoritarian) figure — either Somoza or Sandino—is consistently projected as a panacea.

The commonality underlying *somocismo* and *sandinismo* is quite clearly nationalism. Thus, it should come as little surprise that several of Somoza's ardent supporters within the *vanguardia* later drifted over to *sandinismo* because it also offered a species of bourgeois nationalism, but without the oligarchical garb. The bourgeoisie saw in Sandino's political project the possibility of emancipating itself and the petite bourgeoisie, or of finally gaining control of the political and economic systems. Other members of the *vanguardia* apparently were taken by Sandino's anarchocommunism, perhaps not being fully aware of the consequences of their stance.

Despite early enthusiasm for conservative authoritarian politics among *vanguardia* members, not all continued in the same tradition. A reading of the poetry of Joaquín Pasos and Manolo Cuadra reveals the contradictions plaguing the movement. Both poets apparently flirted with fascism at an early age, but their later poetry bears the seeds of *sandinismo* and the socialist ideas of the FSLN. Cuadra, in fact, joined the Partido de Trabajadores Nicaragüenses (PTN, the Nicaraguan Workers' Party), which later evolved into the Socialist Party (*Poesía política* 9). In the case of Pasos particularly, it appears to be quite likely that he was more attracted to the anarchist tendency within *sandinismo* than to the communist influence.[10] Cuadra articulates a more consciously socialist ideology in "La admonición gritada en las esquinas" (Admonition yelled on the street corners):

> Que no haya división, que no haya casta
> de rico y pobre entre la pobre gente.
> Es la hora roja del iconoclasta:
> Hora del llanto y del crujir de dientes.
>
> Hora de huevos podridos y gengibres
> y de mujeres con los brazos en jarras;
> hora de pueblos libres
> que al fin han soltado sus amarras.
> (*Poesía política* 54)

> [That there be no divisions, no castes
> of rich and poor among the poor people.

It is the red hour of the iconoclast:
An hour of weeping and gritting one's teeth.

Hour of rotten eggs and *gengibres*
and of women with their arms in pitchers;
Hour of free peoples
Who have finally untied the rope that binds them.]

Here Manolo Cuadra calls for an end to class division by challenging the system that perpetuates antagonism. Unlike Pablo Antonio Cuadra and José Coronel Urtecho, he moves beyond nationalism as a political solution, calling instead for socialism and for armed struggle. Red refers to socialists and to the blood they shed in battle. In less explicit political language, Joaquín Pasos defines the ideological beliefs of the *vanguardia* movement. On the one hand, he speaks out against U.S. imperialism in poems such as "Canción de proveeduría" (Song for providing) and "Desocupación pronta, y si es necesario violenta" (Sudden unemployment, and if necessary a violent one). On the other hand, he assumes an oppositional nationalist stance. While there are socialist symbols in this poem, the last four verses, in particular, resonate in a more anti-imperialist, nationalist tone. In that respect, he evokes many of the political interests of a bourgeoisie that demanded self-determination to such a degree that they supported the quasi-populist candidate Anastacio Somoza for president. In the following poem, Pasos dresses nationalism in avant-gardist humor, play, and irony, as if the poet were mocking the bourgeoisie even as he assumes their role:

Los aviones
estadounidenses
salen a repartir
bombones
a los inditos nicaragüenses.[11]

[The North American
airplanes
leave to distribute
bonbons
to the little Nicaraguan Indians.]

We know from *Poemas de un joven* (Poems by a young man, posthumously published in 1986) that this Indian poet identifies with his native people. Here, however, he assumes a non-Indian point of view in order to coyly mimic the paternalistic mentality of imperialism. By employing the diminutive "inditos" and playing with the word "bombones" — describing bombs as bonbons — the speaker implies that these instruments of human destruction are gifts for children. The reader is immediately distanced from the speaker's cynicism and senses the violence that is a part of imperialism. In "Revolución por el descubrimiento del mar" (Revolution through the rediscovery of the sea) Pasos also burrows his way into bourgeois consciousness and plays out its ideological contradictions:

> [uno] siente pasar el viento de una revolución
> cada diez años sucede lo mismo
> dos o tres pájaros son los que comienzan el movimiento
> que es apoyado por todos los pájaros de la comarca
> y que termina siempre en un invierno copioso,
> pero ahora la cosa es distinta, dicen los chocoyos. (40)

> [one feels the wind of a revolution pass by
> every ten years the same thing happens
> two or three birds start the movement
> that is supported by all of the birds of the region
> and that always finishes in a duplicate winter
> but now the thing is different, so say the *chocoyos*.]

The political allegory is quite clear. The birds (the campesinos) are organizing and preparing for armed conflict, but the speaker does not seem too concerned because every ten years or so they have been known to repeat these disturbances. As in the previous poem, the speaker assumes the perspective of the antagonistic class, the bourgeoisie, and his political näiveté points to this class's social isolation: "he oído hablar de revoluciones en Nicaragua, / pero yo no sabía lo que era una revolución, / sólo supe que los liberales y conservadores eran / babosos" (40) (I have heard them speak of revolutions in Nicaragua, / but I didn't know what a revolution was, / I only found out that the liberals and conservatives were / fools). The speaker is not able to sublimate the conflict that is exploding around him. Rather, this "useless" revolution — as Cuadra calls it in the final verses of the poem — becomes bottled up in his consciousness:

> los que hicieron esta inútil revolution — inútil como todas
>   las inútiles revoluciones nicaragüenses —,
> pero que estalla fuera y dentro de mí con la violencia de
>   cien mil pájaros migratorios

que yo trato en vano de calmar mientras sonrío y me
    pongo a leer. (41)

[those who made this useless revolution—useless like
    all useless Nicaraguan revolutions—,
but that explodes outside and inside of me with the violence of
    one hundred migrating birds
that I try in vain to calm while I smile and I
    begin to read.]

The revolution causes reverberations and commotions that reach and disturb the person who would rather quietly escape from the outside world. Perhaps Pasos was trying to convey vividly the ideological levity that characterized his earlier life, when he was secretary of protocol under Somoza. According to Ernesto Cardenal, his alliance with the far right was short-lived, and he soon decided to join the opposition: "Joaquín Pasos era muy nicaragüense y muy humorista y fue uno de los principales opositores de Somoza usando únicamente como arma el humor y la risa" ("Prólogo," *Poemas de un joven* 16) (Joaquín Pasos was very Nicaraguan and a grand humorist and was one of the principal opposition leaders against Somoza, using humor and laughter as his only weapons). As a member of the left-leaning faction within the *vanguardia*, Pasos—after having traversed a purely nationalist position—began to distance himself from those within the movement who had either held onto *somocismo* or taken a liberal (petit bourgeois) stance.

While absolutism as an ideology was an integral part of the early *vanguardia* political orientation, as time went on, these poets, most notably Manolo Cuadra and Joaquín Pasos, saw the need to abandon the neofascist direction in which they were headed and that is written into the *vanguardia* manifesto: "Emprender la conquista del público apoderándonos de su atención por medio de golpes de estado artísticos, del escándolo intelectual, de la crítica agresiva, de la batalla literaria, de la descarada exposición de arte moderno" (*Torres* 170) (To begin the conquest of the public by overpowering their attention through artistic coup d'états, through intellectual scandals, through aggressive criticism, through literary wars, through the insolent exposition of modern art).

The language of this manifesto is indicative of the political movements of the historical period, which included internal divisions within the bourgeoisie, threats to bourgeois economic and political hegemony by the Soviet Union, the organization of labor unions and left-wing political parties (as well as polarized, authoritarian alternatives), and qualitative leaps in capitalist modernization. Like most politically conservative European artistic tendencies of this time ("pure" poetry, for instance), the Nicaraguan *vanguardia* aimed at creating a separate realm, establishing a technologically "new" art that would keep pace with the First World. They hoped that their art would liberate Nicaraguans in the aesthetic domain as Sandino was to free them in the political domain. Art during this period in Nicaragua was grossly inflated, until it was essentially deified, until it became a force that persuasively acted upon material conditions:

> [Estamos] dedicándonos con todo empeño y valentía, si es necesario con heroísmo, a la creación de la poesía nacional, del teatro nacional, de la pintura, de la escultura, de la música y de la arquitectura nacionales, sin tomar en cuenta el mal gusto de los ricos, los prejuicios de los académicos, las burlas de los pedantes y la indiferencia de los pobres. Desconocemos la palabra imposible; queremos hacer uso de todos los medios, *hasta de la dinamita y del fusil literarios para emprender nuestra revolución incurenta, que es más noble, más gloriosa, que las sangrientas revoluciones partidaristas*, más útil que las obesas hartazones comercialistas. (*Torres* 171, my emphasis)

> [Dedicating ourselves in a determined and courageous way, if necessary, heroically, to the creation of national poetry, national theater, painting, sculpture, music and to national architecture without taking into account the bad taste of the rich, the judgments of the academics, the deceit of the pedants, and the indifference of the poor. We don't recognize the word *impossible*. We want to take advantage of all the means, *even literary dynamite and guns, in order to carry out our inward-flowing revolution, which is more noble, more glorious than the bloody partisan revolutions*, more useful than the tired, obese merchants.]

This statement indicates the contradictions living on in the *vanguardia*'s political and aesthetic position. While members of the Nicaraguan avant-garde now plainly dissociate themselves from these days of reactionary militancy, having since become strong supporters of "liberal democracy," the relics of the past give testimony to the intersection of politics and aesthetics in the 1920s and 1930s, in addition to providing an understanding of Anastacio Somoza's rise to power and of the broad coalitions that contested his rule. What is also pertinent in the manifesto is the militaristic terminology that is employed and the way that it prefigures the armed repression of the dictatorship.[12] Yet the military struggle takes place in language and does not occur in the sociopolitical realm. The rhetorical revolution, as Cuadra indicates, is more glorious than actual political battles. The *vanguardistas* are calling for a type of pure poetry that somehow is autonomous from the political realm but absorbs its technological and aggressive language. This posture helps to explain their collusion with authoritarianism.

This aesthetic and political stance in Nicaraguan letters has noteworthy antecedents: namely, the renowned *modernista* poet Rubén Darío.

Cuadra's Poetics in the Latin American Context

Any understanding of the poetics of Pablo Antonio Cuadra requires some knowledge of his relation to Rubén Darío, a central figure of Nicaraguan and Latin American poetry. This comparison reveals an "anxiety of influence" felt by Cuadra and the *vanguardistas* in relation to Darío's highly innovative and provocative poetic corpus. In the terms of Harold Bloom's lyrical Freudianism, we could say that Cuadra "swerved" in order to avoid the shadows of his precursor, creating his own poetics. By partly discarding Darío's highly learned verse in favor of what Jorge Eduardo Arellano has called neo-populism, the younger poet established a new direction in Nicaraguan poetry. Arellano misjudges Cuadra's literary achievement, however, by considering him only as a populist poet,[13] for his unique contribution to Nicaraguan poetry and his status in Latin American literature depend upon a sort of dialogic relation between poetry and ideology. He is neither a populist nor a "learned" artist, but rather is representative of a process that took place in Latin American literature as early as the 1940s, in which, as Carlos Monsiváis has observed, high culture appropriated the forms and language of low culture.[14] As a result of incorporating both, Cuadra perhaps brings into question both poetic tendencies, while simultaneously shedding light on his own ideological "flexibility." Rather than exclusively employing the formal devices and language of high culture, he attempts to recuperate the oral tradition and blend it with his classical poetic tradition. Yet Cuadra does not fully break with modernist representation (or "high culture") either, because his poetry obscures the sociopolitical and collective past.

While this modernist discourse could be seen as part of Rubén Darío's poetic practice, it is even more prominent in Cuadra. As I noted earlier, this interest in popular culture on the part of the *vanguardia* consciously responded to the sociopolitical unrest of the 1930s. Sandino's campesino uprising ostensibly inspired the artists to lend their support to what they perceived to be a nationalist revolution. Pursuing Sandino's mission in the realm of art, they adopted popular language and customs and attempted to recover their national roots. Cuadra and José Coronel Urtecho were the initiators of this poetic movement, Cuadra having been the more successful in implementing this theoretical stance in the actual practice of poetry. Both felt a need to consider the magnitude of Rubén Darío's esoteric poetry in this search for a model.

Contrary to his romantic predecessors, Darío rationally and meticulously constructed his poetic discourse, including classical references and adding musicality, alliteration, and, above all, harmony to his verses. During a period of burgeoning industrial capitalism, the exaltation of the scientific method, the displacement of the countryside, and the acute alienation of the subject, art commonly took for its subject changes in world production. One thinks of the hope that radiates from Diego Rivera's murals of the working class or Fritz Lang's haunting portrayal of the oppressive ills of the metropolis. Yet, as Walter Benjamin has eloquently shown in his analysis of Baudelaire, the open contradictions of this socioeconomic period are also recorded in a dialectical fashion in art. The *modernista* poetry of Rubén Darío, as well as that of his successor, Pablo Antonio Cuadra, reveals the complexity of the formation of consciousness during this historical moment. The tensions between religion and science, the emergence and stratification of the industrial proletariat, and the division between the countryside and the city, for instance, were all manifested, in a mediated form, in the social imagination.

Both Darío and Cuadra opted for a reification of nature, of the countryside, while paradoxically attempting to both include and transcend regional space. On the one hand, this universalist impulse coincided with the development of the world economy and of the international bourgeoisie, and, on the other hand, it negated the local or national exploration that they carried out. Similarly, both artists injected their verses with a deific harmony and unity, while still representing dichotomies that were a part of the everyday life of the bourgeoisie. Angel Rama has noted this in the case of Darío:

Hacia donde mire, el poeta registra el desorden del universo, la injusticia de la sociedad, la subversión de los valores, una desarmonía generalizada que parece regir a la propia naturaleza y permitiría enjuiciar incluso a Dios. Lo que el poeta ve es la contradicción que se ha instaurado en la sociedad, al separarse dos órdenes que estaban unidos y que se siguen enseñando como unidos: por un lado las creencias tradicionales, los modos externos o públicos, las palabras y los ritos que componen los valores de una sociedad y por el otro los comportamientos reales de quienes ejercen aquellas mismas creencias, modos y palabras. Como fue norma del tiempo, observa la contradicción desde un ángulo moral, más que social, pues era la moral el único absoluto que parecía firme después del temporal antirreligioso del positivismo, para medir el funcionamiento de los seres humanos.[15]

[No matter where he looks, the poet registers the disorder of the universe, the injustice of the society, the subversion of values, a general lack of harmony that appeared to govern nature and would allow them to judge God himself. What the poet sees is the contradiction that has been established in society when two orders separate that were once united and keep showing themselves as united: on the one hand traditional beliefs, the external or public modes, the words and rituals that make up the values of a society and on the other hand, the real behavior of those who exercise those same

beliefs, manners, and words. As a norm of the day, he observes the contradiction from a moral angle, rather than a social one, because morality
was the only absolute that seemed to be intact after the antireligious moment of positivism, in order to measure the way human beings functioned.]

The poet projects an idealism and harmony onto this world in conflict, where
the disintegration of so many nineteenth-century conceptions of the subject
is being absorbed. In the case of both Darío and Cuadra, the assimilation of
the changes is inscribed in their poetry as a superimposed (bourgeois)
representation. This is particularly true in the case of Cuadra. In *Poemas
nicaragüenses* he begins, on a formal level, to include in his verses popular
legends, songs, and folklore, which complement the thematical recording of
a peasant revolt. Cuadra transgresses the parameters of classical poetry and
appropriates popular culture in his verses. This general thrust contrasts with
the strictly idealist tendencies in his poetry, to which I briefly alluded earlier.
Darío did write socially conscious poetry in his later works, but much of his
production is metalinguistic and self-referential. He relies almost exclusively
on his idealistic representation of the world as an enclosed structure com-
parable to Hegel's Absolute Spirit.

Cuadra's poetics, then, affirms both the political nature of art, especially
during the 1930s and 1940s, and a rupture with literary formalism. He does
not solely delve into the intricate details of language, as Vicente Huidobro,
for example, was wont to do, nor does he infuse his poetry with the political
militancy of Pablo Neruda or the later César Vallejo. Instead, the Nicaraguan's poetry seeks to describe the historical roots of Latin American identity
and to explore its roots in language. In that respect, Cuadra aligns himself
with Octavio Paz as a philosopher attempting to explain Latin American
subjectivity in an age of imperialism. With this essentialist approach comes
the peril of generalization. For instance, as in Paz's works, Cuadra suggests
that the pre-Columbian past looms over the present and is somehow intrinsi-
cally embedded in indigenous life today.

An Overview of Cuadra's Poetic Work

In 1983 the publishing house Libro Libre in San José, Costa Rica began to
publish Pablo Antonio Cuadra's complete works in consultation with the author.[16] Publishing not only his previous books but also poems that appeared
in a variety of journals but had never been compiled in a book form, they have
nearly created a different configuration of Cuadra's work. This means that, as
with other distinguished poets, most notably Jorge Luis Borges and Octavio
Paz, the reader must reexamine the historical coordinates and take into con-

sideration the possible rewritings and omissions in the act of reading. Having outlined the boundaries, I will now briefly explain the importance of Cuadra's books of poetry as they relate to history and to his own biography.

The first volume to appear in print includes *Canciones de pájaro y señora* (Songs of birds and women, 1927–31; available only in manuscript form before) with his first actual book of poetry, *Poemas nicaragüenses* (1930–33). Both of these works can be regarded as being at the heart of the vanguardist literary and political project, that is, they attempt to work popular forms (the *corrido*, for instance) into the poetic body itself. Far ranging in their topical selection, the poems in this book include love poems, which occupy the first section, children's fables, in the second part, and openly political poetry in the final segment of this volume. The theoretical thrust of *Canciones* is summed up in the first verses of "Ars poética":

> Volver es necesario
> a la fuente del canto:
> encontrar la poesía de las cosas corrientes,
> cantar para cualquiera
> con el tono ordinario
> que se usa en el amor (88)

> [It is necessary to return
> to the source of the song:
> to find poetry in daily things,
> to sing for anyone
> with the ordinary tone
> that is used in love]

Written in 1930, this poem reflects the mood of the times at least as far as the *vanguardistas* are concerned. The concerns that surface in this poem are clearly related to the need for a type of populism that will not alienate the masses. No mention is made here of campesinos writing poetry or generally participating in cultural production, but it is suggested that those who do create—the avant-garde—should take this sector of the population into account. Significantly, this artistic plan comes into effect at the exact moment at which Sandino has begun fighting in the mountains, having given up on the intellectuals altogether (as I mentioned earlier). Hence, the bourgeois intelligentsia apparently realizes that the oligarchy will only continue to accumulate economic and political power at the expense of the bourgeoisie and the campesinos, and that the latter are essential to any class alliance against the oligarchy. Thus a type of "populist" appropriation of the campesinos' political, economic, and — in the case of the *vanguardia* — cultural power is seized and later consolidated and betrayed by Anastacio Somoza.[17]

This explains why one finds in Cuadra's first two books of poetry an apparent political and artistic ambivalence. On the one hand there is an appeal to popular or campesino culture and the anti-imperialist or nationalist poems that punctuate the poetic corpus ("USMC" and "Intervención" in *Canciones* and "El viejo motor" and "Poema de momentos" in *Poemas*). On the other hand, the poet's own commitment to anti-imperialism is clearly more linguistic than it is political.[18] Indeed, one of the last poems in *Canciones*, "Mis dos pies" (My two feet), in a confessional style, spells out Cuadra's political dilemma very clearly: "El pie de Pablo trae el camino de la tradición / El pie de Antonio abre el camino a la liberación" (104–5) (Pablo's foot brings with it the road to tradition / Antonio's foot opens the road to liberation). Throughout Cuadra's poetry, and not just in this first volume, the traditional (oligarchical) ties vie with the ideas of the new bourgeoisie, and the poet's ideological stance fluctuates between the two.

The next two books of poetry represent an inward stage of Cuadra's life. In both *Cuadernos del sur* (Notebooks from the south, 1935) and *Canto temporal* (Temporal song, 1943) the poet is clearly battling with himself and with the meaning of life. The first poems in *Cuadernos* testify to the speaker's extreme sense of alienation; he seems unable to bear what he perceives as "la soledad inmensa de historia" (the immense solitude of history). As Cuadra travels abroad, geographical space takes center stage while the individual, although demarcated, is swallowed up in its overwhelming presence. Part of this sense of alienation could be a result of the poet's being lost in a maze where creativity is nowhere in sight (see "Nubes andinas" [Andean clouds]). This hopeless situation is subsequently interrupted by his appreciating the "mystery" of South American nature and of the Creator ("Inauguración" [Inauguration]). Although he will record his struggle for meaning poetically, personally, and politically, Cuadra will not emerge from this crisis until after World War II in his return to religion in *Libro de horas* (Book of hours, 1946–54). In *Canto* Cuadra's personal and political crisis becomes even more acute, reaching its climax in poem IV and then giving way to traditional Catholic imagery. It is through this return to Christianity, to morals, and to a martyrlike role as poet ("Dadle al poeta — dirían — la palma del martirio"), 48 [Give the poet — they would say — the palm leaf of martyrdom]), that Cuadra is able to give meaning to human existence.

The third volume in Cuadra's complete works includes *Poemas con un crepúsculo a cuestas* (Poems with dusk on my back, 1949–56), *Epigramas* (Epigrams, 1957–63), and *El jaguar y la luna* (The jaguar and the moon, 1958–59). The first of these is even more introspective and self-congratulatory than the three previous books. Among the self-indulgent poems it includes are "Auto sonet," "The Angel" (Cuadra himself), and "Pablo and Antonio." Having come out of his existential crisis, the poet here seemingly swings to the opposite extreme: he is a martyr, religiously devout. Written coterminously with Cardenal's *Epigramas*, Cuadra's poems also focus on the objective of attacking the tyrant (Anastacio Somoza) and differ little from Cardenal's. The most important of the works contained in the third volume is *El jaguar*. The poet did extensive research and reading on the ancient Central American Mayan and Aztec civilizations in order to craft his poems. By intercalating Mayan and Aztec mythology with contemporary history, Cuadra attempts to resurrect his interest in remembering Nicaraguan historical roots and popular culture while denouncing the cruelty of *somocismo*. Thus, for instance, he portrays both the ancient Aztecs and contemporary Nicaraguans as searching out a freedom that they are being denied. However, for all his praise of these ancient civilizations, of the common people ("Una nueva cerámica india" [A new Indian ceramics]), and of the historical tradition, history itself becomes a species of myth that is more ephemeral than it is a real, palpable process that has had a tremendous impact on contemporary life in Nicaragua. So Cuadra indicates in a poem dedicated to the hieroglyphs on a Mayan temple: "In the hieroglyph / of pure existence / my signs / come from oblivion / and head toward the ineffable" (71). In spite of this, it is important to observe that in Cuadra's poetic work, *El jaguar* marks a qualitatively different type of poetry that relies on historical research.

Perhaps the most significant volume published to date is *Canto de Cifar y del mar dulce* (Cifar's Song and the sweet sea, 1969–79). Returning to the epic tradition as the basis for his poetry, Cuadra expresses himself through carpe diem, political, and metapoetical themes. As is all too common in Cuadra's work, his love poems tend to equate a woman directly with nature so that she often becomes the object of pleasure as she stands in symbolically for reproduction, purity, lust, and so forth. ("La doncella" [The fair lady] is a case in point). His poetry also begins to take on some anti-imperialist overtones; his attacks concentrate on the abuse of power and the yearning for freedom (see for example "Oda al viento de septiembre" [Ode to the September wind]). Sexism can be discerned in Cuadra's symbolism: woman is night, she is mysterious, ephemeral, the muse. It is the metapoetic tendency that receives most of the attention in *Canto de Cifar*: "Sé que es eterno / o poesía / lo pasajero" (119) (I know it is eternal / or poetry / this fleeting moment).

Esos rostros que asoman en la multitud (Those faces that become visible in the crowd, 1964–75) constitutes one of Cuadra's most committed efforts to align himself with the common person, as the title itself indicates. As political tension mounts in Nicaragua and then, in 1972, the earthquake devastates the capital, Cuadra feels impelled to denounce political injustice, whether it is U.S. imperialism ("USMC," 28) or *somocismo* ("Catalino Flores", 52). Unlike his earlier poetry in this respect and also in its narrative form, *Esos rostros* gains maximum expression as the voice of the liberal opposition to the oligarchy. This major part of the book (by the same title) leads into a series of homages to various poets, to the artist Joan Miró, and, significantly, to Leonel Ruga-ma.[19] In the "homenajes" Cuadra utilizes a vanguardist narrative type poetry that places weight on thematic continuity and on spatial distribution.

Other than *Tun—la ronda del año* (Tun—as the year passes, 1988), which I will analyze in greater depth later in this chapter, his most recent work is *Siete árboles contra el atardecer* (Seven trees against the sunset), written during the tumultuous years of 1977–78. This work joins *El jaguar y la luna* as an extension of Cuadra's research on Mayan civilization in light of the historical events of this time. Here Cuadra finds in the ancients the seeds of popular liberation from domination. Perhaps the most powerful of these poems is "El jícaro" (The head), which is dedicated to the memory of Cuadra's dear friend Pedro Joaquín Chamorro, editor-in-chief of *La Prensa* and a well-known liberal leader of opposition to Somoza. Employing Mayan historical imagery, the poet portrays his assassinated friend as a martyr who is resurrected in the midst of the mounting opposition to authoritarianism. A similar thematic interweaving between the Mayan past and contemporary Nicaragua is achieved in "El cacao" (Cacao), in which Cuadra recreates the genealogy that stretches from the Mayan cultural meaning of cacao to the Spanish exploitation of it as money after the conquest to the dance for dollars on Wall Street. This collection of poems was first published in Caracas, Venezuela, in 1980 to honor the Nicaraguan revolution. Although they were written before the revolution and Cuadra could not have predicted the outcome that would cause him to leave the country in voluntary exile, it is interesting to turn to the editors' preface to this volume to understand what political stance Cuadra and the editors took with respect to the revolution ex post facto. This should provide us with the insight needed to analyze a representative work such as *Tun—la ronda del año*:

No se vislumbraba todavía el giro que iban a tomar quienes cogían las riendas del poder, pues aún ocultaban los designios de instalar una dictadura totalitaria, a la cual se enfrenta hoy en día Cuadra con la misma entereza y dignidad con que lo hizo contra el autoritarismo somociano.

[There was no foreshadowing yet of the about face that those who took hold of the reins of power were about to take, they were still hiding the plans they had to install a totalitarian dictatorship, which Cuadra faces today with the same integrity and dignity as he did against Somozan authoritarianism.]

Tun—la ronda del año: **The Liberal Humanist's Universal Impulse**

> *This is the most purely political phase, and marks the decisive passage from the structure to the sphere of the complex superstructures; it is the phase in which previously germinated ideologies become 'party', come into confrontation and conflict, until only one of them, or at least a single combination of them, tends to prevail, to gain the upper hand, to propagate itself over the whole social area—bringing about not only unison of economic and political aims, but also intellectual and moral unity, posing all the questions around which the struggle rages not on a corporate but on a 'universal' plane, and thus creating the hegemony of a fundamental social group over a series of subordinate groups.*
>
> Antonio Gramsci, "Analysis of Situations: Relations of Force"

Pablo Antonio Cuadra's essentialist poetic theory is among the most influential in Nicaragua today, although its impact had been steadily waning during the revolution. Before 1979, Cuadra directed the journal *El Pez y la Serpiente* as well as *La Prensa* and its literary supplement, the principal forum of Nicaraguan literature. The country's leading writers published poetry, short stories, and essays in this supplement during the Somoza reign. Other groups, such as Gradas and Praxis, did take a more radical political and aesthetic stand than Cuadra, but they did not have the resources for supporting and sustaining a journal or for starting a newspaper. Thus, Cuadra's *La Prensa* became the center for literary dissemination in the country. Since the revolution, two other newspapers, *Barricada* and *El Nuevo Diario*, have been established (both including literary supplements), and two principal publishing houses, Editorial Nueva Nicaragua and Editorial Vanguardia, were promoted by the revolution.

So far I have attempted to situate Cuadra in the social position (status) that permitted him to make his poetic voice heard and to be in the extremely powerful position of, essentially, deciding the direction that poetry was to take under *somocismo*. As a liberal, he believed that a variety of oppositional aesthetic expressions should surface, given the severity of the political system, and in times of political tension he helped publish an assortment of different types of poetry, even poetry that was openly critical of *somocismo*.

In the previous section I examined Cuadra's seminal yet perplexing role in the *vanguardia*, the way the founding of an aesthetic movement—contemporaneous with the late avant-garde in Europe—became entrenched in reactionary politics, and the manner in which the political was embedded in "aesthetic" space. Interestingly enough, poetry strongly assimilated the ideological oscillation of the political movements of the day. This ideological ambiguity can be seen clearly in the early Somoza, figurehead for the ascending bourgeoisie. On the one hand, he sided with Sandino's anti-imperialist praxis; on the other, he began to annex power and—in order to concentrate state and economic power to an even greater extent—he collaborated with the interests of the United States government and private enterprise in Nicaragua.

Especially after his involvement in "La generación traicionada," it appears that Cuadra moved in the general direction of liberal politics. Yet his poetry in this postmodern period (that is, since the 1960s), including his writings since the revolution, tend to deal with prerevolutionary concerns. The poet, for instance, is projected as a gifted, romantic figure who searches for the ineffable essence of human beings through an equally tenuous medium—the poetic word. Unlike Ernesto Cardenal's, Cuadra's poetic speaker observes and describes from a distance; he is a messianic "torre de Dios" (tower of God) who feels compelled to trace the historical origins of Mesoamerican peoples, exalting the figure of the campesino and the countryside, mythically placing value on the word's ability to transcend the materiality of life. After being revised and edited in the 1980s, *Tun—la ronda del año* nonetheless retains much of the thematic interest found in his earlier work. In fact, this book could be described as a concise compendium of Cuadra's poetry from as early as 1938 to as late as 1987, since most of the poems were rewritten in the 1980s. For that reason alone, *Tun—la ronda del año* is the most pertinent work for an examination of Cuadra's poetic practice.

The Creation of a Poetic Persona

I have suggested that what takes place formally and thematically in Cuadra's poetry is a gap between the poetic speaker and the people and history he describes. This rift between the subject and the world, according to the poet, can be rather satisfactorily narrowed via the poetic word. Indeed, for Cuadra, poetry explores the self, writing, and the world that it attempts to apprehend. Writing poetry is seen as a philosophical-religious act of entropically recording the subject's pursuit of the object. Cuadra resorts to this metaphysical practice on many occasions in this book. In the last stanza of the first poem, for example, he sets the tone for the volume:

> ¡En las playas inéditas
> las muchachas futuras te invocan,
> poeta! Ellas sueñan:
> —Si el ardiente exilado arribara, si sus ojos
> miraran, de ola en ola, la sangre inscribirse en la arena,
> si al menos en los últimos vientos
> como un eco escuchara el clamor de los héroes:
> la vehemente aventura,

la hermosa hazaña vedada a la voz venidera,
guardaría en su canto.[20]

[On the unedited beaches
the future young women invoke you,
poet! They dream:
— If the ardent exile were to arrive, if his eyes
were to look at, from wave to wave,
        blood inscribing itself on the sand,
if at least during the last winds
like an echo he were to hear the clamor of heroes:
the vehement adventure,
the beautiful labor tied to the coming voice
he would save his song.]

These verses are preceded by a rather didactic inquiry: "Vencedores del caos, ¿quién / forjará la palabra / que los haga vencer el olvido?" (Conquerors of chaos, who / will forge the word / that will allow them to defeat oblivion?). What stands out in this text is the rhetorical question and the answer provided therein. The poet assumes the role of a martyr who receives his calling — to dedicate his life to deciphering the unknown. Following this path in one's life is described as both a "vehement adventure" and a "beautiful labor" and is associated with heroism. If Cuadra describes the poet's task as metaphysical, the world he is searching for is an equally romantic ideal: "¿por qué (gritaban) eligieron el riesgo / y se empeñaron en despejar el misterioso signo?" (19) (Why [they cried] did they choose to take the risk / and to determine to clear up the mysterious sign?).

Cuadra's exegesis of naming as "magical and hermetic" (in his article on the *vanguardia*) resurfaces in a poem written thirty-two years later. Clearly distancing himself from Nicanor Parra's concrete poetry, Cuadra instead places himself in line with José Lezama Lima's metaphysical, hermetic poetry. Art, in many ways, thus goes beyond history itself and becomes an autonomous, ideal realm. Cuadra is not content, however, to let his verses operate just in this sphere. Rather, conceiving of poetry (human beings' creation) always entails contemplating nature (God's creation) and the role human beings have to play in it. In "Mayo: Oratorio de los 4 héroes" (May: Oratory of the 4 heroes), Cuadra synthesizes nature and art, then fuses them with history. As nature awakens from its dormant state, so does poetry:

En Mayo es el vuelo nupcial de los insectos.
En el calor de Mayo la lengua incuba
las palabras nuevas. En Mayo termina el reino

del amarillo y comienza el reino del verde.
El gusano se hace mariposa. La estrella
desciende a tierra y se hace insecto. (47)

[In May the nuptial flight of the insects takes place.
In the heat of May the tongue incubates
new words. In May the reign of yellow ends
and the reign of green begins.
The worm becomes a butterfly. A star
descends to earth and becomes an insect.]

Significantly, nature releases new words from their incubation, much as caterpillars become butterflies and stars become insects. By relating language to nature's seasonal metamorphosis and what we might call metaphorical metamorphosis (the association of stars with insects), writing takes on a natural, organic, creative function in the universe. It is important to point out here that writing mysteriously springs from and unites the material and the ideal, as the speaker reminds us in a phrase reminiscent of the Spanish poet Jorge Guillén: "las cosas se van haciendo nombres" (48) (things slowly become names). Immersed in nature, poetry blossoms forth and finds its locus in social justice. Interestingly enough, this transition in the content takes place as the language becomes more politicized:

— *Yo disparo cañones por palabras.*
Defiendo nombres para que no sean sustituidos.
Disparo para que un niño escriba siempre:
Sébaco, Santiago, Camoapa, Momotombo, Colibríes. (48)

[—*I shoot cannons for words.*
I defend names so that they are not replaced.
I shoot so that a child will always be able to write:
Sébaco, Santiago, Camoapa, Momotombo, Colibríes.]

At this stage, Cuadra's verses are infused with what would appear to be military or revolutionary rhetoric: "shoot," "cannons," "defend." While these words point in this political direction, however, they seem to be alluding to a linguistic, as well as a political, conflict (i.e., to national liberation). Later on we run into similar imagery:

— *Esta espada escribe una República.*
De la boca del hombre que afirma su espíritu

ha nacido esta espada. Enciende el fuego
del verbo.
Esta espada defiende el sustantivo. (49)

[*The sword writes a republic*
From the mouth of a man who affirms that his spirit
has given birth to this sword. He ignites the fire
of the verb.
This sword defends nouns.]

Coming from the mouths of human beings, writing and fighting are inextricably interlocked. But it is actually the struggle that gives life to the word: the sword "writes" and "ignites the fire of the verb." Rather than materializing writing, however, Cuadra seems to be textualizing revolutionary struggle. In the last seven stanzas of "Mayo," poetic exploration, nature, and *sandinismo* (of the nationalist variety) are interwoven, establishing a strong and interlinking textual bond between them. The first clear political marker appears following the stanza cited above: "En mayo regamos nuestras palabras con el llanto de los oprimidos" (49) (In May we water our words with the weeping of the oppressed). Like Darío before him, Cuadra cannot separate his poetic from his political struggle. But it is important to underscore the fact that he is no way advocting revolutionary communism; rather, like Darío and the bourgeoisie itself, Cuadra is concerned about national autonomy (much as he promotes aesthetic autonomy). It is in that context that he denounces U.S. imperialism by quoting Darío's famous verse: "¿Tantos millones de hombres hablaremos inglés?" (50) (Will so many millions of men speak English?). He also mentions Sandino four verses later. From this moment on, the poet—echoing Vallejo—and the guerrilla are purposefully interchanged:

—Niños, nos dice la maestra:
¡Hay que ponerse de pie!
¡El guerrillero ha puesto una emboscada
a las palabras que oprimen, ha derribado
los nombres que avergüenzan! (50)

[*Children, the teacher tells us:*
Up on your feet!
The guerrilla has devised an ambush
for the words that exploit, he has overthrown
shameful names!]

The questioning of the official story by the guerrillas/poets at the end of the poem makes it appear as though Cuadra were advocating open aesthetic commitment. We may recall his supporting Sandino's nationalist (anti-imperialist) struggle during the *vanguardia* years and, thus, speculate that this poem was written during the 1930s. It is interesting that the rest of the poems are dated, while this one is not. This text seems to provide evidence of Cuadra's support for Sandino, as well as for the 1979 insurrection. Nonetheless, as we shall see, this poet maintains a critical distance from the revolution, continually insisting that it follow a "politically democratic" course. As I will note, "political democracy" translates into bourgeois democracy and does not entail any overturning of the economic system (dependent capitalism). Consequently, one cannot help but feel that the homage Cuadra pays to Sandino is provisional—that it applies to Sandino's national liberation struggle, but certainly not to his anarchocommunist leanings.

That political position is represented allegorically in all of the poems in *Tun—la ronda del año*. The dialectical relation between freedom and power is the most prominent sign of Cuadra's liberal ideology. Throughout this volume, animals embody different forms of power. Lizards are slimy and evasive; elephants, overbearing and pushy; and sharks, ferocious and unforgiving. All are wrapped up in the all-consuming quest for power, and the Sandinistas figure, by this point in history, among those targeted. However, "Agosto: Apólogo con elefante" (August: Apologist with elephant), which was written or rewritten in 1981–82, celebrates the 1979 victory, as the people dethrone the powerful leader:

> Los poetas preguntaron: ¿es lúcida
> o es ciega la potestad que rebasa nuestras formas?
> Porque el tiempo iba pesando, denso y paquidermo
> Y su peso era un arma. Y su tamaño un reino.
> Y mendigaba como todo rey.
> Extendía su trompa imponiendo el tributo
> demoledor de su desmesura.
> Los sembradores dijeron: "Pisotea nuestras milpas".
> Las vivanderas del mercado: "Destruye nuestros tiangues".
> Y el parroco abrió el Libro
> donde Eleazar, hijo de Sauro—el Macabeo—
> mató con hacha al mamút de Siria
> y pereció aplastado por su masa. (75)

> [The poets asked: Is it lucid
> or blind, the power that overflows our forms?
> Because time weighed, it was dense, it was a pachyderm

And its weight was a weapon. And its size a kingdom.
And he begged as all kings do.
He extended his trunk imposing his tribute
demolishing his own insolence.
The farmers said: "He steps on our fields."
The employees in the market [said]: "He destroys our market."
And the priest opened the Book
where Eleazar, son of Saurus—the Maccabean—
killed the mammoth of Syria with an axe
and died smothered by his weight.]

The first stanza, cited above, is particularly illuminating because it portrays the poet as leader (as inquisitive philosopher), power overcome by its own corruptness, and the disenchantment of different sectors of the society with the Somozan status quo. Contrary to what we might expect, Cuadra does not dwell on the guerrillas' reaction to *somocismo,* but rather transcribes the resistance on the part of farmers, small-scale entrepreneurs, and the church. All of the groups joined in violently overthrowing the dictatorship:

> Con gritos
> con piedras
> con antorchas
> la multitud lo echó del pueblo
> al cenagoso páramo.
>
> Costó vidas su muerte.
> Como antaño aplausos
> levantó aleteos y chillidos
> de aves agoreras.
> Y lo vimos hundirse por su propio peso
> fangoso sol arcaico
>   deforme
>   y extranjero. (75–76)

> [With cries
> With stones
> With torches
> the multitudes kicked him out of town
> to the muddy plain.
>
> His death cost lives.
> As in yesteryear applause

brought forth fluttering and chirps
from fortune-telling fowls.
And we saw him sink under his own weight
miry archaic sun
deformed
and alien.]

Once again, in the concluding verses of this poem, there is a general description of the "people" rising up against Somoza—incarnated in the elephant—the last vestige of the oligarchy. As the most apparent representative of the oligarchy, Somoza, like the class he stands for, in this age of advanced capitalism, is an anachronism (an "archaic sun," "deformed" and "alien"). But there is no reflection here of a future campesinos' and workers' state, because that is not part of Cuadra's vision for the new Nicaragua. Indeed, his disenchantment with the Sandinistas shortly after the revolution was a result of the hesitancy he felt as the FSLN implemented its programs. In order to prove this assertion, it would be helpful to turn to the cornerstone of his liberal ideology: the notions of freedom and power.

Allegorical Poetic Projection

Steven White has addressed the relation between history and myth in Pablo Antonio Cuadra's *Poemas nicaragüenses* (1934), in particular their coincidence with the apogee of the *vanguardia*.[21] For White the "Edenic impulse itself in the early works of both poets [Cuadra and Supervielle] and the ways that Cuadra undercuts and refutes the myth of the peaceable kingdom" are what makes Cuadra's poetry universal and, by extension, highly worthy ("Modern" 72). Identifying this universal impulse is significant, but we need to take this further and ask just what effect this transhistorical or utopian desire has upon lyrical representation. Concretely, in writing globally, certain discursive patterns or territories that imply ideological judgments are delineated. For instance, claiming that freedom and power are two major thematic focal points in Cuadra's work is not enough; these concepts need to be defined in their poetic and historical context. The Nicaraguan poet defines power as monstrous and self-centered; it is both evil and omnipresent. The poet's lifelong task is constantly to undermine or avoid it, and to stand with the powerless. At first glance this depiction might appear to be quite similar to Cardenal's explicitly ethical representation of power. Yet, according to Cuadra himself, his poetic journey follows a path different from Cardenal's, for his old friend succumbed to the sway of power by becoming a Marxist and subsequently judging his old friends and peers:

What could be called "the Cardenal problem" came much later. When he went to Cuba, he became very enthusiastic about Communism and entered an accelerated process of Marxism that carried him, in my opinion, to a dangerous politicization of his religious faith. I call it "dangerous" because politicizing religion immediately produces fanaticism.[22]

Unlike Cardenal, Cuadra refuses to partake in "extreme" ideological ventures, but instead seeks to remain "autonomous." Rather than choosing an official post or a position in the government, the elder poet opts for being a critic of governmental policies that, in his estimation, deviate from democratic political ideals. While Cuadra criticizes Sandinista actions that he feels are undemocratic, he does not appear to be openly opposed to socialism:

Ideally, a socialist system should function democratically. We're completely open to a process that is not demogogic, but systematic and gradual: we never opposed the process of socialization and agrarian reform. What we do oppose is a state that grows on us like a monster. We never want giants again, whether they are called Stalin, Mao, or Fidel. The history of the twentieth century is too telling for us to allow to go on erecting these absolute powers that end up crushing all of man's liberties. And to impede the monstrous growth of the state or of power, we know of only one antidote: democracy. (White, "An Interview" 28)

This concern with power recurs in all of Cuadra's poems. "Septiembre: El tiburón" (September: The shark) addresses a number of different forms of political power that have threatened Nicaragua over the years. One of those signs of aggression is imperialism:

John Davis entró con ellos por el río
y cruzó el Lago en bongo y cayó sobre Granada dormida.
Sonaron a rebato los campanarios
pero ya el humo de los incendios
levantaba coronas de buitres sobre la ciudad destruida.
Así conocimos el inconfundible ruido de los imperios:
el hierro,
el crepitar de ciudades
y un ceniciento aullido de perros. (84)

[John Davis jumped in the river
and crossed the lake in a canoe and fell upon a sleeping Granada.
The bells rang in alarm
but the smoke from the burning

attracted crowns of vultures over the destroyed city.
That is how we learned of the unmistakable sound of the empires:
the steel,
the crepitating of the cities
and an ashen howl of the dogs.]

The people, however, rose up to face and defeat this imperial figure, only to meet others later:

Los trozos de encajes en los espinos guiaron a los indios
y le armaron una emboscada y lo coparon
y lo descuartizaron y lo quemaron y esparcieron al viento sus cenizas
Pero va
   y vuelve. (84–85)

[The pieces of material on needles guided the Indians
and they set up an ambush and they captured him
and they cut him to pieces and they burned him and spread his ashes in
   the wind
But he leaves
   and returns.]

The poem recounts the imperial dreams of grandeur of Gallardillo, Coxon, Harris, Nelson, Sharp, Bourmano, Shepard, Walker, and others hungry for power. In the last section of "Septiembre," regarding an anniversary of the 1979 revolution, Cuadra describes a bearded, egotistical character, a sort of Fidel Castro as Agamemnon. Like the other instruments of power, "—Va y vuelve—dije yo.—Explota / su poder de adaptación. Depreda / en un reino usurpado" (88) (—He leaves and returns—I said. He exploits his power of adaptation. He embezzles a usurped kingdom). The penultimate stanza ostensibly makes reference to the continual recurrence of power, embodied by the shark. An anecdote quoted further on, however, seems to offer a solution to dealing with force:

> Bajó el muchacho al río para lavarse
> cuando saltó del agua un gran pez que
> quería devorarlo. Tobías gritó, pero el
> ángel le dijo: "Agarra al pez de las
> agallas y tenlo sujeto". Y el muchacho
> se apoderó del pez y lo arrastró a
> tierra. Entonces le dijo el ángel:

"Abre el pez, sácale la hiel, el corazón
y el hígado y tira sus entrañas, porque
su hiel, su corazón y el hígado te servirán
para remedio." (91)

[A young man went down to the river to wash himself
when a great fish jumped out of the water
and wanted to devour him.
Tobías yelled, but the
angel told him: "Grab the fish by the gills and
hold him still." And the young man
overpowered the fish and brought him to
shore. Then the angel told him:
"Open the fish, remove his bile, his heart,
and his liver through his entrails, because
his bile, heart, and liver will cure you.]

The remedy offered at the end of this narrative poem is to dismember power completely, to decenter it. By disarming force and being suspicious of its concentration in society, Cuadra appears to tell us, we can keep democracy alive. Thus, his aesthetic project resembles the postmodern tendency to accentuate differences and undermine totalizing impulses. If this insatiable questioning of politicoaesthetic constructs seems radical, we would do well to remember that difference has a central role to play in bourgeois culture. Cuadra posits art as universally transcendent, encompassing various discourses, to be sure, but all of them carefully regulated and then drained of their conflictive energy. Otherwise it would not be so convenient to dismiss "political" or "bad" art in the name of aesthetic autonomy. There is little room in his theory for class and gender, except as discursive imaginations that describe, not ideology's intersection with material reality, but rather the subject's realization of his or her own human limitations. Given that threshold, and following Cuadra's liberalism, the subject must surrender his or her will to divine power. Yet it is precisely in this vigilant social–democratic position that we can find a healthy skepticism that does not allow revolutionary ideology (such as *sandinismo*) to become stagnant. Cuadra states in an interview that the

scribe writes what he's told to write or he uses a formula, and that's that. But the person who carries the sacred fire inside like a torment knows the harm it does. The only reader, the only critic, valid for the poet is his own creative "I". All interference—more so if it's political—and all criticism foreign to the demands of his work are castrating. (White, "An Interview" 30)

His ideology is quite transparent. Art is not a social act; rather, it romantically emerges as a cathartic desublimation of the individual. Once the sociopolitical process "transgresses" individual territory, then — we are to infer — art immediately ceases to be autonomous and becomes political ("An Interview" 29–30). Cuadra clearly negates the political content of his own work, while neatly assigning art and politics to different realms. His transcendental poetry, which aspires to a critique from outside, is not able to sustain the borders that would theoretically separate him from the inside.

Following his logic, to become overtly committed to the political sphere is to sacrifice the critical autonomy of art. He alleges that Pablo Neruda, for example, was guilty of "substituting political for aesthetic criteria."[23] If he dismisses aesthetic engagement offhand, preferring to minimalize any "political" art, it is apparently exceedingly difficult for him to uphold "freedom" as a ubiquitous concept, despite his attempts to do so:

> We produced politicized art, but it was an art that was expressed with freedom, even when it could have cost us our lives. Its belligerence was born of freedom — freedom engaged in struggle. Freedom also gave birth to authenticity. As we shall see later, this authenticity, which gave Nicaraguan literature a high standing in Latin America, did not know how to sustain itself in the hour of triumph — when the Revolution was confiscated and the right-wing dictatorship of Somoza was deceitfully and treacherously replaced with a dictatorship of the left. ("Poetry" 285)

This "confiscation" that Cuadra addresses is curious indeed. For it is apparent that the poet here appropriates "freedom" and gives it a definition emanating from his liberal imagination. Freedom, thus conceived, is divorced from politics. Any art that promotes ideological transformation has evidently stepped outside the boundaries assigned to it by classical aesthetics. What the Sandinistas have posited, according to Cuadra, is the abandonment of the people's "freedom." The government has imposed its ideology on the heretofore autonomous region of aesthetics, and "so began the struggle of an ideology against a culture. But that ideology has had to impose itself, little by little, through a strange kind of costume ball. Never declaring the truth, always denying or disguising it" ("Poetry" 286). Thus, Cuadra suggests that the revolution operates through deception, rather than being supported by the majority of the people; he overlooks the FSLN's overwhelming electoral victory (67 percent) in 1984 and the reports of a thousand international journalists and official observers who certified the results.[24] Clearly, for this poet, desire takes precedence over reality; since he himself did not support the revolution, he denied the FSLN's popular backing through the 1984 elections.

Cloaking his ideology in abstract, elitist, and nostalgic terms, Cuadra calls for a "humanistic Republic," yet he never defines exactly what that entails. He yearns for a life that permits a poet to "see his vehement dreams of justice and his radical need for freedom satisfied" ("Poetry" 289). Although the political program underlying Cuadra's beliefs is not clearly articulated, his poetry and his life express utopian ideals designed to minimize repression in society while simultaneously defending a bourgeois culture once under seige and now in a hegemonic position in Nicaragua.

We can note, then, the general direction the liberal wing of the *vanguardia* took in the poetry of Cuadra, while the left-wing heritage will become embedded in the poetry of his archrival, Ernesto Cardenal. Cardenal will abandon the nationalist political and the populist poetics of Cuadra in favor of a committed political stance as a liberation theologian and as a poet of exteriorism, or concrete poetry.

CHAPTER 3
POETRY AND "SPIRITUAL MATERIALISM": ERNESTO CARDENAL

Ernesto Cardenal stands with Octavio Paz and Nicolás Guillén as one of the most renowned poets in Latin America. His works, translated into more than fifteen languages, show some influence of Ezra Pound and Thomas Merton and also draw heavily on liberation theology. Early in his career Cardenal developed a poetic theory, *exteriorismo*, that owes much to Pound's insights. According to Cardenal, he, like Pound, is ostensibly more concerned with communicating with the layperson than with the erudite;[1] his poetic form is clearly more accessible than Pound's. His montage techniques are designed to reveal the dynamics of social reality that the average campesino lives. Cardenal uses many of Pound's formal devices, but Pound's poetry calls attention to these techniques in a way that Cardenal's does not. Additionally, Cardenal shares Pound's distaste for the capitalist system, even though the Nicaraguan poet's critique is from the Left, while Pound's was from the Right.

Since the Cuban revolution, Cardenal has explored common ground between Christianity and Marxism, and his poetry has been profoundly affected by these two systems of thought. Undoubtedly, the poet's political consciousness grew into a more radical Weltanschauung in the heat of the late *somocista* era. Before joining the FSLN, he seriously deliberated about the issue of nonviolence, refraining from supporting armed insurrection until the last years before the revolution. This background may explain why in his poetry Cardenal has a propensity to suggest utopian solutions for the society as a whole, as though the Solentiname community—as a replica of early Christian communities—could provide a pacific national example. In such a social paradigm, the violence of class conflict and the division of labor—in Nicaragua as well as internationally—become hazy, and the real inner workings of history tend to recede into a utopian project. It would be overstating the case, however, to maintain that Cardenal thus slips into a pure utopian socialism, because the bulk of his writings represent—in an even more determined and laborious way—a return to a dialectical materialist poetics that, through its formal devices, manages to submerge itself in the depths of human (and thus social) relations.

Reading Marxism through a Christian lens has led to a reinterpretation of theology itself, to deconstructing and then reassembling such integral components of religion as sin, faith, resurrection, and salvation. Instead of locating these states solely within the individual, liberation theologians project them back to the social sphere, or, more accurately, they never leave the social realm: they are social properties. These religious concepts can be considered as emerging from the conflict between classes and from imperialist expansion. What is interesting in Cardenal is his ideological representation of socialism as deriving from collective subjectivity and from its struggle for self-determination. I am referring here to what I will call "spiritual materialism," or the attempt by liberation theologians such as Cardenal to integrate Marxism and Christianity on philosophical grounds. In this chapter I maintain that the negotiation between these two epistemologies, whatever their affinities may be, can potentially lead to idealism or to a type of utopianism that posits subjectivity over objectivity instead of grasping the two as dialectical.

Cardenal's "spiritual materialism," is, as I will argue throughout, welded to exteriorism — likened to photomontage and film techniques by Robert Pring-Mill, Marc Zimmerman, and Jorge H. Valdés — which activates the senses.[2] In particular, Cardenal's "materialist" visual perspective organically ties seeing with thinking critically and acting; thus, his poetic methodology is a species of praxis. As in the case of Cuadra, a key indicator of this ideological or political analysis is the poetic speaker and his relation to his poetic, autobiographical, and sociohistorical setting. It is in these areas that the alienating division of labor both in society and in poetry crumble to the ground, for Cardenal's way of seeing penetrates the glitter of bourgeois society and its vestiges in revolutionary Nicaragua and works at presenting a more complete and humane vision of whole beings.

In the poetry of Ernesto Cardenal, Latin America found a new relation between art and ideology, not only in form, but also in content. Before Neruda's *Canto general* (1950), and even after it had made its initial impact on literature, poetic language did not easily retreat from a highly metaphorical world. Thus, the critics tended to herald poets who wrote elliptical, erudite, or convoluted verses. By publishing *Canto general*, Neruda contested the very criteria employed to judge his earlier abstract poetry; he openly challenged the concept of "political" art by speaking more overtly of the sociohistorical circumstances that led to a division of classes, to human beings' exploitation of one another, to the creation of private property, and so on. In essence, as Adorno once remarked of Brecht, he unveiled the dominant ideology that disguised the material relations of capitalism. Even in what many have called his didactic poetry, however, Neruda remained within the domain of poetic discourse, while at the same time resisting it. For instance, although this great Chilean poet wanted to reduce the distance between form and content by writing in the oral tradition and by addressing tangible historical and political issues, a reading of *Canto general* reveals a rich, socially metaphorical repertoire. In this he differs from Cardenal, who claims to have rejected metaphorical poetic expression, and from Vallejo, who felt that poetic language symbolically expressed human existential and utopian experiences and who expressed himself through radical formal innovations. Cardenal and Neruda are united, however, in their belief that poetry is a terrain in which to condemn the inhumanity of capitalism through a critical realist medium. This mode of representation furnishes them with the tools to reveal more organically and profoundly the internal contradictions and processes of social development. Objective reality, then, is not external to the artistic enterprise, but rather willfully an integral component of aesthetic form and content whether the artist wishes it to be so or not. In the case of Neruda and Cardenal, the social connection between thinking and acting (praxis) is emphasized, and the objective connections between social phenomena become the salient features of their poetry.

From Existentialist Temptation to Social Commitment

Ernesto Cardenal's early poetry—particularly *Epigramas* (Epigrams, 1962)—is dominated by self-consciousness.[3] When the political appears, it centers almost exclusively on one odious figure: Somoza García. Among the mostly personal and political poems are some youthful, romantic ones. These epigrams, akin to Neruda's early poetry (*20 canciones de amor y una canción desesperada* [20 songs of love and a desperate song]), are suffused with the poetic persona. This has as much to do with the poet's own youthful self-absorption as with the historical moment, between 1952 and 1956, in which they were written. Indeed, his writing could hardly avoid post–World War II skepticism, which in philosophy translated into existentialism.

The poetic milieu in Nicaragua in which Cardenal was immersed, the so-called generation of the 1940s, which also included Ernesto Mejía Sánchez and Carlos Martínez Rivas, was heavily influenced by the contemporary literary currents in Europe. Martínez Rivas, for instance, conceived his *La insurrección solitaria* (Solitary insurrection) in Paris while in the company of the surrealists and Octavio Paz, but he had arrived in Europe in the early 1950s, precisely at the apogee of existentialism.[4] Cardenal had also traveled to Paris during the same period and was undoubtedly exposed to the "virtues" of existentialist and late avant-gardist art. Indeed, in the specific instance of Nicaraguan politics during this period, *somocismo*'s oligarchical stranglehold on the nascent bourgeoisie seemed unbreakable. No formidable, united resistance could be mounted against the dictatorship at this time. Thus, a political vacuum opened up and existentialism stepped in to fill the void. Cardenal's *Epigramas* emerged out of this period.

An examination of his contemporaries' works reveals a preoccupation with the angst of the time and, I might add, the insensitivity to the role of women's emancipation. In *La insurrección solitaria* (first published in 1953 in Mexico),[5] Martínez Rivas conceived a profoundly influential and paradigmatic book of poetry. Amidst a wave of French, Spanish, and German existentialism, his poetry both affirmed and attempted to destroy the self. Given the decline of religion as a world ideological force, the deception of Stalinism, the push for massive industrialization—which included a further deepening of factory regimentation (of Taylorism in the United States, for instance)—and the disastrous consequences, particularly for the Europeans, of the two World Wars, a general feeling of despair took hold of imagination, and the individual's importance appeared to decline. Under the guidance of the writings of Martin Heidegger, Albert Camus, and Jean-Paul Sartre, the most commonly acknowledged philosophical and aesthetic proponents of existentialism, Martínez Rivas, Cardenal, and Mejía Sánchez began to produce seminal works in their poetic corpus. Following the *vanguardia*'s flirtation with fascism, the distressing results of Somoza's rule in the political arena, and the development of a Nicaraguan bourgeoisie, the poets in the 1950s saw little meaning in their aesthetic enterprise:

> Pero él fue solamente un pintor. Uno
> entre los otros espantapájaros, minúsculos
> en medio del gran viento que choca contra el cielo,
> empeñados en añadir un paso más a la larga cadena,
> ocupados en cambiar la Naturaleza, como las estaciones.
> Rehaciendo y contrahaciendo el rostro del mundo. El
> rostro del vasto mundo plástico, supermodelado y vacío.
>
> (*Insurrección* 90–91)

> [But he was only a painter. One
> among many scarecrows, minuscule
> amid the great wind that fought the sky,
> determined to add one more link onto the long chain,
> busy changing Nature, like the seasons.
> Remaking and countermaking the face of the world. The
> face of this vast, plastic world, overmodeled and empty.]

In these verses Martínez Rivas expresses his distaste for the growing industrial world that has made existence meaningless. Van Gogh as artist (and subject) in these expressionist stanzas loses much of his identity, as he is engulfed in a vast, empty modern world. Far from invoking Cuadra's heroic image of the poet struggling to leave an imprint on society, this artist is an anti-hero, an individual undercutting himself, "struggling himself" out of existence. Unlike his European contemporaries, however, this poet does reserve a site for eternal hope (incarnated in the Virgin Mary). Through a strange, but recurring, vision of women as metaphysical, the poet is able to find meaning in life. Consequently, material life per se is characterized as senseless chaos, while women and the Virgin Mary (envisioned as the near-Absolute) transcend the "banality" of existence and occupy the ideal realm:

> Por él vamos, Yadira, y te miro
> como un gorrión saltar de estrella a estrella.
> Subir de astro en astro. De cometa en cometa.
> Y más allá. Más alto. Más arriba,
> ya por las últimas orillas del cielo,
> en donde va tu cuerpo, quemándose en el aire,
> con rumbo hacia un seguro porvenir de lucero. (29)

> [Along it we go, Yadira, and I look at you
> as a sparrow jumps from star to star.
> To climb from heavenly body to heavenly body.
>   From comet to comet.
> And beyond. Higher. Above,
> now near the last shores of the sky,
> where your body goes, burning itself in the air,
> headed for a sure future as a morning star.]

Given the crisis of the historical moment, in "El Paraiso Recrobrado" (Paradise recovered) the poet would rather contemplate perfection and purity in the universal realm, which he finds in the image of a woman. The authentic, carnal Yadira, from his hometown, literally disintegrates and ascends beyond empirical life to a nebulous, heavenly domain. Catholicism is apparent in this revisiting of philosophical dualism of mind and body, in which the woman clearly is associated with the body. Her body metaphorically incarnates such ineffable qualities of the soul as purity, love, and wholeness and serves as a vehicle for man to realize these immortal yearnings.

Unfortunately, representing women as "woman," in strictly metaphysical terms, denies them individuality and subordinates their identities to male interests. Another contemporary of Cardenal, Ernesto Mejía Sánchez, has satirically characterized this subjugation of women in a critique of the concentration of power:

Una vez más me será dado lo mío. Otra vez
el señor dirá y se le obedecerá. Otra vez
lucirá las armas. Ofrendará un toro a su pueblo.

Estoy sola en mi casa. No tengo prisa. Haz,
haz lo que quieras. Toma lo que quieras.
El señor está en su casa. El señor sólo
debe desear . . . El señor.

Ven, hija, para que premie tu sumisión,
El César pide que le ordenes servirte. Así
las cosas en su punto justo, al caer
la tarde da comienzo la noche donde ella
brilla, moneda al fin, y sus brazos
y piernas no hacen sino servir.[6]

[Once again what is mine will be given to me. Once again
the man will say something and he will be obeyed. Once again
he will brandish his arms. He will offer·a bull to the people.

I am alone in my home. I'm not in a hurry. Do,
do what you want. Take whatever you'd like.
You, sir, are at home. The man should
only desire . . . the man.

Come, daughter, so that I may reward your submission,
Cesar asks that you tell him to serve himself. That way
things are in place, when the sun
sets it gives way to the night where she
shines, coin after all, and her arms
and legs do nothing except serve.]

Contrasting the will to power with submission is one of the principal themes
in "Sunday Afternoon." Yet the reader cannot help but notice that (the)
woman is described as a prostitute. She is physically available ("her arms and
legs do nothing except serve") to serve (the) man's every desire. Furthermore,
if she provides him with "appropriate" wish fulfillment, he offers her com-
pensation in the form of cash. In fact, the speaker equates her with money
("where she / shines, coin after all"). It would be difficult to find a more scath-
ing critique of the collusion of prostitution, exploitation, patriarchy, and
capitalism. Another dimension of this poem is its possible allegorical function: the woman becomes a Nicaragua dominated by the United States. Mejía
Sánchez also projects a metaphysical, eternal role for women:

de todo lo que niego y lo que afirmo,
a vuestra sombra memorable quiero
morar oscurecido eternamente.

Una tras otra, páginas amigas
como mujeres que el amor desnuda
el ojo va cubriendo su desvelo.

Páginas olvidadas, mare nostrum,
páginas nuevas para el ojo limpio,
las vírgenes a oscuras desveladas. (43–44)

[of all that I negate and affirm,
in your memorable shadow I want
to live darkening eternally.

One after another, friendly pages
like women that are undressed by love
the eye slowly covers its sharpness.

Forgotten pages, mare nostrum,
new pages for the clean eye,
in the darkness the virgins are unveiled.]

As in the poem by Martínez Rivas, women passively and ineffably await men's initiatives. Here woman is a virgin, so pure that she becomes timeless, barely recognizable.

Mejía Sánchez denounces partriarchy in capitalism, simultaneously acknowledging his own complicity in it. Shortly after the Cuban revolution, for example, he honestly affirmed his bourgeois background and the implications of his ideological position on capitalism. In the final verses of "Libertad de pensamiento" [Freedom of thought] we find the impressions of an individual who is a member of this privileged class and is struggling with his support for the revolution:

Yo no tengo nada contra los negros ni contra
la repartición de la tierra; pero no estoy
conforme con la sumisión de las letras negras
de la imprenta ni con el despilfarro de balas
rojas de odio. El capitalismo está sentenciado.
Yo moriré con él, dicen, y muchos más morirán.
¡Pobres de nosotros, y sin haberlo gozado! (117)

[I don't have anything against blacks or against
dividing up the land; but I am not

comfortable with the submission of black letters
off the press nor with wasting
red bullets of hate. Capitalism is sentenced.
I will die with it, they say, and many more will die.
Poor us, and without having enjoyed it!]

This discussion of Martínez Rivas's and Mejía Sánchez's poetry is designed
to show the subjectivist tendency of the poetry of this generation, to demonstrate that in the absence of a dialectic between objectivism and subjectivism
we encounter an unbalanced fetishism of the latter. As result of this introspective journey, these personal relations — expressed in heterosexual relations in this generation's work — manifest an almost religious supplementation for the decay of bourgeois life on an international scale. In the process
of creating this ideology, women become an iconic form of salvation in a
world "void of meaning."

As I mentioned, Cardenal's *Epigramas* (1962) also appears to be quite introspective, in spite of his political portrayal of Somoza García.[7] Although
the book was commonly perceived by Nicaraguan poets and critics to be a
powerful statement at a moment of political repression, it becomes apparent
that Cardenal's portrayal of Somoza differs little from Cuadra's nationalist
position. We are to understand that the oligarch must capitulate to the nascent bourgeoisie. The justification for this reading lies in the speaker's individual consciousness: it pervades almost every poem in the volume, and it
is in need of frequent reassurance. As a book of poetry, *Epigramas* is highly
significant because it reveals Cardenal's ideological position at this stage of
his life, before he begins to commit himself to social justice:

> Al perderse yo a ti tú y yo hemos perdido:
> yo porque tú eras lo que yo más amaba
> y tú porque yo era el que te amaba más.
> Pero de nosotros dos tú pierdes más que yo:
> porque yo podré amar a otras como te amaba a ti
> pero a ti no te amarán como te amaba yo. (17)

> [Having lost you, you and I have both lost:
> I because you are what I most loved
> and you because I was the one that loved you most.
> But of us both, you lose twice as much as I:
> because I will be able to love others as I loved you.
> But they will never love you like I loved you.]

The end to this affair — so brilliantly recorded by juxtaposing the pronouns *tú* and *yo* so that they might easily be confused — grammatically and thematically finishes with parallel constructions contrasting only in *ti* and *yo*. Apparently distressed by the breakup, the speaker jealously claims that the love he offers is greater than any that any other (male) can offer her. He devalues her, however, in order to salvage his own ego: he will be able to love others as he loved her, whereas she will not be able to find someone to love her as much as he loved her. This is one among many love poems intertwined with poems about alienation, domination, control, and the all-consuming figure of Luis Somoza Debayle. These poems manifest poetic, but not political, complexity.

In his "political" epigrams, Cardenal depicts the dictator as plundering the Nicaraguan economy while encouraging the presence of U.S. financial interests. Yet what clearly distinguishes this early poetry from his later work is that the thematic nodes do not center on sociohistorical factors, but rather on Somoza as an individual. This relation between the personal and the political can be seen in this famous poem:

> De pronto suena en la noche una sirena
> de alarma, larga, larga,
> el aullido lúgubre de la sirena
> de incendio o de la ambulancia blanca de la muerte,
> como el grito de la cegua en la noche,
> que se acerca y se acerca sobre las calles
> y las casas y sube, sube, y baja
> y crece, crece, baja y se aleja
> creciendo y bajando. No es incendio ni muerte:
> > Es Somoza que pasa. (30)

> [The siren of a long, long alarm
> sounds in the night,
> the mournful howl of a
> fire siren or of a white ambulance of death,
> like the cry of the *cegua* at night,
> which comes closer and closer over the streets
> and the houses and rises, rises, and lowers
> and rises, rises, lowers and goes away
> rising and lowering. It is not a fire nor a death:
> > It is Somoza that passes by.]

Somoza becomes the ubiquitous symbol of repression. There is little doubt that the political is visible in these poems, but the speaker and his personal relations occupy at least as much space as the oppressive conditions. By focusing as much attention on the individual as on society, the young, romantic Cardenal seems to be equating personal with political passion. This early stage of his life commitment necessarily includes both spheres:

> Me contaron que estabas enamorada de otro
> y entonces me fui de mi cuarto
> y escribí ese artículo contra el Gobierno
> por el que estoy preso. (20)

> [They told me you were in love with someone else
> and so I went to my room
> and I wrote this article against the government
> which is why I am now in prison.]

In these verses the speaker is awakened politically by his lover's leaving him, and it is this event in the personal sphere that moves him to write the article. The last eight poems of *Epigramas* underscore the romantic, even existentialist, theme of individual alienation. Silence and emptiness overcome the speaker until he seems to be drowning in them.

It is worth noting that *Epigramas* is also Cardenal's most problematic book with regard to his representation of women. These poems underscore the "romantic" clashes that afflict both man and woman. It is the male speaker, however, who frequently gains the upper hand:

> Tú que estás orgullosa de mis versos
> pero no porque yo los escribí
> sino porque los inspiraste tú
> y a pesar de que fueron contra ti:
>   Tú pudiste inspirar mejor poesía.
>   Tú pudiste inspirar mejor poesía. (22)

> [You who are so proud of my verses
> but not because I wrote them
> but rather because you inspired them
> and in spite of the fact that they were (written) against you:
>   You could inspire better poetry.
>   You could inspire better poetry.]

In this poem the woman is characterized as vain and ephemeral; she is the muse the poet has been awaiting. Claudia, Ileana, and Myriam all serve as sources of poetic inspiration. Nowhere in this book do we find a portrait of the life of a woman that deviates from this traditional role. Cardenal's later work differs in its depiction of gender. In *Vuelos de victoria* (Flights of victory) the romantic passion seems to have subsided and women are integrated into the poet's portrayal of the revolution. The change is apparent in the poetic documentation of the National Guard's brutality in "Las campesinas del Cuá," in spite of the conventional image of the mother as *patria*:

> Muchos han oído estos gritos del Cuá
>   gemidos de la Patria como de parto.
> Al salir de la cárcel Estebana García con cuatro menores
> dio a luz. Tuvo que regalar sus hijos
> a un finquero. Emelinda Hernández de dieciséis
>   las mejillas brillantes de llanto
> las trenzas mojadas de llanto . . . (16)

> [Many have heard those cries from El Cuá
>   whimpers of the Homeland like giving birth.
> Upon leaving jail Estebana García with four minors
> gave birth. She had to give her children away
> to a farmer. Emelinda Hernández sixteen years old
>   bright cheeks from having cried
> her ponytails wet from crying . . .]

The poem documents the experiences of the women in the village El Cuá, their cooperation in the armed struggle, and the horrible physical pain they endured as a community at the hands of the National Guard. Further, Cardenal carefully records the resistance of Cándida, Amanda, and Emelinda. This poem is followed up with a more explicit testimonial poem, in which women of El Cuá explain the destruction of the community and the torture and assassination of the townspeople (57). By engraving these testimonies in public memory, Cardenal contributes to compiling a women's history of *somocismo* and of the revolution.

Compared with others of his generation, Cardenal shifted out of formal and thematic self-absorption and filled the emptiness with social commitment. His poetry in the intervening years, after *Epigramas* and before *Vuelos*, builds progressively and resolutely toward a final epistemological union of Marxism and Christianity.

But this concern with class and gender in his later poetry is nowhere to be found in *Epigramas*. It was not until Cardenal spent time in Gethsemani, Kentucky, with Thomas Merton that his consciousness began to awaken and he moved beyond the limitations of bourgeois nationalism and introspective poetry. It was in Colombia, though, that he gained an appreciation for liberation theology and began to plan Solentiname—a Christian base community on the island of the same name. Of greatest import in the period following his early work, however, is Cardenal's political and philosophical growth, which took a qualitative leap after he visited Cuba and then published *En Cuba*. For it is in this historical and geographical context that he began to piece together the epistemological union of Marxism and Christianity, and it is this new Weltanschauung that encompasses his later work.

The Intervening Works

Epigramas, then, is the youthful, romantic, and liberal stage of Cardenal's political and cultural development without the more overt Christian and Marxist inflections that can be observed from 1973 to the present. His epigram on Adolfo Báez Bone carries through, as Cardenal himself has commented, to a higher level of political consciousness, to "Hora cero" (Zero hour),[8] written just after the April 1954 Conspiracy—in which Cardenal was involved—and published in its entirety in 1959.[9] In this poem his own political participation interlocks with a nationalist struggle for liberation, albeit in the interests of the bourgeoisie. Beginning with the exploitation of Nicaraguans by U.S. multinationals such as the United Fruit Company and then studying the heroic resistance of Sandino to U.S. imperialism, the poem then moves into a description of the April Conspiracy and ends with a sinister and callous portrait of Somoza. Not only does a qualitative leap mark a divide between his prior political outlook and this more comprehensive one, but also, in tandem, his poetry begins to acquire the characteristics that make his later poetry unique.

In the formal realm, "Hora cero" is a collage of such features as:

1. *contrasts or conflicts*, which fan out into a wide variety of political, economic, linguistic, and social areas (light/dark, humanization/dehumanization, collective/individual, labor/capital, historical data/government cover-up, English/Spanish);

2. *structural shifts*, which provide intercalated commentary on the main body of the poetic text (remarks by the third-person narrator concerning the historical narration of events, insertion of verses from a song Sandino's army sang in contrast to the narration);

3. *repetition or choral effect*, which underscores the poem's thesis as it contrasts with the position espoused by the poem's antagonists ("and he [Sandino] was neither a military man nor a politician" in order to affirm his very ordinary background and "So that there are cheap bananas / And so that there are cheap bananas"

to point out the irrational roots of the capitalist system in its exploitation of the banana workers and to show how the crisis of overproduction functions);

4. *conjunctions*, which are used decisively in reinforcing the basic conflicts between labor and capital: *o* (or) and isolated nouns become a mode of expression for the irrationality or whimsical spirit of the "free market," while *y* (and) links a series of events that tie the exploitation of Nicaraguan workers to U.S. imperialism;[10]

5. *structural balance or the balance of fragments*, which allows Cardenal to depict the interworkings of capital's exploitation of the banana workers in contrast to the workers' resistance and oppressed conditions.

These formal techniques are directly fused to thematic concerns; they allow Cardenal to present a broad, murallike representation of U.S. imperialism, Somoza, and Sandino's nationalist opposition to both. Thus, the territory is much more extensive in "Hora cero" than in the earlier *Epigramas*. While his poems are much more exhaustive in "Hora cero" than in *Epigramas*, his subsequent works will cast a much larger net on social, political, historical, theological, and philosphical issues. At this stage, Cardenal has not, for example, fully come to grips with materialism, he has not carved out a philosophical position that highlights the complementarity of Marxism and Christianity.

Cardenal's next two books of poetry, *Gethsemani, Kentucky* (1960) and *Psalmos* (1964), are products of the poet's religious conversion. The first of these works is a series of poems based on his experiences as a Trappist monk with Thomas Merton in Gethsemani from 1957 to 1959. On the whole, the poems are shorter and the information less densely presented than in "Hora cero." Nonetheless, Cardenal does include precise data—about multinational corporations and radio ads, for example—that are counterposed to the alternative way of life of the Trappist monks, whose values deny the mores of multinational capitalism. In opposition to the waste that capitalism generates (described in "Como latas de cerveza vacías" [Like empty beer cans]), the poet turns to the fullness of life via mystic introspection (found in "En Pascua resucitan las cigarras" [The locusts resuscitate at Easter]).[11] It seems quite evident that Cardenal's conversion to the mystic tradition stands in stark contradistinction to the global expansion of U.S. imperialism. One can now envision clearly the evolution that takes place between this conversion and his work with the Solentiname collective, 1965–1977, in the midst of and in opposition to the oligarchy and the military's collaboration with the economic and political interests of U.S. multinationals.

The blueprints for a utopian community in Solentiname were modified somewhat, stripped of much of their idealism, when Cardenal lived in Cuernavaca, Mexico, in 1959–60 and later in Colombia with the liberation theologian Camilo Torres. While the poems in *Gethsemani* concentrated on the poet's communion with God in contrast to the alienation and destruction of capitalism, in the poems collected in *Psalmos* a radical shift allows Cardenal, through Torres's teachings, to appreciate the affinities between Christianity and socialism. In this work, formally similar to the biblical Psalms, the poet pleads with God through the voice of the oppressed to intervene on their behalf. But these are not just the cries of the oppressed of biblical times, they are also the invocations of the proletariat, of Jews who were persecuted in Nazi concentration camps, of animals, of the victims of gangster shootouts. During his stay in Colombia, Cardenal acquires the ability to delve into the complexity of this oppression and to portray it in a much more palpable, sociohistorical way.

From 1965 on, his poetic career and conscious understanding of objective reality are even more acute. In his next two works, *El estrecho dudoso* (The uncertain strait, 1966) and *Homenaje a los indios americanos* (Homage to the American Indians, 1969), Cardenal utilizes many of the formal features in "Hora cero" to rewrite Nicaraguan and continental American history from the point of view of the oppressed. Thoroughly researched and documented, both works present this history in a narrative and not a strictly poetic form. In employing this narrative technique, which harks back to epic poetry, Cardenal is able to cite the conquistadors' chronicles as well as historical sources—such as Bartolomé de las Casas's writings—that do not see the world upside down. Concreteness and precision are certainly the most salient characteristics of both *El estrecho* and *Homenaje*. These heavily researched works on the different dimensions of colonialism prepare Cardenal for his later forays into the analysis of imperialism and stand apart from his previous work because of the tremendous breadth of his poetic representation.

Another important advance in Cardenal's poetry comes with the publication of *Canto nacional* in 1973. In terms of its political commitment, this book of poetry is probably equaled only by *Psalmos*. For it is in this work that the Marxism he had been studying seriously at least since his trip to Cuba in 1970 fuses with the liberation theology he had been advocating since his residence with Camilo Torres in Colombia. A natural progression takes place in his oeuvre. Compiling all the elements of his poetry that have made it so profound—his detailed historical research, his knowledge of plant and animal species, the formal devices of "Hora cero"—Cardenal creates a tour de force that provides a sweeping analysis of the class struggle in Nicaragua. Above all, he stretches beyond mere exposition and endorses the FSLN's role in that struggle.

One of the interesting formal techniques in *Canto* is Cardenal's use of the abrupt intercalation of verses in contrast to the narrative flow of books like

Estrecho dudoso. It is as though Cardenal were trying to communicate the need for revolution through poetic form, as though one could see the sparks flowing from the sharp divisions among the classes. Throughout the poem we find powerful references to the class conflict: "Tierra que nos han robado / Banqueros, dinastía Somoza, compañías, nos la han robado / y la roban cada día" ("Land that they have stolen from us / Bankers, Somoza dynasty, companies, have stolen it from us / and they steal it every day").[12] In addition to describing the class confrontations, Cardenal inscribes the struggle within the boundaries of nationalism. Hence, the FSLN's fight also sets the autochthonous against the alien (U.S. imperialism).

Unlike in his early work, here Cardenal does not just denounce Somoza Debayle as an evil individual and the oligarchy as greedy. Rather, he transcends the limitations of this liberal stance by going to the heart of the class struggle: labor versus capital. In that respect, *Canto nacional* and his explosive "Oráculo sobre Managua" (Oracle above Managua) represent a higher development in Cardenal's understanding and expression of the revolutionary struggle in Nicaragua, and this conscientization—Paulo Freire's term—also entails a leap in his poetic abilities.

Written in the same year as *Canto*, "Oráculo sobre Nicaragua" is a biographical poem dedicated to the young revolutionary and poet Leonel Rugama and, by implication, to the revolutionary struggle itself. More than any other work that we have examined thus far, "Oráculo" prefigures the type of poetry Cardenal writes after the revolution. Here we find him searching into the deep recesses of material and spiritual life in order to confirm the validity of revolutionary struggle. The poem's most prominent elements are descriptions of the nature and motion of energy, biblical references that complement evolutionary theory, and portraits of Leonel Rugama's life and his involvement in the famous standoff with the National Guard.

In relation to his previous poetry, the most singularly important formal (and thematic) feature may be the scientific research, for it is clear that Cardenal's ideology has steered toward a greater understanding of historical materialism and of scientific socialism. This poem and his later works, *Vuelos de victoria* (1985) and *Cántico cósmico* (Cosmic song, 1989), always create a nexus of liberation theology, revolution, and the motion or energy of the universe. For Cardenal, these three elements synthetically fuse into a totality that explains a great deal about objective reality. They are also mutually complementary within the totality that the poet represents:

> Hacer concreto el Reino de Dios.
> Es una ley establecida por la naturaleza
> —que ninguna molécula puede retener permanentemente
>   más energía que las otras—.[13]

[To make the Kingdom of God something concrete.
It is a law established by nature
—that no molecule can permanently retain
    more energy than the others—.]

Thus, in this lengthy historical poem, imperialism goes against the natural course of the universe, whereas revolution proposes to follow its development (*"Texaco, Standard Oil* . . . Los monopolios / se extinguirán como los dinosaurios del Jurásico," 215 [Texaco, Standard Oil . . . The monopolies / will become extinct as the Jurassic dinosaurs]).

Leonel Rugama stands at the intersection of the universe, the revolution, and Christianity, becoming a modern-day saint or martyr. As is customary in Cardenal's later poetry, the poet wants to honor this martyr with an epic homage and to rewrite history from the perspective of those who, to Cardenal's mind, are carrying history foward. The poet accomplishes this through a dialogue in which he speaks with Rugama. It is not, however, just a dialogue that he is having with the young martyr, but also a eulogy because Rugama was killed defending the progress of humanity:

Vos buscabas la comunión, la
    comunión con la especie.
Después de todo morir por los demás
no fue acto de análisis científico sino de fe.
    La praxis de la Pascua. (223)

[You were looking for communion, the
    communion of the species.
After all dying for everyone else
was not the product of scientific analysis but rather of faith.
    The praxis of Easter.]

Here we must clearly note the religious overtones. Cardenal's scientific research acts as a buttress and does not interfere with his liberation theology. Hence, despite his interest in exploring virtually every facet of evolutionary theory, Cardenal, as one would suspect, still holds that it is faith that impels human beings—and the universe, for that matter—to act. In the case of Rugama this view is logical because he was a seminarian in Acahualinca, but in similar instances, as we will see in *Vuelos de victoria*, the martyrs, whether they are atheists or not, are considered to be saints.

One final aspect of "Oráculo" that deserves mention is that Cardenal meticulously describes the final shootout between three young FSLN members—Rugama among them—and Somoza's National Guard (228–31) by relying on articles from *La Prensa* and the comments of people from the neighborhood to communicate this event visually and to magnify it in the class struggle. This "objective" report is combined with Cardenal's own observations on Rugama's life, his explanation of the movement of the universe, and his denunciation of capitalism as a system that "prohibits us from loving [one another]" (225).

Throughout the poem, Cardenal focuses on Rugama's life because, in many ways, it parallels his own. It is perhaps even more important because Cardenal, at this point, had not fully engaged himself in the struggle, but was contemplating such an act. In ending this section on the middle stages of Cardenal's poetry, it would helpful to scan at least briefly Rugama's major poetic work, *La tierra es un satélite de la luna* (The earth is a satellite of the moon, published posthumously in 1978) and take stock of the thematic and formal parallels between the young Rugama's work and Cardenal's poetic corpus.

Leonel Rugama, the "Militant Saint"

In the preface to Editorial Nueva Nicaragua's 1983 edition of *La tierra es un satélite de la luna*, José Coronel Urtecho correctly observes that, for all their ideological and political differences, Ventana—a group that was essentially the literary wing of the FSLN—and the *vanguardia*—known for its fascist leanings—actually held at least three things in common: technical experimentation, exploration of the indigenous past, and political involvement. Leonel Rugama's verses are emblematic of these tendencies.[14] A young member of Ventana, Rugama dared not only to write poetry, but also, more significantly, to spill his blood for the revolutionary cause. Since few, if any, had set that sort of precedent, Rugama has achieved a monumental status, along with Carlos Fonseca, as the exemplary revolutionary in Nicaragua. According to Coronel Urtecho, for instance, Cardenal and Rugama are "los dos grandes poetas revolucionarios que han tenido eco" (15) (the two great revolutionary poets that have had an echo).

What gives Rugama these credentials is precisely the fact that he is both an excellent poet *and* a revolutionary. Some of the poetry collected in *La tierra* is written in the midst of revolutionary activity, while other poems were published in *Taller* (a journal established at the University in León) and in *La Prensa literaria*. As Beverley and Zimmerman point out in their study of his role as both poet and revolutionary within Ventana, Rugama follows in the footsteps of those in this literary group who urged people not just to represent the struggle, but also to join it.[15] In a sense, then, Rugama, along with

Cardenal—although Rugama clearly exercises some political influence over Cardenal—can be credited with being the poets most active in creating a revolutionary subjectivity and consciousness.

In two of Rugama's well-known political and poetic invocations, "Como los santos" (Like the saints) and "La tierra es un satélite de la luna" (The earth is a satellite of the moon), one can begin to comprehend why it is that this poet was more keenly aware than others of the type of revolution that needed to take place. In the first of the poems Rugama calls out to the oppressed in order to get them congregated. In the process, he describes the conditions of the marginal population and of the working class:

> aseado chófer particular
> engrasado taxista
> camionero polvoso
> busero gordo
> soldador borracho
> zapatero remendón
> judío errante afilador de cuchillos
> > de hachas
> > machetes y tijeras. (61)

> [tidy private chauffeur
> greasy taxi driver
> dusty truck driver
> fat bus driver
> drunk welder
> shoe repairer
> wandering jewish knife, ax
> > machete and scissor
> > sharpener.]

After naming almost every conceivable profession or quasi profession, the speaker addresses them in an autobiographical manner, speaking to them of his commitment to "kill the hunger that kills us" (65). The last stanza seems to indicate that this poem was written just before he joined the guerrillas, thus committing his life to the cause:

> las imágenes de los santos
> de los santos que han muerto matando el hambre
> y en la mañana imito a los santos. (66)

[the images of the saints
of the saints who have died killing hunger
and in the morning I will imitate the saints.]

Having verbally committed himself to the revolution, Rugama briefly recounts the deeds of certain inspiring revolutionaries (among them Sandino
and Che Guevara). As in Cardenal's work, the revolutionary figures are not
only saints, they are also inscribed in the history of the Nicaraguan people.
Both poets make these heroes come alive again in the oral tradition of the oppressed. Rugama's ideological structure is founded on liberation theology
and Marxism. The subjects that emerge from the interstices of these systems
of thought are the oppressed and the proletariat, the very subjects of the
revolutionary struggle according to Rugama.

His poetry is similar to Cardenal's not only in terms of the thematic layers,
but also in formal devices. Like Cardenal, Rugama employs repetition to
emulate ordinary speech, and he uses colloquial language as he does so. In
order to highlight the most significant thematic nodes (the condition of these
marginal workers, for instance), Rugama arranges the pictorial space of the
poem much as the elder Cardenal does. Conjunctions accentuate the labori-
ousness of the tasks that the workers must carry out and thus point to the
misery of their condition and the historical need for revolution in order to
overcome these exploitative circumstances. But most significantly, Rugama
is able to record the most minute details of everyday life and to describe them
in the common language of the worker. This is what makes him, along with
Cardenal, a practitioner of praxis even in his poetic vocation. As Coronel
Urtecho puts it, Rugama is an expert in "poetic agitation."

In the remainder of this chapter, I would like to gather together the different strings of thought that I have seen in these intervening stages of Ernesto
Cardenal's and very briefly in Rugama's poetry. What follows is an in-depth
look at the formal and thematic features I alluded to in my discussion of
Vuelos de victoria.

The Ethical Dialectic of Individual and Society

In liberation theology, traditional Christian concepts such as sin, faith, salvation, and resurrection are reworked and redefined in relation to social class,
race, and (to a lesser degree) gender. Since the rise of the bourgeoisie in the
late eighteenth century, the church had reinforced these notions—in the
Paulist tradition—as "private property" belonging to the soul. Historically,
individuals devoted themselves to personal relationships with God. Libera-

tion theologians have argued that privileging such an interpretation suppresses a social reading of these concepts (faith, sin, etc.).

Contrary to the laissez-faire approach, liberation theology returns to the primitive communism found in, for example, Acts, Matthew, Mark, and Luke.[16] In response to the exploitation of labor, the extraction of raw materials and surplus value, and the violence perpetuated by U.S.-trained militaries, among many other things, an increasing number of theologians see capitalism as highly detrimental to the people of Latin America. Particularly since the Cuban revolution, José Miranda, Gustavo Gutiérrez, and other liberation theologians have drawn parallels between Marxism and Christianity, and have seen the two epistemologies as compatible agents for social change. Following in that tradition, Cardenal's poetry redefines traditional theological concepts not as pertaining solely to the hypothetically isolated individual, but rather as expressing the dialectical process enacted when the individual commits himself or herself to the community. Thus, the once static or ossified concepts regain an active spirit of engagement in social and political life.

The Reelaboration of Faith as Praxis

Against an exclusive conception of faith as vertically structured, Ernesto Cardenal's *Vuelos de victoria* (1985) aims at synthesizing the duality of materialism and idealism (the division between mind and body). Faith moves vertically and horizontally, making it clear that God is among humans and operates through them. This position stands in stark contrast to a feudal, hierarchical structure that ostensibly emulates a divine order in the universe. Cardenal's poetry points to socialism—that is, to a social system that attempts to break down class structure, to empower people with more decision-making possibilities, to distribute wealth more equitably, to provide everyone with free health care, education, and housing, and so forth. Poetry is active and dialogic in the present, consistently providing the reader with expectations that social circumstances are going to improve. In a manner reminiscent of Ernest Bloch, Cardenal projects a future utopia that attempts to recover the prehistoric desire for collectivity. Like Bloch he valorizes the impending recognition of the material authenticity of human beings' social nature; he calls for an organic, rather than a destructive, relation between beings. His outlook is *concrete*, even though he too is a "Marxist philosopher of religion," as Fredric Jameson remarked of Bloch.

Thus, transforming the material conditions of capitalism in such a way that human beings are able to fully share in the act of production and the surplus value that the economic system creates is an integral part of faith. Cardenal distinguishes between a ruthless and exploitative system that no amount of tinkering can substantially change and the more humane system that was being created by the Nicaraguan people and that proved to be more fulfilling in spite of the hardships. This dichotomy is spelled out in the structure of *Vuelos de victoria*.[17] The first part of the book is entitled "Antes de la victoria" (Before the victory) and the second part "Después de la victoria" (After the victory). Although the first section constitutes a smaller portion of the book — five poems, as compared to forty in the second part — Cardenal never ceases to refer to the *somocista* years. Instead of focusing on a fetishized, individual belief system, Cardenal expresses faith as collective hope and realization, seen from the perspective of an individual speaker. In place of bourgeois moralism, the reader now becomes aware of the constant dialectic between the speaker and the world. It is worth recalling that Cardenal's earlier poetry (especially *Epigramas*) tended toward introspection: the speaker was detached from the collective (at least, there was no community in sight) and social analysis was reduced to placing blame on the individual. From "Hora cero" onward, the speaker is positioned in a highly complex and organized system of exploitation. "La llegada" (The arrival) as contrasted with "Otra llegada" (The other arrival) in the second part of the book describes a materialist faith that casts reality in a humanizing light while the sociohistorical conditions of *somocismo* continue to warp human potential. In the first poem, the speaker's faith or dream anticipates the revolutionary changes — Cardenal actually foresees the qualitative leap that will take place in 1979 because of his keen awareness of the contradictions plaguing Nicaragua during this prerevolutionary period and his involvement in revolutionary change. The second poem represents the fulfillment of this prophetic vision, the material confirmation of Cardenal's faith. The first section of the poem seems to foreshadow revolutionary change:

Bajamos del avión y vamos nicaragüenses y extranjeros
revueltos hacia el gran edificio iluminado — primero
Migración y Aduana — y voy pensando al acercarnos
pasaporte en mano: el orgullo de llevar yo
el pasaporte de mi patria socialista y la satisfacción
de llegar a la Nicaragua socialista — "Compañero" . . .
me dirán — un compañero revolucionario bien recibido
por los compañeros revolucionarios de Migración y Aduana
— no que no haya ningún control, debe haberlo
para que no regresen jamás capitalismo y somocismo —
y la emoción de volver otra vez al país en revolución
con más cambios cada vez, más decretos de expropiaciones
que me cuenten, transformaciones cada vez más radicales
muchas sorpresas en lo poco que uno ha estado fuera

y veo gozo en los ojos de todos—los que quedaron
los otros ya se fueron—y ahora entramos a la luz
y piden el pasaporte a nacionales y extranjeros
pero *era un sueño* y estoy en la Nicaragua somocista
y el pasaporte me lo quitan con la cortesía fría
con que me dirían en la Seguridad "pase usted"
y lo llevan adentro y ya no lo traen (seguramente
estarán telefoneando—seguramente a la Seguridad
a la Presidencial o quién sabe a quién) y ahora
todos los pasajeros se fueron y no sé si voy a caer preso
pero no; regresan con mi pasaporte al cabo de una hora
la CIA sabría que esta vez yo no fui a Cuba
y estuve sólo un día en Berlín Oriental
por fin yo ya puedo pasar al registro de Aduana
solo yo de viajero en la Aduana con mi vieja valija
y el muchacho que me registra hace como que registra
sin registrar nada y me ha dicho en voz baja "Reverendo"
y no escurca abajo en la valija donde encontraría
el disco con el último llamado de Allende al pueblo
desde La Moneda entrecortado por el ruido de las bombas
que compré en Berlín Oriental o el discurso de Fidel
sobre el derrocamiento de Allende que me regaló Sergio
y me dice el muchacho: "Las ocho y no hemos cenado
los empleados de la Aduana también sentimos hambre"
y yo: "¿A qué horas comen?" "Hasta que venga el último avión"
y ahora voy a ir hacia la tenebrosa ciudad arrasada
donde todo sigue igual y no pasa nada *pero he visto*
los ojos de él y me ha dicho con los ojos: "Compañero." (11–13; my emphasis)

[We get off the plane and Nicaraguans and foreigners walk along
in a scrambled manner toward the big illuminated building—first
Immigration and Customs—and I am thinking, passport in hand, as we get
closer about: the pride of carrying
my socialist homeland's passport and the satisfaction
of coming into a socialist Nicaragua—"*Compañero*" . . .
they will say to me—a revolutionary *compañero* who is well received
by his revolutionary *compañeros* at Immigration and Customs
—not that there shouldn't be any control, there should be
so that capitalism and *somocismo* never return—
and the emotion of returning once again to our country in revolution
with more changes taking place, more decrees of expropriations
that they tell me about, even more radical transformations
many surprises in the little time that one has been away

and I see the joy in the eyes of all—those who stayed
the others already left—and now we enter the light
and they ask for national and foreign passports
but *it was a dream* and I am in Somozan Nicaragua
and they take my passport with cold courtesy
with which they will tell me in Security Headquarters "come in"
and they take it inside and don't bring it back (they most
certainly are telephoning—most likely the Secret
Service or who knows who) and now
all the passengers are gone and I don't know if I'm going to be taken prisoner
but no; they return with my passport an hour later
the CIA probably knows that this time I didn't go to Cuba
and I was in East Berlin only one day
I can finally go through the checkpoint at Customs
I am the only passenger left in Customs with my old suitcase
and the young man who searches pretends to search
without searching anything and he has said to me softly "Reverend"
and he doesn't dig deep down in the suitcase where he would find
a record with Allende's last call to the people
from La Moneda interrupted by noise of bombs
which I bought in East Berlin or Fidel's speech
about the overthrow of Allende which Sergio gave to me
and the young man says to me: "It's eight o'clock and we employees in Customs haven't eaten dinner we are also hungry"
and I replied: "When do you eat?" "After the final plane arrives"
and now I'm going to go out into the dark, leveled city
where everything is the same and nothing happens *but I have seen*
his eyes and he has said to me with his eyes: "Compañero."]

We assume that the speaker has, in fact, arrived at Augusto Sandino Airport
in revolutionary Managua, but "it was a dream and I am in the Somozan Nicaragua" interrupts his delightful experience, as well as our smooth reading.
But in these verses the language indicates what effect revolutionary changes
would have on the subject: the new society fills Cardenal with pride because
he is an integral part of it (that is why he employs the possesive "mi"). From
this moment onward, however, Cardenal confronts the dehumanizing and
distorted character of social relations under Somoza's dictatorship: the all-
too-frequent experience of having his passport and his belongings exces-
sively checked. The last two lines return to the initial reality with an insistence that describes the materiality of Cardenal's faith: "and now I am going
to go out into the dark, leveled city / where everything is the same as before

and nothing happens but I have seen / his eyes and he has said to me with his eyes: '*Compañero.*' "

In "La llegada," as in the whole of Cardenal's poetry, his ideological formation depends on the human body as the maximum source of communication. It is particularly vision, Cardenal's different way of seeing—to put it in John Berger's terms—that unites his poetic corpus. Yet his poetry underscores the fact that this visual capacity does not emanate from a single subject (as bourgeois fetishism does), but rather enunciation naturally springs forth from collective agency. On the one hand, of course, the perspective is still Cardenal's, but what he sees—his very conscious framework—is authenticated by his recognition of the need for collective, political change. ("La llegada" ends with precisely this connection: "but I have seen / his eyes and he has said to me with his eyes: '*Compañero.*' ") Vision, then, for Cardenal is a privileged domain that reveals both the uniqueness of each individual and the universal bonds that make human beings one. In this poem, those proverbial mirrors of the soul—the eyes—serve as confirmation of material and ideal communion. As the poet imagines a socialist Nicaragua he "sees joy in the eyes of all," but the present reality in the poem—the historical coordinates of *somocismo*—then confronts what is, in fact, a dream. No matter. Dreaming for Cardenal entails a preemptive imagining of a more humane society where the fetishization and objectification of human beings vanishes into the historical past. Indeed, in this historical case, it is not just the poet's dream, but also that of the Nicaraguan people. As the reader will notice throughout *Vuelos de victoria* and in "La llegada," seeing can be a weapon for envisioning different types of complex social relations or for ignoring the immediate demands of *somocismo* in the name of a metaphorical way of interpreting reality, as the young man at Customs does as he pretends to register (another type of seeing) when he is not registering at all. For Cardenal, then, the senses—the very dehumanized, natural elements of our bodies—are humanized, used to their ultimate subversive potential as revolutionary weapons against the political machine of *somocismo* and, in fact, of capitalism itself.

This paradoxical humanizing of the senses in an inhuman environment comes out of Cardenal's religious background as the biblical commandment to love your neighbor as yourself, which is not seen as a calling to be kind and respectful toward your neighbor in one-on-one encounters, but rather is invoked as an allegory for the collective responsibility of socialism. By endowing this biblical commandment with a new, amplified significance with a social dimension, Cardenal strips it of bourgeois, individualist interpretation. Further, the idealism he posits is enmeshed in the materialism of the world and not divorced from it. That is, faith (as a potentially intangible substance) arises from or never fully leaves the physical world. It is this philosophical position that constitutes, as I will suggest in this chapter, an irreparable contradiction and that partly shields Cardenal's interpretation of objective reality.

An even clearer example of this notion of faith emerges in the poem "En el lago" (In the lake). In this context, the Kingdom of God is omnipresent, extending its light through evolution and revolution. The speaker draws parallels between the expansiveness of the universe and its concentration in one particular galaxy. Contemplating the universe leads the speaker to reflect on the place of this world in it and on the faith that human beings have, which permits them materially to change the world:

> Vengo de ser interrogado por la corte militar
> y pienso en los inmensos mundos sobre nosotros
>   una sola galaxia
>   (si la Tierra fuera como un grano de arroz
>   la galaxia sería como la órbita de Júpiter).
> Y pienso en el compañero "Modesto" en la montaña;
> de origen campesino; no se sabe su nombre.
> Luchan por cumplir nuestro destino en la galaxia. (19)

> [I come from being interrogated by the military court
> and I think of the immense worlds above us
>   only one galaxy
>   (if the Earth were like a grain of rice
>   the galaxy would be like the orbit of Jupiter)
> And I think of the *compañero* "Modest" in the mountains;
> from a peasant background; no one knows his name.
> They are fighting to carry out our destiny in the galaxy.]

Seeing in this poem can be interpreted as collecting data — the actual physical act of internalizing the world in images — and, metaphorically, as envisioning a different way of life that is more in keeping with our human nature. In these verses, the poet moves formally from seeing to thinking and then to remembering, and thematically from observing the wonders of the universe in Solentiname to the guerrillas who are fighting to "fulfill our destiny in the galaxy." When he is writing the poem, however, that destiny has not yet been fulfilled — it is a prerevolutionary poem. So, as in the example of "La llegada," the poet's thinking or imagining does not correspond *directly* to the reality in which he is living; rather, Cardenal constructs a more humane society based on the historical present and past. This world view rests not only on human nature on earth, but also on the evolutionary and revolutionary logic of the universe.

Faced with the torture of children, men, women, and the elderly, to which the speaker gives testimony in the following five verses, he upholds faith in love over destruction, revolution over dictatorship. But this is a rational faith, based on a prefigured rationality of the universe that is not distinguished from the Creator: "The Kingdom of God radiating light years." Consequently, the scientific and the religious cannot so easily be separated from each other; in fact, they feed off each other. It is as though Cardenal—in a manner reminiscent of Thomas Aquinas—aware as he was of the threat that science could pose to Christianity, persistently burrowed his way into science and searched for that fissure in rationality in which he could place his faith. Thus, instead of steadfastly clinging to the creation story in Genesis, he can, based on his materialist theology, affirm the materiality of human beings—that we are, in effect, atoms—while still retaining his belief in the Creator. Hence this comment: "Y la vida / ¿no será como la luz?" (And life / is it not like light?).

What he is doing, in fact, is exploring the historical and universal implications of "you are the light of the world," which, for Cardenal, must include the interweaving of all creatures of the universe, the natural material of the universe (the planets), and the Creator. And this investigation leads the reader back to vision once again, to the senses, which have the potential to absorb and act on this universe:

> ¡Tan lejos en el espacio-tiempo!
> Mundos que nos llegan sólo como luz.
> Pero la luz no toda la vemos. En el arco-iris
> tras la violeta está invisible el ultra-violeta
> Y está otro ultra tras el ultra-violeta
> ya es la zona del amor. (20–21)

> [So far away in space-time!
> Worlds that arrive to us only as light.
> But we don't see all the light. In the rainbow
> behind the violet stripe is an invisible ultraviolet
> And there is another ultra behind the ultraviolet
> that already is the area of love.]

Cardenal suggests that the more complex—and apparently chaotic—the universe becomes, the more it actually begins to jell, at which point the poet maintains that we encounter "the zone of love." In what could seem a paradoxical ideological maneuver, it is in the universe that the poet finds the justification for a collective way of life: "Pero el centro de la Vía lactea no es una estrella mayor / sino una concentración de estrellas" (But the center of the Milky Way is not a major star / but rather a concentration of stars). In the sociopolitical domain of Nicaraguan life, this translates into the comment that this distance could separate the universe from this world and estrange humans from their existence, but instead it gives their lives meaning. In concert with the vastness of the universe, of creation, the revolution fulfills its loving role, as it affirms both difference and unity. For instance, the Cuban revolution is compared to a concentration of disparate stars:

> Son como mil mundos los que yo miro
> pero los astrónomos pueden ver como un billón.
>   "Amar la evolución".
> En Cuba escuelas, policlínicas, círculos infantiles
> proliferaban como hongos después de la lluvia. (21)

> [There are some thousand worlds that I am seeing
> but the astronomers can see about a billion.
>   "Love evolution."
> In Cuba schools, clinics, daycares
> proliferated like mushrooms after a rainfall.]

Loving evolution simultaneously entails loving revolution. Thus, to love means to recognize, appreciate, and enhance human potential on earth, which implies affirming the wholeness of the universe in our every act. The association of revolution and evolution penetrates every aspect of these verses. They are not only related phonetically, but also linked in the structural relations within the verses and in their thematic message. The institutions that "naturally" grow in Cuba—which are human confirmations of humanity and universality—are compared to the mushrooms that sprout up after rains. This new (socialist) way of seeing, thinking, and acting is perceived as a more complex and richer development of humankind, a new stage in evolution. Finally, what is of import is that here socialism for Cardenal is thoroughly scientific and not utopian; socialist transformation becomes an organic turn in human history. Once again, while Cardenal at times appears to argue convincingly for scientific socialism, the utopian tendency within his thought never completely vanishes. In fact, in the final analysis, the utopian proves to be much stronger than the scientific. The scientific side wins out in this poem, however: "La gravedad no es sino la curvatura del universo / esto es, su anhelo de unión" (Gravity is nothing but the curvature of the universe / that is, its longing for union). In his liberation theology, to have faith means to work toward material conditions that will benefit all. A vision of the universe as movement, change, and love follows naturally:

En nuestro pequeño rincón, la revolución planetaria
    una humanidad sin clases
      aquello
por lo que gira el planeta alrededor del sol.
    ¡La unificación
    del universo! (21–23)

[In our small corner, the planetary revolution
    a humanity without classes
      that
which makes the planet revolve around the sun.
    The unification
    of the universe!]

Through their "small corner" passes the energy of the planet, negating the division of humanity (into classes) and asserting, instead, the unification of humankind. After the insurrection Cardenal transforms his faith into the very life of the revolution, so that it is an expression of the energy of the galaxy. Often the hazy blue suggests that Nicaragua is in the Kingdom of God or at a stage of communism (also conceived as heaven); thus, the transformations in revolutionary Nicaragua are interpreted as affirmations of the movement of the universe. This "spiritual materialism" is represented in "Meditación en un DC-3."

Recalling a line from Novalis, "To touch a naked body is to touch the heavens," the speaker begins to disentangle its significations:

    ¿Pero si no creen en el cielo?
Es claro que no es la bóveda azul atmosférica
    eso es siempre la tierra
y el ir volando en un DC-3 en el cielo de la patria liberada
es la tierra.
Pero la infinita noche negra
de las estrellas, con nuestra Tierra llena de humanos que se aman
y todas las demás amorosas Tierras
        es el cielo
      es el Reino de los cielos. (101)

[But what if they don't believe in heaven?
It is clear that it is not just a blue atmospheric dome
    that is always the earth
and flying in a DC-3 in the sky of the liberated homeland
is the earth.

But the infinite black night
of stars, with our Earth full of human beings who love one another
and all of the rest of the loving Earths
            is heaven
            is the Kingdom of the heavens.]

In these lines the speaker plays on the double meaning of "cielo" as both sky
and heaven, referring to the belief in heaven and the parallel concept of flying
in the sky. He seems to be distinguishing as well between existence and essence, which explains why he capitalizes "tierra" (earth) in two lines, while
not capitalizing it in two earlier ones. The earth is given meaning when humans love one another and thus reaffirm their Creator's love for them. And
this love is communicated via the senses of the body and especially when
those human senses are liberated, that is, when they are no longer subjected
to objectification as they are in capitalism. Hence, according to Cardenal, the
union of the material and the spiritual is a manifestation of God's perfection
and of communism:

besuquear un bebé,
pareja con caricias profundas,
apretón de manos,
palmadita en el hombro,
lo humano tocando lo humano,
la unión de piel humana con piel humana
es como tocar el Comunismo con el dedo compañeros. (my emphasis; 101)

[to kiss a baby,
a couple with profound caresses,
a shake of hands,
a slap on the shoulder,
someone human touching someone human,
the union of human skin with human skin
is like touching Communism with our fingers compañeros.]

Kissing, caressing, shaking hands, and patting someone on the shoulder are
physical expressions that unite human beings and that, paradoxically, allow
them to transcend conventional physical existence communally. We might
say — recalling Marx's memorable comment in the Eighteenth Brumaire — that
there the phrase goes beyond the content, here the content goes beyond the
phrase. For it is specifically in this last line of the poem where the materiality

of the form is fused with the energy of content. The very act of touching accrues a collective—and thus natural—signification when it is united with communism. As Terry Eagleton has acutely noted in commenting on the meaning of this passage from the *Eighteenth Brumaire*:

> The content of socialist revolution, by contrast, is excessive in all form, out in advance of its own rhetoric. It is unrepresentable by anything but itself, signified only in its "absolute movement of becoming," and thus a kind of sublimity. The representational devices of bourgeois society are those of exchange-value; but it is precisely this signifying frame that the productive forces must break beyond, releasing a heterogeneity of use-values whose unique particularity would seem to refuse all standardized representation. It is less a matter of discovering the expressive forms 'adequate to' the substance of socialism, than of rethinking that whole opposition—of grasping form no longer as the symbolic mould into which that substance is poured, but as the "form of the content," as the structure of a ceaseless self-production.[18]

Further, by capitalizing Marx's term for a utopian society, Cardenal implies that communism can be equated with the Kingdom of God as a sacred human creation. As an instrument of creation, as a development of consciousness, faith seeks to restore the collective relationship of human beings with the universe. In the words of Gustavo Gutiérrez, faith

> proclaims that the brotherhood which is sought through the abolition of the exploitation of man by man is something possible, that efforts to bring it about are not in vain, that God calls us to it and assures us of its complete fulfillment, and that the definitive reality is being built on what is transitory. Faith reveals to us the deep meaning of the history which we fashion with our own hands: it teaches us that every human act which is oriented towards the construction of a more just society has value in terms of communion with God—in terms of salvation; inversely it teaches that all injustice is a breach with him. (238)

Gutiérrez employs rather abstract terminology ("justice," "injustice") to define the role of faith as he interprets it in the Gospel. In *A Theology of Liberation* (1971), however, he, like Cardenal, makes it clear that the closest approximation to the Kingdom of God on earth is socialism. The danger is that Cardenal was almost resolutely uncritical of the revolution, and consequently the scientific socialism that is a vital part of his ideological position is met by resistance from a utopian socialist tendency, and the end result is that the latter frequently comes out on top. It is certainly idealist and perhaps dishonest to claim that Nicaragua was on the road to communism. The poems in the revolutionary period tend to picture the revolution as salvation or as heaven or as communism, as the last poem underlines.

One could speculate at this point about Cardenal's own participation in the revolutionary struggle in 1979 and wonder whether his *political*—and not military—association with the FSLN proves, in the end, to be detrimental to his ideological formation, or whether his pacifist background has somehow blocked all passage to revolutionary process as a painfully self-critical act. Or we may hypothesize that Cardenal's ideological stance does not differ so radically—it is not in fact more honestly Marxist—from the Sandinistas', in which case, the gap opening up between the poet's utopian and materialist versions of socialism would generally mirror the historical and political contradictions in which the FSLN found itself by 1990. Cardenal, however, would represent a more radical—yet utopian—wing of the FSLN.

Salvation and Resurrection in Revolution

It is doubtful that Ernesto Cardenal's mentor, Thomas Merton, would have agreed with Cardenal's synthesis of Marxism and Christianity (although he might have been sympathetic);[19] and it was only following some practical political experience (including the *somocistas'* destruction of Solentiname) that Cardenal did finally advocate armed struggle. Even before that, however, Cardenal clearly integrated the Christian concepts of salvation and resurrection with the Marxian ones. The heroic proletarians that Marx and Engels evoke in the *Communist Manifesto*, for example, must "undo the chains that bind them" because they can create a new society that will liberate them from their oppressive circumstances. This message is not unlike that of liberation theology. In the enigmatic Jesus Christ, the liberation theologian sees a revolutionary who shed his blood for the good of others; in liberation he recovers the meaning of freedom through revolution (against the Roman empire), and in resurrection he finds a martyr who lives on in the consciousness of the people.

Cardenal incorporates these concepts into a number of poems in this volume; for instance, into "La compañera del guerrillero." In addition, this poem brings to mind the universality of such a struggle:

> Ella era la compañera del guerrillero
>   —aunque el guerrillero estuviera casado—
> y cuando él fue matado ella entendió por primera vez
> lo que antes había oído y no entendía:
>   "la tierra que guarda los huesos queridos." (69)

[She was the guerrilla's *compañera*
   —although the guerrilla was married—
and when he was killed she understood for the first time
what she had heard before and not understood:
   "the earth which preserves loved bones."]

Although this poem does not contain overt religious references, it does communicate allusions to Christian paradigms. The death of her lover awakens an understanding in her; it moves her consciousness. Unlike an existentialist interpretation of death, this one describes a renewed significance: he is not cast into oblivion, but rather is retained by the earth and at the same time buried in her heart. His being is enmeshed in another human being, giving her new life, and he, by implication, is now a natural part of the earth. The guerrilla's death provokes a new understanding of life and the struggle that is based on natural, historical evolution, so that his death deepens her commitment to defending life:

Ella tiene un amor enterrado en su corazón,
y unos huesos enterrados en un rincón de esta tierra
contra la invasión yanki, contra
   los contra,
porque ella era la compañera del guerrillero.

[She has a loved one buried in her heart,
and some bones buried in a corner of this earth
against the Yankee invasion, against
   the contra,
because she was the guerrilla's *compañera*.]

Thus, he fights because he loves other human beings and because he wants to affirm his organic bond with the environment. As in other poems about resurrection, his remains take on a significance that transcends their mere material existence: they are equated with love, and her heart is likened to the earth. And this love becomes the driving spiritual force that allows the defense of the revolution to be carried out. As the language play indicates, this revolutionary love will overcome the U.S.-supported forces (the contra) in a negation of the negation—"contra los contra."

What is discomforting in this poem is the telling position of the woman. The message points in at least two directions. It is not clear whether the *compañera*'s role is merely to provide moral support for the male guerrillas or whether she is to join the struggle. Equally vague is the speaker's reference to her as the guerrilla's mistress. On the one hand, we could interpret this as a violation of individualistic morality, and on the other, we could surmise that infidelity or promiscuity is socially acceptable for men, but not for women. (She apparently is faithful to her married lover.) Moreover, she is a guerrilla's anonymous lover whose existence, we are to infer, cannot be separated from his. Thus, the guerrilla (man) is active, whereas she is passive. By positing this reductive and essentialist opposition Cardenal seems to ignore the central role that women played in the revolutionary struggle—not as secondary but as primary agents in the toppling of Somoza's Nicaragua.[20]

"A Donald y Elvis" (To Donald and Elvis) presents a vision of liberation and resurrection similar to the one in "La compañera del guerillero." Cardenal begins by calling his *compañeros* from Solentiname sacred. They are holy because they fought for others, fought with the FSLN in the revolution, and are now remembered by a school and a library constructed in their names. Like Christ, Cardenal suggests, Donald and Elvis worked to better humankind, but were assassinated by the authorities. And also like Christ, they have been not only commemorated in buildings where the public congregates, but also resurrected in the consciousness of the community:

> Cuando vi los huesos desenterrados de los dos
> te recordé Donald diciendo en la misa de Solentiname
> que la resurrección no eran las quirinas saliendo de las tumbas
> sino la supervivencia de la conciencia en los otros. (92)

> [When I saw the bones of the two disinterred
> I remembered Donald saying in mass in Solentiname
> that resurrection was not the quirinals leaving the tombs
> but rather the survival of consciousness in others.]

The sanctity of their lives remains in the community because they committed themselves to it. Cardenal counters the degradation of the human body in capitalism with a valorization of the body that does not allow a division of mind and matter. His theology affirms afterlife when one gives one's own physical self fully for the community:

> Así también la Revolución tiene sus reliquias y mártires.
> La voz campesina de Felipe guardada en un cassette
>   también es sagrada.
>   La otra de las tres islas grandes es la Felipe Peña.
> Donald, Elvis, y Felipe que murió sin tumba,
>   ustedes ahora son santos. (93)

[The Revolution also has its relics and martyrs.
Felipe's campesino voice preserved on a cassette
    is also sacred.
       And the other one of the three big islands is Felipe Peña.
Donald, Elvis, and Felipe who died without a tomb,
    you are now saints.]

Resurrection in Cardenal's poetry recuperates the collective nature of human beings not only through a spiritual recollection, but also vis-à-vis the body, which is seen as the body of Christ — all of humanity is one. As in the previous poem, the martyrs are not cast into some heavenly otherworld, but rather are fully integrated with nature:

Dios quiera que yo algún día fuera sagrado como ustedes.
Para la eternidad todo lo de ustedes ha quedado grabado
hasta cualquiera de sus gritos jugando fútbol.
El lago de Nicaragua reflejando el cielo
    es todo de ustedes.
El cielo que en el agua se refleja
    es de ustedes.

[God willing that I some day am sacred like you.
For eternity everything about you has been recorded
even any of your yells as you played football.
Lake Nicaragua reflecting the sky
    is all yours.
The sky that is reflected on the water
    is yours.]

In this poem, the poet visually reconstructs the physical presence and the acts of Donald and Elvis in such a way that they will never leave the community; everything they did is recorded and engraved in the memory of others. Committing their acts to public memory is another way in which Cardenal uses the senses to their maximum potential; this way of seeing overshadows any attempt to erase or destroy it. Also key in these verses is his centering on the double meaning of "cielo," exposing its material and ideal signifieds. Donald and Elvis are at the same time immanently a part of this world and transcendentally "beyond" it, in the universe, since they gave their lives for the community. Gustavo Gutiérrez has elaborated on this concept of salvation:

The true agents of this quest for unity are those who today are oppressed (economically, politically, culturally) and struggle to become free. Salvation—totally and freely given by God, the communion of men with God and among themselves—is the inner force and the fullness of this movement of man's self-generation which was initiated by the work of creation.[21]

The Dialectics of Sin

As I noted earlier in this chapter, Cardenal's *Epigramas* depict, almost exclusively, the role of individuals as lovers (Cardenal himself) or sinners (Somoza García). His poetry since that period has located individual sin in its dialectical relation with the social milieu that aids in forming the subject. In his famous poem on Marilyn Monroe, what stands out is not the personal tragedy in and of itself, but the world in which she lived. One could rightly argue that his later poems are more of an indictment of the dehumanization (hence, sin) of capitalism than the moral flaws of individual subjects.

In Cardenal's renowned narrative poem "Oración por Marilyn Monroe" the enigma that surrounds her as a Hollywood star and her subsequent objectification in the movie industry as a seductive, passive territory waiting to be conquered are analyzed in detail. Rather than a heroic tale, it is a story about alienation in industrial capitalism. She changed her name:

(pero Tú conoces su verdadero nombre, el de la huerfanita violada
    a los 9 años
y la empleadita de tienda que a los 16 se había querido matar)[22]

[(but You know her real name, the name of the orphan that was raped
    at the age of 9
and the young store employee who at 16 wished she had killed herself)]

Behind the makeup, the reader encounters a Marilyn fighting to survive. She alone is not the sinner; in many ways she is the victim of a system that exploits her natural beauty:

Pero el templo no son los estudios de la 20th Century Fox.
El templo—de mármol y oro—es el templo de su cuerpo
en el que está el Hijo de Hombre con un látigo en la mano
expulsando a los mercaderes de la 20th Century Fox
que hicieron de Tu casa de oración una cueva de ladrones. (65)

[But the temple is not the 20th Century Fox studios.
The temple—of marble and gold—is the temple that is her body
in which the Son of Man stands with a whip in his hand
driving out the moneychangers from 20th Century Fox
who made Your house of prayer a den of thieves.]

The image of her body (exterior) as gold and marble is set against the spiritual (interior) fire of Christ driving out the merchants who made God's temple a den of thieves. In another ironic move, Cardenal captures the linguistic emblems of exchange value—ivory and gold—which describe so precisely how Marilyn Monroe's skin and hair became mere products on the market. As the liberation theologian states in the following lines, the sinners are those who institutionally violate human sanctity (both body and soul). This "logic" of capitalism differs sharply from the "love your neighbor" of socialism:

Señor
en este mundo contaminado de pecados y radioactividad
Tú no culparás tan sólo a una empleadita de tienda.
Que como toda empleadita de tienda soñó ser estrella de cine.
Y su sueño fue realidad (pero como la realidad del tecnicolor). (65)

[Father
in this contaminated world of sin and radioactivity
You will not blame a young store employee.
Who as every young store employee dreamt about becoming a movie
    star.
And her dream came true (but the truth of technicolor).]

It is through a prayer, a dialogue with God, that the speaker is given the moral pretext to begin analyzing the life of this individual. The speaker envisions what the Creator's reaction will be: "You will not blame . . . ," and becomes His mouthpiece, as the difference between the speaker and the interlocutor is erased. Hence, this poem is as much about Cardenal's theology as about the destructiveness of capitalism. Dreaming—as the fulfillment of one's species being—comes up again as it differs from an artificial, inhuman environment (technicolor) that places appearance over essence. As commodities in the capitalist system, both Marilyn Monroe and the earth are degraded to the point that all that we see is a façade: the reductive appearance of what they have become. The commodity, as Marx wrote in the *Grundisse*, pits the value of things against their substance.[23]

Unlike his early depiction of Somoza, Cardenal emphasizes that Monroe is to be forgiven along with "us." Thus, what at first sight appears to be the fault or sin of the individual is quickly transferred to the collective realm. We are to blame for having allowed the accumulation of capital and the exploitation of individuals in multinationals like 20th Century Fox, as well as for having abandoned Marilyn when she felt alienated. In short, we shunned our duty to care for another human being and instead fostered the reign of the commodity—the primacy of appearance:

> Perdónala Señor y perdónanos a nosotros
> por nuestra 20th Century
> por esta Colosal Super-Producción en la que todos hemos trabajado.
> Ella tenía hambre de amor y le ofrecimos tranquilizantes.
> Para la tristeza de no ser santos
>   se le recomendó el Psicoanálisis.
> Recuerda Señor su creciente pavor a la cámara
> y el odio al maquillaje—insistiendo en maquillarse en cada escena—
> y cómo se fue haciendo mayor el horror
> y mayor la impuntualidad a los estudios.

> [Forgive her Father and forgive us
> for our 20th Century
> for this Colossal Super-Production in which all of us have worked.
> She was hungry for love and we offered her tranquilizers.
> For the sadness of not being saints
>   psychoanalysis was recommended to her.
> Remember Father her growing dread of the camera
> and the way she hated the makeup—insisting that she put her own
>   makeup on for each scene
> and how the horror grew larger
> and greater her absences from the studios.]

The narration continues by recounting the increasing objectification she felt as she began to "unravel" until one day she was found dead in her bed, still clutching a telephone receiver. In the final four verses of this section, her resistance to and rejection of the artificial world to which she used to respond are mounting. Her increasing opposition to her own commercialization manifests itself structurally within these lines via the repetition of "and," the enumeration of nouns such as "dread," "hate," and "horror," and her insistence that she be in control of herself rather than be doctored up by someone else, a "fresh" commodity. Cardenal uses this final scene as an allegory for her life:

Fue
como alguien que ha marcado el número de la única voz amiga
y oye tan sólo la voz de un disco que le dice:
WRONG NUMBER.
O como alguien que herido por los gangsters
alarga la mano a un teléfono desconectado. (66)

[It was
as though someone who has dialed the number of his only friend
and hears only the voice of a recording that says:
WRONG NUMBER
Or as though someone injured by gangsters
extended his hand toward a disconnected telephone.]

With this allegory Cardenal emphasizes the way functional objects and material benefit in capitalism have gained more importance than the life of human beings. Monroe connects with no one because human beings do not respond to her human condition, but rather let her deteriorate. The assistance that she was offered in the previous verses—tranquilizers and psychoanalysis—prove that the society is incapable of imaging and counteracting its own destructive powers against its members: in response to a social problem, it offers only individual alienation. In this poem Cardenal implies that we cannot cease to be accomplices of this destruction because it is a *social* phenomenon to which only social solutions can apply.

This portrayal can be read as the opposite of a number of poetic biographies that appear in *Vuelos de victoria*. One of the most compelling is a dialogue between the speaker and Laureano in the eulogistic poem "Viaje muy jodido" (A screwed-up trip). The speaker attempts to allow Laureano to speak through him, and then makes his own observations about this character's life. Laureano was interested in Marxism but had no intellectual training; he was a Christian, although he flirted with agnosticism. In a symbolic union of the two epistemologies, Laureano said, "Ya no creo en Dios ni en ninguna de esas mierdas. / Creo en Dios pero para mí Dios es el hombre" (123) (I no longer believe in God nor in any of that shit / I believe in God but for me God is man). Moreover, he—like Cardenal—negated the power of death over life:

> fuiste sobre todo mi hermano
> hermano bastante menor en años
>   pero sobre todo compañero
> ¿esa palabra te gusta más verdad?
>   La que más amabas después de la palabra Revolución.
> Compañero Sub-Comandante Laureano,

Jefe de los Guarda Fronteras:
Digo junto con vos, que nos vale verga la muerte. (125)

[You were above all my brother
a much younger brother
    but mainly a *compañero*
You like that word more don't you?
It's the one you liked the most besides Revolution.
Compañero Sub-Commander Laureano,
    Head of Border Patrol:
I say with you, that we don't give a fuck about death.]

The dialogic character of this poem as form, and the material resurrection of Laureano as content, negate the disappearance of the poet's dear friend. And this dialogic nature becomes ever more credible as Cardenal reassembles his own memories of this young man that relate to the collective struggle that combines Marxism and Christianity. Cardenal considers Laureano to be transcending the limits of his physical being—or at least to be fulfilling his human powers—because, unlike the sinner, he worked for the betterment of humanity and represented the natural processes of evolution and revolution. Thus, according to Cardenal, he occupies a space in eternity, as one who existed and continues to exist:

No has dejado de existir:
Has existido siempre
y existirás siempre
        (no sólo en este,
        en todos los universos).
Pero es cierto,
una sola vez viviste,
        pensaste,
            amaste.
Y ahora estás muerto.
Es estar digamos como la tierra, o la piedra, que es lo mismo,
"la piedra dura porque esa ya no siente".
Pero no, nada de piedra dura,
    sí estás sintiendo,
    más allá de la velocidad de la luz
        del final del espacio que es el tiempo,
totalmente consciente,
        dentro de la conciencia

vivicísima
de lo existente. (125–27)

[You haven't ceased to exist:
You have always existed
and will always exist
            (not only in this one,
        in all the universes).
But it is true,
you lived only one time,
                you thought,
                    you loved.
And now you are dead.
It is like being like the earth let's say, or a stone, which is the same thing,
"the hard stone because that one no longer feels."
But no, none of that hard stone,
you are feeling,
beyond the velocity of light
    from the end of space which is time,
totally conscious,
        within the very live
consciousness
    of that which exists.]

These lines are the culmination of a crescendo in which—in a concrete style—Laureano comes to life as he has fused his purpose in life with that of others. This is borne out formally in the poet's momentary isolation of Laureano's life—"only one time"—but then his life becomes a "living" part of the universe, where the intentions of all material being clearly outweigh the relative insignificance of one single member of that universe. As a Christian Marxist, Cardenal sees capitalism as a stagnating and even destructive social organization that acts against the natural unity of the universe, that holds up a false image of human nature as centered upon the destiny of the individual and does not focus on humankind's integration into the cosmos. The capitalist way of life, then, is tantamount to a negation of the living, sensuous consciousness of the universe—embodied in the Creator. The opposition between the loving nature of the universe and the decaying face of capitalism is so starkly drawn in this poem that readers—once they have visualized Cardenal's rendering of reality—are pushed to act to change the status quo. In short, seeing in Cardenal's poetry always involves a complex act of probing and of thinking things out, at which point one is so keenly aware of the true existence of things lying behind their appearance that one must act.

The interplay of exterior and interior, universe and revolution, can be located in his poetry as it relates to the speaker. For the narrator finds his own liberation and meaning through the lives of campesinos who have fought in the revolution to dismantle a dehumanizing society in order to replace it with one that hopes to minimize inequality and allow human beings to develop their potential. Cardenal's is a an idealistic Weltanschauung that projects into the future because material conditions permit only partial realization of it in the present.

Cardenal's poetry is undoubtedly replenished and even nourished by his commitment to socialism and, thus, to the campesinos. As a recorder of their collective and individual history, he insists on depicting the reality he and they experience in the most detailed way possible via realist form. Yet it is only logical that his mediation means that we are not reading the campesinos' testimony, but rather Cardenal's interpretation of their lives. Hence, his poetic work constitutes his commitment to the struggle for communism, which, in terms of his own class position, is always just beyond his ideological reach in the realm of self-representation. It is this depiction of oneself that we will observe in the popular poetry (chapter 5).

The Conjunctions of Form and Meaning

In contrast to the Barthesian revolution in language, Ernesto Cardenal's poetry attempts to reclaim the referent and, in the case of his homeland, to internalize the revolution through the subject and represent it in a collage of historical events. Cardenal has not, however, dismissed experimentation in language in favor of sloganistic political poetry. The uniqueness of his poetry lies in the relatively balanced distribution of vanguardist typographical techniques, language that simulates speech, and Marxist-Christian ideology. Interweaving these elements leads to interrogating the conventional bourgeois form of presenting reality with the tools of what Cardenal perceives as more empirical reality. In spite of the lucid formal analyses done by Jorge H. Valdés, Robert Pring-Mill, and Paul W. Borgeson, I am not convinced that Cardenal's formal techniques are any different from those of the avant-garde.[24] The film techniques and pictorial images mentioned in Pring-Mill's article can be found in the poetry of Ezra Pound, Rafael Alberti (in *Yo era un tonto*), André Breton, Vicente Huidobro, and others. It is, rather, Cardenal's simultaneous employment of vanguardist techniques, a conversational tone, and his unique world view that contributes something innovative to poetry. Generally speaking, as I have attempted to demonstrate in this chapter, it is his elaborate formal and thematic "way of seeing," based on a Marxist-Christian tour de force, that constitutes Cardenal's most fundamental contribution to Latin American poetry.

Cardenal's poetry expresses a mediated recording of collective conscious-ness through language that emulates ordinary speech, thus seeking to avoid the alienation with which hermetic poetry has been plagued and to return to the oral tradition, so that the poetic word can more closely replicate the spo-ken word. In other words, he seeks to provide poetry with its vital link to action, since, as Walter J. Ong argues, "the real word, the spoken word, is always an event, whatever its codified associations with concepts, thought of as immobile objectifications. In this sense, the spoken word is an action, an ongoing part of ongoing existence."[25] In his poetry Cardenal returns to this active impulse of the oral tradition, in which the senses are acutely en-gaged in reading the poem, much as they would be in interpreting and acting on reality.

"La mano" (The hand) exemplifies both formally and thematically the restoration of the unity of consciousness to which I have referred. It helps to explicate the binding relation that exists between the speaker (in first-person singular) and the collective. The agent that unfolds the poem, is, of course, the hand. The speaker identifies one particular hand and proceeds to examine its intricate parts, marveling that it is "un espacio plano con cinco prolongaciones cilíndricas ágiles / como acróbatas" (a flat space with five ag-ile, cylindrical acrobats). He later describes the great feats that the universal hand has carried out:

> La mano saludaba.
> Aquello que labró el primer pedernal
> lo que hizo rascacielos, libros, telas tractores y violines
> y también estas carrozas,
> una palma y cinco dedos,
> lo que hizo que el homínido pensara y hablara,
> descubriera fuego,
> hiciera estas carrozas revolucionarias,
> hiciera revolución. (129)

> [The hand was waving.
> That which ground the first flint
> which made skyscrapers, books, cloth, tractors, violins
> and also these floats,
> a palm and five fingers,
> which made the hominid think and talk,
> discover fire,
> make these revolutionary floats,
> make the revolution.]

Here the hand is not statically isolated from a social context, but rather more fully developed within a network of actual social relations. The physical appearance and existence of the hand and its labors are reiterated to exalt them: "a palm and five fingers," "made these floats," "make these revolutionary floats." The sum total of that labor is concisely depicted in two verses, one of them indented to add emphasis: "Todo lo que es hecho / todo lo humano de la tierra es hecho por manos" (Everything that is made / everything human on the earth is made by hands). The individual hand that the speaker defamiliarizes is lost in the hands of the multitude, enhancing the force of its social nature. Cardenal then, in concluding, shifts his focus to address the reader:

> Nada más que una mano
>   hermano dame tu mano
> también se nos dio las manos hermano para ir juntos
>   de la mano
> mano a mano
>   de la mano. (131)

> [Nothing more than a hand
>   brother give me your hand
> our hands were also given to us to walk together
>   by the hand
> hand in hand
>   by the hand.]

The repetition of "mano" inculcates it with the physical and historical meaning the speaker has attributed to it. The hand is visually extended to the poet, who, in turn, restores its collective and ethical significations. What is happening in this process is the gradual assimilation of the hand into the revolutionary subject, "her/mano." From there, the speaker redefines the hand in its social context; he establishes its social meaning vis-à-vis the prepositions "a" and "de," literally "hand upon hand" and "holding hands." The poet manages to expose the plurality of meanings that the hand has linguistically as well as a synecdoche for human beings who are naturally bound together. In other words, "mano" functions in the social milieu in the structure of the poem itself *and* allegorically as the source of social labor in the revolution.

The potential for typographical and ideological subjectivity—that is, the privileging of subjective appearance over objective reality—is subverted as collective unity is restored to form and content. It is a process similar to what we find in the poetry of Ezra Pound, in which there is very tight parallelism between medium and theme. Jean-Michel Rabaté has noted this process in Pound's *Cantos*:

> The tension between order and chaos is but the dramatization of the act of intellection, especially when history is the object, since the historical field is one in which meanings are not pre-given, even if facts abound. A voice is needed to give the surplus of meaning which can tilt forward the ideogram toward its volitional aim. The problematics of utterance and enunciation has to be placed in the gap between topographical fragmentation and ideological assertion, in the oscillation between a centre, an axis, and the ever-recurrent risk of dismemberment.[26]

The paradox of Pound's writing, as well as Cardenal's, is that empirical reality is dissected, appreciated in its heterogeneity, and then cohesively fused into a whole. This procedure is manifested in the physical layout of the poem, in shifting focus (between the subject and the speaker), and in thematic composition. Presenting the text in this way gives it a dynamic appearance; it motivates readers to act upon a reality that they can change.

One significant difference between Cardenal's poetry and that of his contemporaries Gioconda Belli, Ana Ilce Gómez, and Pablo Antonio Cuadra is his insistent use of conversational language. In his works, the word not only comes alive and implies action, it also speaks to a wider audience than traditional poetic diction can read. Thus, his poetry appeals to socialist interests, that is, it engages a sector of the population that has been excluded from aesthetic representation: the working class and the campesinos. Moreover, as I pointed out in the first half of this chapter, there is a parallel between structural and ideological presentation in that both inspire the reader to follows the act of reading into the realm of political action. Specifically, in loading his poems with verbs, juxtaposing poetic voices, and structurally uniting disparate characters, he convinces his readers that there is a collective human cause that needs their participation, and that by acting they are fulfilling God's purpose on earth. As I have noted in this chapter, however, from a historical-materialist perspective Cardenal's work—like Belli's—tends to offer enigmatic or overly idealistic solutions to the social contradictions in Nicaragua rather than incorporating these conflicts into his Marxist-Christian worldview.

I have singled out as the most heightened of the senses in Cardenal's poetry vision, which is closely related to a different way of perceiving human relations in capitalism, prompting the reader to conceive of a more humane society: socialism. While vision originates in Cardenal's individual class and gender ideology, he does implicitly test the limits of this particularism in his post-*Epigramas* poetry by showing—both formally and thematically—that all individual interpretations are ultimately collective. Indeed, his ideological position comes out of his own constrained bourgeois background, only to confront the limitations of this ideology as he maps the complexity of the contradictions in bourgeois society. At the same time, however, his political and religious principles—found in his belief in liberation theology—face their own horizons when they are countered with materialism. In short, what I have called Cardenal's "spiritual materialism" proves, in the eyes of historical materialism, to be an oxymoron: a discrepancy on the epistemological level—the evident inconsistency between idealism and materialism—and on a "praxical" level, that is, in the manner in which Cardenal envisioned and worked for socialism in Nicaragua. Cardenal's political and philosophical stance ultimately reflects the oscillations of the FSLN—at times he interprets the intricacies of the class struggle in Nicaragua and at other moments he posits utopian solutions in place of a more rigorous analysis. Thus, throughout his work, even in its late stages, Owen's and Fourier's thought is as likely to resonate as the gripping, conflictive nature of Marx and Engels's materialism.

CHAPTER 4
FEMINIST AND FEMALE SELF-REPRESENTATION IN REVOLUTION

In Nicaragua, as in many other Western countries, the student movement and the women's movement of the 1960s came to represent a threat to the established order. And, as in other parts of Latin America, these radical political developments began earlier than they did in Europe or in the United States. In 1959, the Cuban revolution shook the foundations of imperialism, and its reverberations were felt throughout the Americas. As the Kennedy administration planned the Alliance for Progress in Washington to bolster the "neighboring" economies—to avoid the revolutions in the developing world that Soviet leader Nikita Khrushchev had predicted—student militants began forming what was known as the Autonomy Generation, which would later evolve into the New Nicaragua Movement. This group originally included Sergio Ramírez, Carlos Fonseca, Tomás Borge, and Silvio Mayorga.[1]

Around the same time (1960) that the FSLN was founded, Ventana, a literary movement concerned with posing an alternative to traditional aesthetic production, surfaced in León. Its literary magazine became an innovative alternative to the traditionally bourgeois *La Prensa literaria*. While *La Prensa literaria* claimed to be developing more-authentic art that was devoid of political slogans and demagoguery, Ventana had no qualms about publishing works deemed to be "political." On the second anniversary of the Cuban revolution, for example, the editorial staff—consisting primarily of Fernando Gordillo and Sergio Ramírez—published a special issue on Cuban poetry (Randall, 31). An offshoot of *La Prensa literaria* took an even more conservative stance: as offspring of the *vanguardia*, Roberto Cuadra and Edwin Illescas argued that Nicaraguan literature had been tainted by political interests and that artists should concentrate on technical or literary experimentation. This group, the "Betrayed Generation," held polemical debates with Ventana.

These literary developments coincided with the new political activism. Although the FSLN was newly formed and had not yet carried out any significant political or military maneuvers, the Revolutionary Student Front (FER), founded in 1961 in Managua, was active in the university setting. And these organizational activities set up a base for more radical political praxis. FER, in essence, served as a front for the FSLN, which, at that time, was an

underground organization. Not until the late 1960s and early 1970s, however, did FER truly become embroiled in the more class-oriented politics. By
that stage they began organizing hunger strikes; demonstrations against the
increases in transportation, food, and milk costs; and marches supporting re-
lease of FSLN prisoners.[2]

In this political context the women's movement united into a cohesive
body and feminine and feminist literature came into being. One of the most
influential poets to have an impact in the 1960s, as we will have occasion to
note, was Michèle Najlis. She began her literary career as a "little sister" of
the Ventana movement—having published her first poems in their literary
magazine as well as editing the final issue—and later directed the militant
journal *Taller* with Alejandro Bravo.[3]

The Negotiation of Class and Gender

> *The Feminist struggle is not waged before or after the revolution. Nor does it
> go by unarticulated. The women's struggle is advanced simultaneously and in
> an articulated form as the revolutionary process. Before and after the revolution
> this struggle needs to be addressed. And this struggle must be accompanied by
> male "compañeros" as they too are victims of the "machista" ideology.*
>
> Elsa Tamez, "Theology of Liberation and Revolution: A Woman's Perspective"

As one-third of the revolutionary forces in Nicaragua, women were in-
strumental in toppling the dependent capitalist state. Consequently, their
struggle was seen from the outset as primarily ideological and was not
diverted to a question of "rights" (as it was in the United States, for example);
national armed resistance aimed at overthrowing Anastacio Somoza Debayle
took precedence over the rights of any particular constituency within the
FSLN.[4] Given the wartime conditions in Nicaragua—60 percent of the
budget allocated to the military, compounded by 30,000 percent inflation—
the primary objectives of the revolution changed rather drastically, and the
economic distribution of resources favored military expenditures. In addition, during their years in power, the Sandinistas tried to pay off the tremendous foreign debt that Somoza left them.

In spite of these disastrous economic circumstances, much political legis-
lation favorable to women was passed during the revolutionary period.
Women's organizations grew at a remarkable rate; AMNLAE (the Luisa
Amanda Espinosa Association of Nicaraguan Women), for instance, increased its membership from around 1,000 members in 1979 to 85,000 in
1985.[5] Sexual and racial equality, including equal pay and health benefits,
were written into the law. Prostitution and sexist advertising were banned.
In the political arena, women composed 22 percent of the FSLN's member-

ship, and they constituted 37 percent of the party leadership ("Movilización" 357).

In spite of the seemingly insurmountable economic and military crises, the Sandinistas had the backing of at least three-quarters of the population when they took power. Given that political support, both Maxine Molyneux and Beth Stephens have maintained, more could have been done to correct gender inequities, but many of the changes were postponed or curtailed in favor of national infrastructural projects.[6] While women benefited from the reduction of the illiteracy rate from 52 percent to 13 percent, the establishment of health centers, and the increased schooling, by 1985 the government had still not fully implemented a program to restructure the revolutionary family. Thus, the "double-shift day" was a frequent phenomenon, and 34 percent of all families were headed by single mothers. In addition, according to official sources, women made up 60 percent of the poor in Nicaragua ("Movilización" 357–58).

These circumstances, of course, have had an impact on ideological formations. In poetry the changes and contradictions in consciousness are being represented at the intersection of gender and class, and can be found in the verses of such writers as Michèle Najlis, Ana Ilce Gómez, Gioconda Belli, and Daisy Zamora. By analyzing such representations in the works of these poets, I hope to show that certain territories — the family, motherhood, reproduction — that have in patriarchial societies traditionally been considered female, were being both challenged and reinforced during both *somocismo* and *sandinismo*. In the process, it should become clear that we are dealing with a dispersed female identity and not reductively examining binary oppositions, that we are facing ideologies that — although they may agree on certain fundamental levels — also conflict with one another.

I am operating throughout under the assumption that gender roles and sexuality are social constructs. As we have seen, the definition and formation of gender roles in revolutionary Nicaragua, despite other economic and political demands, was still being contested, revised, and repressed at the time this poetry was written. The poetry records both this ongoing process toward liberation and the Nicaraguan society's collaboration with and minimalization of this emancipation movement. On a broad scale, then, a reading of the poetry of Ana Ilce Gómez, Daisy Zamora, and Gioconda Belli points to the controversial dialogue between feminism and socialism. Are the interests of the feminist movement subordinated to those of the revolution? Is it not possible to guarantee and reinforce women's rights in socialism without sacrificing the ideals of the revolution? And can this not be done in spite of the devastating economic and military imperatives that every revolution seems to face? These are the questions that I analyze in the poetic texts.

Before posing these questions and analyzing the poetry, however, we must begin with one of key historical figures in Nicaraguan women's poetry and in the FSLN itself, that is, with Michèle Najlis.

Najlis's poetry is unique for the late 1960s because she was one of the first women to achieve notice in the male-dominated vocation of poetry and because her work is both experimental formally and committed politically. Her major work before the revolution, *El viento armado* (The armed wind, 1969), has gained the respect of critics and artists precisely because it balances formal innovation with anti-*somocista* (and pro-FSLN) content.[7] The latter is important because her poetry, in this volume, appears to draw on a very broad set of ideological stances that find a common denominator in anti-oligarchical and pronational liberation struggles. Her work crosses the different political factions within the FSLN, from the liberal to the more radical segments, signaling both the widespread ideological currents operating within the FSLN and the elastic nature of Najlis's poetry.

Coming out of the Ventana tradition, Najlis's poetry, even when it gravitates in a more universal and romantic direction, firmly settles on the social bond between human beings. While the first part of *El viento armado* (through page 27) in fact engages in very few references to political militancy or the armed struggle, the social nature of human beings is strongly communicated in every one of these early poems. In "Hay días . . . " ("There are days . . . "), for instance, the presence of the Peruvian vanguardist poet César Vallejo is clearly felt:

> Hay días
> en que los gestos pesan como carga de pobre
> y el movimiento adivinado,
> presentido,
> pasa junto a nosotros como sin vernos.
> La inquietud que hierve en todo el cuerpo
> atraviesa las miradas,
> y el roce de las manos
> —invisible—
> llega hasta el libro que pretendemos leer,
> hasta el poema inconcluso
> hasta el drama en pequeño de todos los días. (17)

> [There are days
> when every gesture weighs like a poor man's load
> and the foretold movement
> anticipated,
> passes near us as if not seeing us.
> The restlessness that boils throughout the body

traverses the looks,
and the grazing of hands
—invisible—
until it reaches the book that we attempt to read,
until the unfinished poem
until the miniature play of every day.]

The reader may be reminded of Vallejo's *Poemas humanos* (Human poems), especially "Me viene, hay días, una gana ubérrima política . . . " (There are days when a very fertile politics overcomes me . . .), or "Un hombre pasa con un pan al hombro . . . " (A man passes by with bread on his shoulder . . .). As in these poems by Vallejo, the anguish of existence is not insurmountable and self-consuming or a sobering individual tragedy, but rather is tempered by the speaker's attachment to others: "every gesture weighs *like a poor man's load.*" The anticipation, in fact, physically arrests those who imagined they had closed off the outside world. It is as though the body could not contain its own social nature, its desire to break out of its artificial isolation. The ostensibly internal or self-conscious act of reading or of finishing a poem becomes, in Najlis's eyes, an open social manifestation (social consciousness). Literary creativity, which is likened to life, includes a multitude of physical and social signs. Passing from the body, where it boils, the restlessness arrives at the book being read, the unfinished poem and then reflects back on the human being who initiated the process. The restlessness becomes socialized in everyday life, the result of external (social) experiences that affect human beings internally (spiritually). The last verse, consequently, encapsulates the private and public at once: a play, or drama, connotes a specific literary genre as well as a social process in our daily lives.

For further proof the reader can notice how the social nexus slowly becomes more concrete as the book progresses. By page 33, for example, the poet flatly states—in another Vallejo-like poem (here the poetic reference is to *Los heraldos negros* [The black heralds]: "Hay golpes en la vida . . . " ["There are blows in life . . . "])—that she wants "to be in all other beings" ("ser en todos los seres"). To explore or discover oneself, the poem argues, is to connect with other human beings.

In the second and most powerful segment of *El viento armado* (pages 27–59), Najlis's themes are more palpably political, and their social ties more explicitly stated. One of the most explosive examples of this increasing commitment is "Nos persiguieron en la noche . . . " (They persecuted us at night . . .). Echoes of Cardenal's protest poetry can be heard throughout:

Nos persiguieron en la noche,
nos acorralaron

sin dejarnos más defensa que nuestras manos
unidas a millones de manos unidas.
Nos hicieron escupir sangre,
nos azotaron;
llenaron nuestros cuerpos con descargas eléctricas,
y nuestras bocas las llenaron de cal;
nos dejaron noches enteras junto a las fieras,
nos arrojaron en sótanos sin tiempo,
nos arrancaron las uñas;
con nuestra sangre cubrieron hasta sus tejados,
hasta sus propios rostros,
pero nuestras manos
siguen unidas a millones de manos unidas. (31)

[They persecuted us all night,
they rounded us up
leaving us no defense except our hands
united to millions of united hands.
They made us spit out blood,
they whipped us;
they filled our bodies with electric shocks,
and our mouths they filled with lime;
they left us with the beasts many long nights,
they threw us into timeless basements
they tore off our nails;
with our blood they covered the rooftops,
and even their own faces,
but our hands
continue to be united to millions of united hands.]

Subjected to the tortures so concisely described here in the preterite tense,
the victims resist and survive by supporting one another. Acting against the
anonymous "they"—undoubtedly Tachito Somoza's National Guard—the
tortured are united with millions of others. By switching to the present tense
in the last verse, Najlis underscores the physical resistance in poetic language.
The speaker's alliance with the victims further fortifies this defiance. She
might be one of the victims or she might be denouncing these atrocities as
one who was indirectly affected by them and who feels impelled to commit
herself to the victims' cause.

In several poems in the middle section of her book, Najlis's engagement
becomes more distinct via her support for the armed struggle. This was a
very perilous stance to take in the late 1960s in Nicaragua:

Ahora que andas por los caminos de la Patria
con el corazón en todo el cuerpo.
Ahora,
con las piernas en el barro
y el fusil — más tarde arado —
junto a tu espalda fuerte.
Ahora,
tal vez de día
tal vez de noche,
piensa que el pueblo es tu victoria
y lucha contigo. (45)

[Now that you roam the roads of the Homeland
with your heart all over your body.
Now,
with your legs in the mud
and your rifle — later plowed under —
next to your strong back.
Now,
maybe during the day
maybe at night,
think that the people are your victory
and that they struggle with you.]

In this homage to the guerrilla, the poet arouses patriotic sentiments in the
(Nicaraguan) reader and welds the guerrilla to the homeland (he wanders all
over the homeland and sinks into its mud). On closer inspection, all evidence
points to the guerrilla's being frozen in a classical heroic posture — much like
the famous photo of Che Guevara in Bolivia — because, in fact, he is dying
in battle. His rifle, we are told, will be buried ("later plowed under") along
with him ("next to your strong back"). So the poet addresses her poem, in
a dialogic fashion, to the guerrilla, asking him in the midst of death to
remember that the people are fighting with him. This is not a call to a specific
friend or comrade, but an evocation of all those who were engaging in the
armed struggle before the revolution. It is telling that Najlis associates guerrilla warfare with men and that it is they who fight for the livelihood of the
homeland. This omission of female guerrillas would seem to suggest that not
many women were involved in the revolutionary struggle in the late 1960s.
Najlis was writing this poetry during a transitional period when the women's
movement in Nicaragua was just beginning to take hold.

This collective vision of the future and the present struggle (in 1969) also
manifests itself in a number of other poems in this section of *El viento armado*.

As in the case of Cardenal's and Belli's works, there is an organic link between the guerrillas and the land on which they fight, and the dead are resurrected and, henceforth, immortal:

> Los muertos
> sostendrán los brazos del combatiente,
> la voz de las multitudes,
> la herramienta del campesino.
>
> Los muertos . . .
> ¿Quién sostendrá las manos de los muertos? (59)
>
> [The deceased
> will support the arms of the combatants,
> the voice of the multitudes,
> the tool of the peasants.
>
> The deceased . . .
> Who will support the hands of the deceased?]

As we will see, the militancy that is expressed in Najlis's poetry is most evidently felt in the poetry of Gioconda Belli, although she will carry it in a
different direction with her representation of eros and the armed struggle.
The Vallejo-like language and poetic structure in the first and last parts of
El viento armado resemble Ana Ilce's poetic quest although, significantly, Ilce
does not hurl herself into political commitment. The majority of Najlis's
poems—in the middle section of the book—combine political and poetic expression as well as engagement. To my mind, that is what makes her poetry
like César Vallejo's late poetry, published posthumously as *España, Aparta de
mí este cáliz* (Spain, take this chalice from me).

Critical Reception and Political Blindness

In *Ceremonias del silencio* (Ceremonies of silence; 1975) Ana Ilce Gómez reveals
not only her personal impressions as a woman living in Nicaragua during the
1970s, but also her society's expectations, inhibitions, and modes of repression. This book speaks to the reader in prerevolutionary historical circumstances under *somocismo*, a period when the women's movement was set in
motion, when Managua was referred to as a city that had "died" after the
earthquake, when the FSLN was gaining ground in spite of U.S. military aid
to the National Guard, and when literary groups such as Gradas and Ventana
became heavily involved in political activity. As it became apparent that the

Somoza regime was vulnerable, the scope of resistance to it spread from the national to the international realm, and women played an increasingly crucial role in working to overthrow the dictator.[8] As this political awareness mounted, female poets began to publish their work: Gioconda Belli, *Sobre la grana* (About the seed, 1974); Yolanda Blanco, *Así, cuando la lluvia* (Like when it rains, 1975); and Rosario Murillo, *Sube a nacer conmigo* (Come be born with me, 1976).

Ana Ilce Gómez's *Ceremonias del silencio* was praised by all those I interviewed in Nicaragua as an excellent book of poetry.[9] Yet, to my knowledge, nothing has been written about this writer's works generally, much less about the ideological content of her verses. Instead, in writing their reviews, critics have lauded Ilce's depiction of the tragedy of life and of amorous relationships, and in doing so, they have set the personal apart from the political. There is a feeling, especially among male poets and critics, that women can write excellent confessional or autobiographical poetry, but that this genre is not "serious" literature. Perhaps this can be explained by saying that these critics unconsciously or consciously see an inverted reality in these works—in other words, they are unable or unwilling to engage the attacks on patriarchy.

One need only examine certain book reviews to understand exactly what space women are being conceded in poetry, which is presumably men's domain. Take, for instance, the case of Daisy Zamora's latest book, *En limpio se escribe la vida*, (Life Written on a Clean Slate) published in the autumn of 1988. For José Coronel Urtecho this book is characteristic of women's poetry in that: "por distintas que sean las formas de que ellas se valen, rara vez dejan de reflejar, de una manera o de otra, la fisionomía física o mental o al mismo tiempo física y mental de la mujer poeta. La mujer más que el hombre, siempre está en su poesía"[10] (as different as the forms that they use can be, they seldom stop depicting, in some way or another, physical or mental physiognomy or simultaneously depicting women's physical and mental time. Women, more than men, are always present in their poetry). One wonders after reading this passage if such a vague definition could not also be applied to men, for it seems logical to assume that men too refer to their own physical and mental composition. But the true weakness in these lines is that they rely on assumptions that are related to the sexual division of labor: women (not men) are in charge of child care, go through a menstrual period, biologically reproduce, and therefore—Urtecho would have us believe—women's art must somehow anchor itself on the body in a way that men's poetry does not. More than this, if it is true that many women *tend* to write more self-consciously than men, then what are the sociohistorical roots that allow for this type of development? For Urtecho nowhere comments more profoundly on the history of such gender divisions. Similarly, in his review of Zamora's recent book, Jorge Eduardo Arellano does unite the personal and political, but he passes over her indictment of patriarchy: "Daisy

Zamora no podía eludir su propia alma combatiente y por eso se lanza, como una intrépida cronista, a encontrarse y a reencontrarse con ese saldo a su favor de activa comprometida con la terrible realidad"[11] (Daisy Zamora could not elude her own combative soul, and consequently she hurls herself, like an intrepid chronicler, toward finding herself and toward reengaging herself with her settled, active commitment with a terrible reality). It is true that reality can be terrifying, especially when one is being exploited daily. Arellano, however, would rather see the poet as an Espronceda-like romantic in search of herself through political commitment (which is viewed reductively, without recognizing its feminist dimension). This selective criticism obfuscates the thematic and formal richness that makes Zamora's poetry, as well as Ilce's, so powerful.

In essence, a reading of Ilce's poems, along the lines proposed by Arellano, deprives the poems of much of their thematic substance and suspends them in a metaphysical world. If one reads her poetry only in this manner, then something is being excluded, discarded, or unconsciously repressed as the poetry is converted into an artifice. As social testimony, Ilce's poems are indictments of class and gender discrimination under *somocismo*, and to ignore the political explosiveness to which her alienation testifies is to misread the very ideological core of her verses.

Ana Ilce Gómez and the Sounds of Silence

One way to misread Ilce's poetry is to patronize it: one might argue that her romantic or idealistic inclinations lead the speaker to yearn for a man. Thus, the solitude that pervades her verses can be perceived as circulating within the realm of the family; that is, within that all-encompassing Oedipal framework that Gilles Deleuze and Félix Guattari have so strongly criticized.[12] In order to justify such a reading, however, one would have to neglect the social nature of the family itself, as a reproducer of ideology in society and a locus of resistance. In essence, one would have to convert the family into something that it is not: an autonomous sphere. As Deleuze and Guattari have eloquently argued, psychoanalysis, by overemphasizing the role of the family, has in fact bolstered traditional gender roles.

My inverted reading sees solitude in Ana Ilce Gómez's writing not as an isolated romantic tragedy, but rather as a manifestation of alienation in Nicaragua during the 1970s. The emptiness and loneliness can be reread in Marxian terms as the alienation of people from their fellow human beings and from their work, their products, and themselves. For Marx, the alienated person is envisioned as an abstraction, that is, as someone who has been isolated in the social realm and, consequently, denied the fulfillment of "species being." In these particular ways, *Ceremonias del silencio* is instructive, for the alienation that the reader detects is filled with social connotations. The narrator's estrangement is not strictly associated with an existential angst, but rather attains social significance in work, socialization, and class and gender formations. In many ways, what occurs in Ilce's poetry is that the social milieu destroys the subject. In "Esa mujer que pasa," the speaker all but disappears from the poem's social context:

> ¿Quién es esta mujer que pasa,
> esta sombra,
> esta noche?
>
> ¿Quién conoce su nombre?
> ¿Quién la nombra
> del otro lado de la nada
> para nada?
>
> ¿Quién es esta mujer que pasa
> y no deja nada de sí?
>
> Sólo su paso rueda en la noche,
> Sólo su voz.[13]
>
> [Who is this woman who passes by,
> this shadow,
> this night?
>
> Who knows her name
> who names her
> from the other side of nothing
> for nothing?
>
> Who is this woman who passes by
> and does not leave an imprint of herself?
>
> Only her steps go 'round the night,
> Only her voice.]

The reader may imagine a skeletal figure that struggles for existence. From the beginning of the poem, she is a shadow turned into night (she is invisible), she is anonymous and does not know why she exists. By the third stanza, in fact, the speaker is a ghostlike character who is apparently alive but leaves no tangible trace of her existence ("does not leave an imprint of herself"). The last stanza does little to define the situation; the reader may still envision a phantom, neither deceased nor living.

A close look at the rhetorical devices identifies the social environment that does not recognize her existence. The repeated "who?" refers to a social body and not to the speaker. The speaker is, rather, the object of neglect. Hence, this poem also addresses itself to a human community that is not concerned with the goodwill of its members.[14]

In "Entresueño" (Dreamland), existence—the affirmation of connection or of species being—is posited in a tenuous gender identification. Here, as before, the subject is feebly delineated. She falls in love, it appears, with a boy or young man who has a "woman-like body" and knees like a female child. He can see, but chooses not to:

> Muchacho
> tienes ojos para mirar
> y no ves nada.
> Ni aún lo temerario
> que puso Eva alrededor de mí.
>
> Muchacho,
> tienes manos para tañer el arpa
> o cuerpo hecho de mujer
> o rodillas de niña.
> Pero tus manos
> son dos alas que vuelan.
>
> Muchacho,
> tu boca es un pozo
> y ahogada estoy.
> ¿Tendré perdido acaso
> de paso un pie en el
> Paraíso?
>
> Mi atadura es tu existencia
> muchacho
> alma de cántaro
> que de tanto ir al agua
> se rompe en cien.
> Ten cuidado
> porque corto es el
> tiempo y nadie sabe
> si mañana,
> si pasado mañana,
> si nunca. (13–14)
>
> [Young man
> you have eyes to see

and you see nothing.
Not even the imprudence
with which Eve surrounded me.

Young man,
you have hands to play the harp
or a body made by a woman
or a young girl's knees.
But your hands
are two wings that fly.

Young man,
your mouth is like a well
and I am drowned.
Might I have placed my foot, maybe,
by chance, in
Paradise?

My tie is your existence
young man
vessel soul
who having gone to the water too much
breaks into a hundred.
Be careful
because time is short
and no one knows
if tomorrow,
if the day after,
if never.]

The young man is clearly not *machista*: he is sensitive ("young man / vessel soul / who having gone to the water too much / breaks into a hundred"), sexually ambiguous (even androgynous), and artistically inclined. Heterosexual desire here is rewritten in a language that is alien to the cultural norms: the speaker loves a young man ("I am drowned") who is not macho.

The language allows for multiple descriptions of the young man. If the verb "tienes" (to have) ushers in the third verse, then the predicate can be structured as follows: (1) "manos para tañer el arpa"(hands to play the harp); (2) "o cuerpo hecho de mujer" (or a body made by a woman); (3) "o rodillas de niña" (or a young girl's knees). However, if the predicate actually hinges on "tienes manos para tañer" (you have hands to play), then playing would refer to his erotic encounters with a lover and to his virtues as a father figure because he is tender with children: [*tañer las*] *rodillas de niña*; [to play the] knees of a girl. But the needed definite articles are missing (el *cuerpo* [*his* body]; las *rodillas* [*her* knees]). The third verse in the second stanza compounds the reader's confusion and forces reexamination of the poem. In Spanish "cuerpo hecho de mujer" can mean either a womanlike body or a body made by a woman. Thus, his body is like that of a woman, his knees like those of a girl. Certainly this is a credible reading that cannot easily be dismissed. Does he flee from her ("but your hands are two wings that fly") because he is homosexual? Does his sexual preference matter? Furthermore, what if he represents, instead, a male image that the speaker desires but cannot find? The last six verses do little to clarify the situation; rather, they brusquely declare that time is short and one must live life to its fullest. If this poem represents desire for an imaginary male, then it appears that that yearning cannot be fulfilled given the existing gender constructions in Nicaragua.

In contrast to this ideal male character, we find the image of a domineering, jealous man in "Estoy sola ahora" (I am alone now). He circles the woman, as an animal would its prey:

> Estoy sola ahora, pero él ronda mi vida afuera.
>
> Das vueltas alrededor de mi cuerpo.
> Sé que estás ahí.
> Sé que siempre has estado en tu pequeño
>   (estrado
> bajo el sol, esperando que yo salga
> —contra viento y marea,
>   (rabioso y terco
> aguardando la hora de mi amor—.
>
> Pero sé que estás ahí donde no estoy,
> donde nunca—mi vida—he estado
> donde jamás me buscaste ni te hallaste
> para trocar tu victoria en mi derrota
>   (y mi muerte
> en tu vida.
>
> Ahora das vueltas alrededor de mi cuerpo.
> Ahora estoy sola.
>
> Muy de lejos de donde tú, en mi eterna
>   (búsqueda
> golpeas irrefrenablemente la puerta
>   (gritando con
> toda tu alma: "¡Sé que estás ahí!"

Donde no hay ya claridad
ni huella alguna que te salve. (33–34)

[I am alone now, but he patrols my outside life.

You circle my body.
I know you are there.
I know you have always been in your small
                                    (drawing-room
under the sun, waiting for me to leave
—come what may
                    (enraged and stubborn
awaiting my love—.

But I know you are there where I am not,
where I never—my life—have been
where you never looked for me nor found me
to exchange your victory for my defeat
                                    (and my death
for your life.

Now you patrol my body
Now I am alone.

Far away from you, who in your eternal
                                    (search
beat unrelentlessly on the door
                                    (yelling with
all your soul: "I know you're there!"
Where there is no clarity
nor any imprint that will save you.]

Misinterpreting love as domination is not just an individual experience; it implies collective repercussions as well. For in this environment it is clear that desire, sensuousness and erotic pleasure are equated with death. The man's role as an animal does not stray far from pornography, in which one individual exercises absolute control over a passive other:

> Virility, or the masculine gender carried by power, requires the denial of the body and its importance, whether this takes the form of control of the body of another or the portrayal of the man in heterosexual male pornography as complete master of his own body and the woman as totally at the mercy of her own desire.[15]

These representations of men circulate both in the speaker's private world and throughout the public sphere. Indeed, the woman in Ilce's love poems continues to combat the image of the *machista* that is depicted in "Estoy sola ahora," since she desires a person who will not indulge in phallic domination. In the majority of these works, the speaker's alienation from her fellow human beings is articulated as unactualized desire. Both men and women are portrayed as alienated from the traditional gender expectations that the culture as a whole values.

The concept of alienation in the poetry of Ana Ilce Gómez encompasses estrangement not only from one's fellow human beings, but also from one's work. In an abstract sense this entails the objectification of the object—in Marxian terms. The product becomes something foreign to the worker who produced it. But Marx also analyzed the alienation of those who must sell their labor power, the alienation of workers in their working conditions, and the alienation that is inflicted upon workers denied the full value of their products (the theory of surplus value). Further, workers cannot control what they produce because it belongs to someone else (the capitalist); consequently, they do not even know what becomes of their product. Only through wages and benefits are they compensated for their production. We can see this conflict represented in "Singer 63." The subject is an anonymous, average seamstress who works long and hard without any respite:

> La señora de ayer
> se llamaba . . .
> No era ninguna extravagancia.
> Clavaba alfileres en los trajes,
> se asomaba a la puerta
> para mirar las nubes. (35)

> [The woman of yesteryear
> she was called . . .
> She was not extravagant.
> She would poke needles in clothing,
> she would peer out the door
> to see the clouds.]

This anonymous "woman of yesteryear" produces until she dies with her fingertips and heart perforated, another cog discarded in the productive process:

> La señora de ayer
> no miró los caracoles muertos ni

las playas maravillosas,
sólo clavaba alfileres en los trajes,
sólo sonreía a medias;
por eso murió con sus dedales
y su corazón repleto de
marcas: Royal 62,
Singer 63, Phillips 64 . . .

[The woman of yesteryear
did not see the dead snails nor
the marvelous beaches,
she only poked needles in clothing,
she only half-smiled;
that is why she died with leather fingers
and her heart was completely pierced with
brands: Royal 62,
Singer 63, Phillips 64 . . .]

She is relegated to anonymity, while the sewing machines are remembered by name. The company for which she works is clearly exploiting her because she cannot enjoy life ("did not see . . . the marvelous beaches"). Over time, she becomes a machine.

The misery of the subject's working conditions is subsequently integrated in Ilce's poetry into a broader, traditionally Catholic view in which the poet sees life as drudgery or punishment. Unlike Cardenal's "heaven on earth," Ana Ilce Gómez's world lacks the earthly fulfillment that is promised by liberation theology. This ideology is succinctly outlined in "Aguamarga" (Bitter water):

Brizna de nada. ¿Quién tiene fósforo por tiniebla
y sostiene en el dedo el palillo moribundo? Yo tenía,
medía, daba el tiempo. Veía la rosa de los cuatro vientos.
La rosa ridícula. (99)

[Empty breeze. Who has a match for the darkness
and balances on her finger the moribund toothpick? I had,
measured, bided my time. I saw the rose of four winds.
The ridiculous rose.]

The first few verses encapsulate her bitter reaction to existence, as though Virgil were purposely guiding her through Dante's hell. There is no invocation of a Creator's name, no specific origin to life. What stands out, rather, is the anguish of living. But the tone changes as the poem continues:

> Pero quien
> hila sobre el viento no obtiene sino la tela frágil como rosa
> del papel carbón. Porque la clave nuestra no es soñar,
> sino esperar el sueño.

> [But whoever
> spins on wind does not get but a fragile material like a rose
> made of carbon paper. Because our key is not to dream,
> but rather to await a dream.]

Unable to live without some raison d'être, she alludes to a dream that human beings must all postpone, presumably until our earthly existence ends. Yet she knowingly or unknowingly contradicts herself while trying to affirm her faith. For what is she doing if not dreaming? She is dreaming that a dream awaits her (heaven). The speaker does, however, attempt to minimize earthly existence by concluding that material life disintegrates, decomposes like the rose (the body, poetry) that turns into ashes (death, silence).

In Ilce's poetry, feeling the dread of life is linked directly to a theological expectation of an afterlife. There is no redemption except in following the example of Christ—that is, in sacrificing oneself for the love of God. Poetry serves as the privileged medium through which she communicates this mission:

> Yo di vida a este canto.
> y heme aquí reducida a polvo.
> Desvencijada,
> rota,
> hambrienta.

> Yo lo tuve dolorosamente,
> le di vida y me mata,
> como cuervo me saca los ojos. (69)

> [I gave my life to this song.
> and here I am converted into dust.
> loose-jointed,
> broken,
> hungry.

I held it painfully,
I gave it life and it kills me,
like a raven it gouges out my eyes.]

Life is metaphorically associated with poetic process. In a manner reminiscent of Vallejo's early poetry, Ilce's, like life, seeks the ineffable Spirit. It is the doomed search for the Creator that allows her surrender, in order to give up her earthly existence to It:

> Al final me llevará
> a la piedra,
> al sacrificio
> donde he de soportar el hierro
> que merezco.

> [In the end it will lead me
> to the stone,
> to be sacrificed
> where I will bear the iron
> that I deserve.]

In spite of her devotion, she expects to be punished for her sins ("where I will bear the iron"). Unlike Gioconda Belli and Daisy Zamora, Ilce speaks of death and self-sacrifice as the only ways out of the misery of earthly existence. In that regard, Ilce's poetry is closer to Cuadra's traditional theological and poetic position than to the "materialist theology" of Cardenal. Her poetry is enlightening precisely because the underlying ideology is traditional Catholicism, and it latently exposes the subjugation of women within this religion in Nicaragua. The misery and alienation of living with macho gender expectations are vividly portrayed in her poetry.

Gioconda Belli: Eros and Revolution

> *A feminine text cannot not be more than subversive: if it writes itself it is in volcanic heaving of the old "real" property crust. In ceaseless displacement. She must write herself because, when the time comes for her liberation, it is the invention of a new, insurgent writing that will allow her to put the breaks and indispensable changes into effect in her history. (97)*
>
> Hélène Cixous and Catherine Clément, *The Newly Born Woman*

"Writing the body"—women describing their bodies discursively—can be a powerful force in appropriating the patriarchal discourse. Writing can never be a solitary or individual act, however: it is always immersed in the social sphere. To use the erotic description of the female body as a tool against patriarchal discourse, which attempts to silence and dominate it, is not in itself a revolutionary act. It must be accompanied by political action that works toward altering the ideology, institutions, and, in the end, economic and political systems promoting patriarchy. Therefore, while writing the body does constitute a rebellious move, it does not directly challenge the structures of capitalist society.

Feminist critics such as Rosalind Jones have indicated that, unless there is a serious critique of Freudian phallocentrism, writing the body can easily fall prey to it. In other words, this branch of feminism may not go far enough in critiquing patriarchy. To posit a "discourse of the clitoris," as Gayatri Spivak has done, does little to deconstruct patriarchal ideological foundation. Rather, it merely provides an alternative vision of the world that is separate but distinct from male discourse, while still operating within its confines.[16] But the most effective means of dealing with Freudian metapsychology is to prove—as Deleuze and Guattari and Luce Irigaray have done—that the cornerstone of psychoanalysis, the Oedipus complex, is not a universal construct. Thus, as Deleuze and Guattari recognize, this concept is pertinent today, but its validity as a theory needs to be questioned. The Oedipal triangle exists as an ideological node that reveals something about our sociohistorical perceptions of sexuality in patriarchy. The members of this triangle are not permanently fixed in time, but rather are subject to constant change. With hindsight we can see that Freud's model is a product of nineteenth-century bourgeois thought and, consequently, is a theory that privileges subjective factors over objective reality.[17] As a theory that continues to wield influence in the twentieth century, and arguably has now become one of the most dominant ways of conceiving of consciousness, psychoanalysis—presumably stripped of relations to social class and the class struggle—has established itself as the hegemonic ideological force on sexuality. As Deleuze and Guattari have convincingly argued, it is not enough to unravel the "materialist" mythology underlying phallocentrism; rather, it is necessary to further demystify its "individual" character:

> It is . . . disturbing to see to what extent Freudian analysis retains from the fantasy only its lines of exclusive disjunction, and flattens it into its individual or pseudoindividual dimensions, which by their very nature refer the fantasy to subjugated groups, rather than carrying out the opposite operation and disengaging in the fantasy the underlying element of a revolutionary group potential. When we learn that the instructor, the teacher, is daddy, and the colonel too, and also the mother—when all the

agents of social production and antiproduction are in this way reduced to the figures of familial reproduction — we can understand why the panicked libido no longer risks abandoning Oedipus, and internalizes it. The libido internalizes it in the form of a castrating duality between the subject of the statement (*l'énoncé*) and the subject of the enunciation, as is characteristic of the pseudoindividual fantasy ("I, as a man, understand you, but as judge, as boss, as colonel or general, that is to say as the father, I condemn you"). But this duality is artificial, derived, and supposes a direct relationship proceeding from the statement to the collective agents of enunciation in the group fantasy. (*Anti-Oedipus* 64)

Once the lengthy task of overcoming phallocentrism is under way, then writing the body becomes an even more radical proposal. When writing the body is seen as a sociopolitical phenomenon and not as an individual manifestation, then feminism and socialism both will have moved toward a more humane social system.

In Gioconda Belli's poetry there is an attempt to move in this radical direction, but not without some complications. Belli's early erotic poetry never ceases to call for armed struggle, and she was personally involved in the political upheaval. After the revolution, her poetry became even more significant because the infrastructure and superstructure were being recreated, and it was precisely at this moment of transition that feminist organizations such as AMNLAE were making their voices heard. In such a context her poetry raises the question of whether women's liberation can take place only in a struggling socialist system. The question is certainly problematic. As Maxine Molyneux has pointed out, socialism has quite frequently postponed the feminist struggle in favor of other, "more vital" demands. In the case of Nicaragua, women's rights, including the banning of pornography and of prostitution, were written into the constitution, but the government did not follow up on what Molyneux calls "women's interests" by consistently putting them into practice. Similarly, in the case of poetry, the eroticization within the boundaries of the subject can only recreate an artificial environment — like the unnatural milieu that psychoanalysis fabricates — that is a distortion of the real, social nature of the body. When the human body can no longer be disengaged from the body politic, then an ideological inversion that allows us to appreciate it not as a "thing-in-itself," but rather as a thoroughly social organism, will take place.

Recreating the Female and Political Body

When Gioconda Belli published *Sobre la grana* (About the seed) in 1974 and, even more significantly, the book that won the Casa de las Américas prize,

Línea de fuego (Line of fire), in 1978, her openly erotic poetry caused an uproar in Nicaragua. While women had frequently written love poems, they had not ventured into description of physical intimacy and intercourse, menstruation, and childbirth. Writers of both genders repressed observations about female bodily functions and thus contributed in many ways to the perception of women as passive. Women were seen (at least until the 1960s) as rather dehumanized sites for men's orgasms. They were perceived as cooperating with the man to give him pleasure. Then it was countered that women indeed do have orgasms and even multiple orgasms. It must have been disturbing for male poets not only that Belli assumed the "privilege" of working in their domain (poetry), but also that she did not walk quietly onto the stage. By eroticizing the female body, she was reclaiming an area of representation usurped by patriarchy. But as Hélène Cixous has argued, this was not sufficient:

> It is not a question of appropriating their instruments, their concepts, their places for oneself or of wishing oneself in their position of mastery. Our knowledge that there is a danger of identification does not mean we should give in. Leave that to the worriers, to masculine anxiety and its obsessional relationship to workings they must control—knowing "how it runs" in order to "make it run." Not taking possession to internalize or manipulate but to shoot through and smash the walls.[18]

Belli's poems in *De la costilla de Eva* (From Eve's rib, 1987) implicitly meet Cixous's challenge by calling for the affirmation of the female body in the body politic. Arising out of a struggle with silence and the once-dominant patriarchal ideology, poetry attempts to define the human subject as active participant in the eros of revolution. In spite of her materialist pretensions, however, Belli reifies this integration of female experience in patriarchy in such a manner that love—whether it be sexual or revolutionary—tends to lose its material roots. For instance, Belli's poetry describes the "magical" substance of erotic pleasure, which at times is linked to armed struggle. This contrasts with her detailed representations of physical love. Nonetheless, as we shall see, neither sexual nor revolutionary love can escape the trappings of romanticism and philosophical idealism.

Her conception of these encounters as magic is evident in the epigraphs, which were taken from Julio Cortázar's *Rayuela* (Hopscotch), and can be traced throughout *De la costilla de Eva*. In fact, the title itself alludes to the Scripture, to a feminist inversion of the biblical question of alterity, suggesting that one of the main preoccupations of the volume is to posit poetry and the revolution as the media that synthesize opposites.

"Evocación a la magia" (Evocation to magic) is paradigmatic of this thematic fusion of feminism, revolution, and the phenomenon of the other. All point to mysterious—and not conscious—ties that bind them together in unity:

> ¿Te encontraré, Mago?
>
> ¿Alguna vez volveré a llorar
> con la cara escondida en las rodillas?
>
> ¿Alguna vez volveremos a los aeropuertos
> sin salas de espera
> de donde salimos como pájaros
> prendidos del tiempo y de la última mirada?[19]
>
> [Will I find you, Magician?
>
> Will I cry again someday
> with my face hidden between my knees?
>
> Will we return someday to the airports
> without lobbies
> from where we left like birds
> seizing the moment and the last glance?]

The speaker begins with the first phrase in *Rayuela*, changing the gender from feminine ("Maga") to masculine ("Mago"), but pursuing the same ontological path that Cortázar explored. Positing an objectified image of gender, as Cortázar does, tends to reinforce the stereotypes that are encouraged by society. Thus, it would seem problematic for Belli to follow the same procedure, merely altering the gender, unless this appropriation of male symbols is accompanied by a critique. As we shall see, Belli's adoption of male images is contradictory.

The first three stanzas suggest that the magical, for the poet, consists of conjectures in a timeless place situated at the limit of eros and thanatos. This specific dichotomy is more clearly elucidated as the reader proceeds to the fourth stanza:

> ¿Te veré acaso cuando otra vez regrese de
> alguna parte
> llorando el amor mojado de la desesperación,
> contándote que yo pensaba ser Scherezada de
>   tus noches
> para que nunca me cortaras la cabeza?

> [Will I see you by chance when I return
> to another place
> crying this damp love of desperation,
> telling you that I wanted to be the Scheherazade
> of your nights
> so that you would never decapitate me?]

As the speaker continues to interrogate "la magia," it becomes more tangible. The reference to a Scheherazade, of *A Thousand and One Nights*, associates the image with eros and links it directly to creation (the narration of stories), in opposition to decapitation. As in the poetry of Ana Ilce Gómez, eros is essentially equated with thanatos. Male domination and hostility are contrasted with intimacy and physical pleasure. For Belli, on the other hand, to grapple with mystery is to struggle with creation and destruction (in their biological and sociohistorical dimensions). Hence, while the materiality of these two features of human existence is magnified, the poet continues to refer to them as ephemeral.

The doubt expressed in this portion of the poem soon changes to affirmation:

> Te encontraré, Mago, en un día sin citas,
> sin premeditación,
> entre las corteses de tu calle o la mía
> con esta misma nostalgia prendida en la punta
>   de los dedos
> doliéndome las ganas de romper el hechizo que
>   nos hicimos
> el tiempo que desconstruimos
> mientras el ojo que no engaña
> te refleja en todas las vidrieras de la vida,
> en los charcos, las bujías, el cansancio,
> en las noches que paso con tu fantasma a cuestas,
> ese que me ama
> como un loco soldado en media Revolución. (*De la costilla* 41)

> [Will I find you, Magician, on a day without appointments,
> without premeditation,
> on your civil street or mine
> with this same nostalgia burning our
>   fingertips
> with a painful desire to break the charm that
>   we formed

the time we deconstructed
while the eye that does not deceive us
reflects an image of you on the windows of life
in the puddles, the candles, the weariness,
during the nights I spend with your phantasm beside me,
the one who loves me
like a crazy soldier in the midst of the Revolution.]

The rhetorical questions at the beginning of the poem are now concrete statements uniting the speaker with magic via the first-person plural. In these verses she boldly asserts that she will find the Magician (the other) on his or her street. What binds them is the spell that they have created together, the nature of which is never fully articulated. This image later metamorphoses into a timeless "fantasma" who loves the speaker and is omnipresent in her life and in the revolution. The nebulous necromancer is the origin and catalyst of poetry, the revolution, and the subject. The problem here, as I indicated earlier, is that this image becomes the uncritical flip side of the male concept of the muse who only exists symbolically. By the end of the poem, then, the physical image of this Magician vanishes, as does the semblance of reality.

"Evocación a la magia" forms part of the first section of the book, entitled "De la fuga" (Of the escape). The poems in this segment convey a nostalgic yearning for the source by attempting to portray language in its relation with the real. Thus, for Belli, material changes take place because of human creative potential, which she considers limitless and virtually indescribable. Writing poetry is one way of exploring creative energy, and making a revolution is another: both derive from a dialectical process of struggling to liberate humankind. Thus, her work shows the constant interplay between the ideal and the material in an attempt to work out a conception of a new revolutionary consciousness. Unlike Cardenal's "concrete poetry," Belli's poetry hovers between the two realms, its language never completely appropriated by either one:

> —ese temblor primario
> que nos acerca al principio del mundo,
>> el lenguaje elemental del roce o el
>> contacto,
>> la oscuridad de la caverna,
>> el hombre y la mujer
>> lamiéndose el espanto del estruendo—
> Reconocer,
> ante el espejo,

la huella,
la ausencia de cuerpos entrelazados
     hablándose.
Sentir que hay
un amor feroz
enjaulado a punta de razones,
condenado a morir de inanición,
sin darse a nadie más
obseso de un rostro inevitable. (21–22)

[—that primary earthquake
that brings us closer to the beginning of the world,
     the elementary language of a caress or
     contact,
     the darkness of a cavern,
     a man and a woman
     licking the fright of their clamor.
To recognize,
before the mirror,
the imprint,
the absence of intertwined bodies
     talking to each other.
To feel that there is
a ferocious love
imprisoned on the edge of reason,
condemned to perish from inanition,
without giving oneself to anyone more
obsessed with an inevitable face.]

In "Permanencia" (Permanence), absence and presence are fighting for existence in these verses as the speaker is attempting to define love. Language takes on traits similar to tactile sensations; both are rooted in something physical, yet their signifiers point to something that cannot be easily described, something metaphysical. Beginning with "that primary earthquake" and continuing with the rest of the verses, the reader can perceive an apparent dichotomy between inexplicable feeling and physical touch. This can be seen in, for example, "licking the fright of their clamor." The "fright" the couple feels is placed amidst two material acts, "licking" and "clamor." In the following verses we encounter similar antinomies. The mirror acts as a key metaphor for love, which is reflected in the couple but cannot be empirically verified. Like the mirror, according to Belli, love leaves an imprint even though it appears materially to be absent, "the imprint / the absence of intertwined bodies / talking to each other."

Thus, language (like sexual union) idealistically extends itself beyond man and woman to a certain degree, while at the same time remaining anchored in material life. The sign is at once represented and deconstructed, the one and the other. Language and the lovers exist as physical entities; but the product of their interaction is ostensibly intangible, inexplicable.

The representation of the body (and, hence, of the poetic persona and the revolution) in discourse begins with "Del renacer" (Of rebirth), the second section of *De la costilla de Eva*. "Rebirth" refers both to the poetic word and to female consciousness in the revolution. In the first segment of "Canto de Guerra" (War song), the speaker deals with the metaphorical apprehension of reality through poetic language, her self-image as a woman, and the idea of utopia. Poetry, the subject, and the revolution are perceived as a heterogeneous totality that resists silence, alienation, and outside agression, that is mediated by eros/thanatos and the armed struggle:

> Vendrá la guerra, amor
> y en el combate no habrá tregua
> ni freno para el canto
> sino poesía naciendo del hueco oscuro
> del cañón de los fusiles.
>
> Vendrá la guerra, amor
> y nos confundiremos en las trincheras
> cavando el futuro en las faldas de la Patria
> deteniendo a punta de corazón y fuego
> las hordas de bárbaros
> pretendiendo llevarse lo que somos y amamos.
>
> Vendrá la guerra, amor
> y yo me envolveré en tu sombra invencible,
> como fiera leona
> protegeré la tierra de mis hijos
> y nadie detendrá esta victoria
> armada de futuro hasta los dientes.
>
> Aunque ya no nos veamos
> y hasta puedan morirse los recuerdos,
> te lo juro por vos,
> te lo juro apretando a Nicaragua
> como niña de pecho:

¡No pasarán, amor
los venceremos! (19)

[The war will come, my love
and in combat there will be no respite
nor a moment for song
but rather poetry being born from a dark hole
of the barrel of arms.

The war will come, my love
and we will be mixed with one another in the trenches
digging the future on the Homeland's lap
deterring the fire at the edge of hearts
the hordes of barbarians
attempting to take what we are and what we love.

The war will come, my love
and I will wrap myself up in your invincible shadow,
like a ferocious lioness
I will protect my children's land
and no one will detain this victory
fully armed with a future.

Although we may not see one another
and some memories may die,
I swear to you,
I swear to you holding Nicaragua
like a young child:

They will not cross the border, my love
we will defeat them!]

In the second part of this book of poetry, the three related bodies—poetry, the human subject, and the revolution—are evoked metaphorically and fused into one. The association between poetry and the struggle is made in the fourth verse in the first stanza. The dark hole refers to the barrel of the gun and, like the cave of "Permanencia" (21–22), it is a metaphor for the mystery of love. And love, as the verses in this poem indicate, is inextricably tied to the revolution and its struggle to exist. As the second stanza makes clear, in the struggle collectivity takes priority over individual considerations. They will hardly recognize one another, they will mix with each other, they will become one group. The last two verses of this stanza pit the "hordes of barbarians" (the U.S.-backed contras) against a united Nicaraguan people.

Hence, the revolution is depicted as the very incarnation of the people's existence, "attempting to take what we are and what we love."

Here, as throughout this book, revolutionary and artistic actions are not presented as rational phenomena, but rather, like love, are articulated as emotional or irrational. It is this tilting of the balance in favor of irrationalism that debilitates Belli's revolutionary commitment and reduces her political stance to that of a utopian socialist. The form of her poetry thus produces a lack of specificity in the content. First, because the origin of creativity in Belli's writing—whether it be revolution, reproduction, sexual intercourse, or poetry—is unknown or magical. Hence, she blocks the path toward a rational understanding of the class struggle, whether it is in the political, economic, or aesthetic realm. Second, in place of class struggle and a more multifarious description of its emotive and real impact on human lives, Belli furnishes an imaginary resolution for real sociohistorical contradictions and glosses over a more precise representation of these forces.

Returning to the poetic process, we see that Belli portrays the speaker as linked with nature, which is both objectified and an integral part of her; and then has her join the collective (the revolution). A similar relational procedure is evident in "Reflexiones" (Reflections):

> He renacido mi corazón de altas montañas,
> de fuego derretido
> de gorriones,
> de lunas con espejo en la cara,
> porque "la lucha es el más alto de los cantos"
> y si yerro, puedo aprender,
> y si desnuda, de amor puedo vestirme,
> y si callada, puedo hablar,
> y todo está en mirar los lagos que circundan
>   la vida
> tomar sus peces,
> tiernamente quitar las algas que algún día
>   se enredaron en el pelo,
> y seguir adelante volando como las mariposas. (55)

> [My heart has been reborn from tall mountains,
> from a melting fire,
> from sparrows,
> from moons with a looking glass on their faces,
> because "the struggle is the greatest of the songs"
> and if I err, I can learn,
> and if nude, I can dress myself in love,

and if silent, I can speak,
and all comes down to gazing at the lakes that engulf
  life
gather their fishes,
tenderly remove the seaweed that one day
  became entwined in my hair,
and continue flying like butterflies.]

What is of interest here is that the poet/woman/revolutionary becomes politically conscious when she is reborn. The first stanza of "Reflexiones" introduces a series of negations that conflict with the speaker's affirmations. In these verses she denounces all that could impede the development of her consciousness as a woman. The inner force of the subject is projected in Fernando Gordillo's famous verse, "the struggle is the greatest of all songs." Clearly, the struggle refers both to her own growth and to the creative potential of human beings in the revolutionary process. As the speaker acts, she becomes ever more entwined in nature and, thus, she formulates a more complete definition of herself and of her milieu. In this case, in fact, the poet appropriates nature's fish and extracts the vitality (the ancient life form: the seaweed) that subsequently gets caught up in her hair (her self). The last verse implies that the speaker and nature have been fused via poetry. Syntactically, the verse indicates that "continue flying like butterflies" is a continuation of "it all comes down to . . . ," and it also seems to suggest that the fish have been transformed into butterflies. The speaker has emerged from the water—like the fish—trying to extract the seaweed (nature) from her hair. Consequently, she appears to be indistinguishable from the object that she pursues.

From a Marxist perspective, Belli's poetry reveals an attempt to render the development toward species being, where the individual is not divorced from nature or from self-expression. She is always affirming her subjective identity in a social setting—in a transitional, "socialist" society—but she ultimately releases her potential to describe these social relations in a more complex way. While Belli does attempt to record her biological and political desires as enacted in order to try to satisfy the self's propensity toward both the individual and the social, they never transcend the limits of desire. What she endeavors to represent is what Bertell Ollman explains as the confluence of these spheres in the development of species being:

Man's species powers of seeing, feeling, thinking, loving etc., are only possible because man labors, eats, drinks and is sexually active, because he manages to stay alive and healthy. Man without any relations to nature is a relationless void; without any specifically human relations to nature, he is an animal; and without his animal relations to nature, he is a dead human being — assuming of course that these relations once existed, or else he would never have been alive to die. If natural powers can be viewed as establishing the framework in which life itself goes on, then man's species powers express the kind of life which man, as distinct from all other beings, carries on inside this framework.[20]

This process of human realization and integration is partially borne out in poetic form. Shifting from the first-person singular to first-person plural essentially corroborates the thematic changes I outlined earlier; moving to the inclusive first person, for example, invites the reader to participate in collective imagination, even as the speaker herself is integrated into it. Yet the poetic form itself militates against any more detailed account of the individual's social nature and her social relations. For the social relations, I would argue, are never the focus of her poetry since the root of these relations is deemed to be "magical" and, consequently, cannot be reflected — in the Lukácsian sense. Rather, they appear as metaphorically distant representations.

This is true even when Belli's poetry turns to the revolutionary process, which is the focus of the next section. This segment of the book portrays commitment to actively working in the revolution as an antithetical paradigm of Nicaraguan life during and since that historical event: "Este tiempo de muertes, / es tiempo también de valorar la vida" (This time of death, / is also a time to value life). The speaker is directly incorporated into the revolutionary process:

> de pulirnos como cristal fundido en este puro
>   fuego de la Revolución
> tomándola amorosamente
> sin negarle ni uno solo de los poros,
> darnos . . .

> [to sculpt ourselves like blown glass in this pure
>   fire of the Revolution
> taking it lovingly
> without negating any of the pores,
> give of ourselves . . .]

In her idealist fashioning, eros and thanatos are the catalysts that unite the pores of the body (revolution, poetry, the subject). According to Belli, this recreation of consciousness gives the individual the capacity to transcend herself by — seen from the Althusserian point of view — interpellating herself with the revolutionary process. As a result of acknowleging the collective and acting in it, the individual experiences a qualitative leap in consciousness.

The concluding segment expresses the constitution of the poem's themes: the revolution is one heterogeneous body. The poet and her word are christened with new meaning in this social context:

> en estas tardes en que la patria amenazada
>   nos hace poemas
> desde esas caras, esos fusiles, esas manos
> que nos miran como diciendo:
> Hermano, mientras yo muero, ¿qué estás
>   haciendo vos?

> [during these afternoons in our threatened country
>   poems are being made
> by those faces, those arms, those hands
> that look at us as if saying:
> Brother, while I'm dying, what are
>   you doing?]

As Belli's poem acknowledges, one body, composed of many faces, hands, and weapons, creates a "transcendental" or collective human consciousness: the revolution. While one can empathize with the anger and frustration that permeates the poem, the question still remains: has the complexity of the revolutionary struggle been depicted faithfully? One is tempted to maintain that this version of the revolutionary struggle—in contrast to that of the campesinos who fought in it and wrote their own documentary poems in the midst of it—makes up for its lack of empirical detail with subjective sensations. Indeed, Belli's representation is firmly entrenched in subjectivity, so much so, in fact, that the real dynamics of the revolutionary struggle are not allowed the space that they would need in order to candidly record the movement of historical, political, and economic forces.

Sexual Liberation in the Revolution

> *Esta Revolución interna,*
> *esta Insurrección solitaria de C.M.R.*
> *contra el desamor de flores marchitas,*
> *y la construcción*
> *no sólo de nuevas relaciones de producción*
> *sino de nuevas relaciones de amor.*

[This internal Revolution,
this Solitary Insurrection by C.M.R.
against the indifference of trampled flowers
and the construction
not only of new relations of production
but also of new relations of love.]

Gioconda Belli, *"Problemas de la transición"* (Problems of the transition)

If there is a parallel between revolutionary struggle and sexual liberation, it is valid insofar as they are both ongoing processes, a type of fluid, continuous movement. Thus, as we have noted in "Evocación a la magia" and subsequent poems, when Belli refers to "magic" it is not in connection with a given fixed state of being or concept, but rather with a dialectical process.[21] Her poetry suggests that desire in a new revolutionary society should allow a multiplicity of forms of sexual expression and that patriarchal taboos must be broken. Just as new relations of production come to the fore, as she comments in "Problemas de la transición" (Problems of the transition), so must there be new sexual and love relations. Throughout *Línea de fuego* and *De la costilla de Eva* she insists on total liberation from sexual repression. And these thematic nodes in the text are more heavily reinforced in these poems, in which she concentrates on libidinal liberation. In contrast to the sections analyzed earlier, in *Línea de Fuego* she recovers much of her interest in detail. In "Evocación lluviosa" (A rainy evocation), for instance, she apparently refers to the repressive Somozan apparatus that negated full human potential. The individual is trapped in her emptiness and feels as though she is in a hostile and alien city, where her liberating desires are negated. The revolution, then, provides the individual with explosive happiness, an irrepressible and animal-like euphoria — in short, the means for freeing herself:

Esta soledad, este vacío indefinible que va creciendo
en lugar de la alegría, es como estar perdido en una
ciudad hostil y extraña haciendo y diciendo lo que no
sentimos, ni deseamos, añorando la explosiva felicidad,
la euforia irreprimible y animal que invadía los
sentidos como grandes flores que reventaban en las
entrañas, salían por los ojos, por la boca, embelleciendo
el transcurrir de la vida en mil y una formas hermosas. (70)

[This solitude, this inexplicable vacuum that keeps growing
in place of happiness, it is like being lost in a
hostile and alien city doing and saying what we do not
feel, nor desire, awaiting the explosive joy,

the unrepressable and instinctual euphoria that invaded
our senses like large flowers that burst forth in our innermost
recesses, projecting out of our eyes, out of our mouths, beautifying
the passing of life in a thousand and one embellished forms.]

This poem differs greatly from poems in *De la costilla de Eva* such as "Amor en dos tiempos" (Love at two moments), in which she describes the body in terms of desirous, open, sexual passion. The unleashing of the forces of desire—endemic to her idealism—is accompanied by a parallel procedure in language, where she excludes punctuation and syntax:

> Mi pedazo de dulce de alfajor de almendra
> mi pájaro carpintero serpiente emplumada
> colibrí picoteando mi flor bebiendo mi miel
> sorbiendo mi azúcar tocándome la tierra
> el anturio la cueva la mansión de los atardeceres
> el trueno de los mares barco de vela
> legión de pájaros gaviota rasante níspero dulce
> palmera naciéndome playas en las piernas
> alto cocotero tembloroso obelisco de mi perdición
> tótem de mis tabúes laurel sauce llorón
> espuma contra mi piel lluvia manantial
> cascada en mi cauce celo de mis andares
> luz de tus ojos brisa sobre mis pechos
> venado juguetón de mi selva de madreselva y musgo
> centinela de mi risa guardián de los latidos
> castañuela cencerro gozo de mi cielo rosado
> de carne de mujer mi hombre vos único otra vez
> llamame pegame contra tu puerto de olas roncas
> llename de tu blanca ternura silenciame los gritos
> dejame desparramada mujer. (91)

> [My piece of sweet almond *alfajor*
> my woodpecker plumed serpent
> hummingbird pecking my flower drinking the honey
> testing my sugar touching my earth
> *anturio* the cavern the mansion of sunsets
> the thunder of the seas sailboat
> legion of birds seagulls grazing sweet medlar
> palm tree awakening beaches on my legs
> tall, trembling coconut tree obelisk of my loss
> totem of my taboos laurel weeping willow

foam against my skin blanketing rain
cascade in my riverbed zeal of my travels
light of my eyes breeze over my breasts
playful deer from my jungle my home and sea coral
sentry of my laughter guardian of my heartbeat
castanet bell pleasure of my rose heaven
of women's flesh my man you the only one again
call me hold me against you port of raucous waves
fill me with your white tenderness quiet my cries
leave me a scattered woman.]

Belli specifically names heterosexual intercourse and its two principal sexual organs, the penis and the vagina; they are codified in a variety of different metaphors. Each erotic sign — flower, cavern, *alfajor*, woodpecker, medlar, and weeping willow — has a number of meanings that are rooted in the popular musical tradition in Latin America. The entire body enters into this physical dialogue. The speaker accentuates her full emotional and physical investment in the act through possessive adjectives. She does not represent this union as the woman's giving the man pleasure, but rather her joining him in a mutual physical celebration. As intercourse awakens her body, it brings her sensitive carnal areas to life. And Belli depicts mutual orgasms as the simultaneous fusion and dismemberment of the self:

Campanas sonidos ulular de sirenas
suelto las riendas galopo carcajadas
pongo fuera de juego las murallas
los diques caen hechos pedazos salto verde. (91)

[Bells sounds ululating mermaids
I let go of the reins I gallop laughter
I remove the walls from the game
the dams break into pieces I jump erotically.]

Referring to the enclosures — the figurative prison cells, cities, closed doors, and caves — that are now torn asunder, she breaks the chains of restrictions. Instead of imagining the body as a limitation, reinforced by social repression, it becomes the source of emancipation. The reader who follows the thematic symbols cannot help but read this intertextually, since the physical organism serves as metaphor for the body politic. As a reading of "Fronteras" (Borders) indicates, passionate affairs lead to a passionate politics:

Sin embargo
estas querencias nos dejan otras patrias en la piel,
nos abren fronteras
aprendemos el amor de otros pueblos
nos sentimos menos solos en el mundo.
Por esta noches y estas mañanas
vos habitarás la patria de mis montañas
yo habitaré tus rascacielos. (87–88)

[Nevertheless
these desires leave other homelands on our skin,
they open up our borders
we learn love from other peoples
we feel less alone in the world.
For these nights and these mornings
you will inhabit the homeland in my mountains
I will inhabit your skyscrapers.]

The significance of making love goes beyond its individual boundaries and extends to a love for humankind, and this altruistic gesture establishes a homology between the individual and the social body. He "inhabits" her body, which is likened to her homeland, Nicaragua.

Feminism's engagement with revolution is not, however, without contradictions in Belli's poetry. They include the "militarization" of some of her erotic verses, as well as an awkward attitude toward reproduction. In view of the devastation that took place in all phases of life as the revolution confronted the U.S.-backed contras and as armed struggle continued to be an essential part of everyday life, it is logical to assume that this militarization had a tremendous ideological impact on Nicaraguans. Belli's poetry painfully records the contradictions between her wanting to represent a more peaceful and creative world and the need to honor those who gave their lives for the revolution. In poems such as "Anoche" (Last night), for instance, the male lover resembles "un combatiente desnudo" (79) (a naked combatant). Intercourse is degraded to a violent, bellicose experience:

te veía esgrimir tus armas
y violento hundirte en mí
Abría los ojos
y todavía estabas como herrero
martillando el yunque de la chispa
hasta que mi sexo explotó como una granada. (79)

[I saw you brandish your arms
and submerge yourself violently into me
I opened my eyes
and you were still like a blacksmith
hammering the anvil of the spark
until my sexual organ exploded like a grenade.]

The poet here takes on a schizophrenic role. Part of her searches for a loving solution to this continual assault on human life, but this defense of eros can be sustained only through thanatos. Yet it is exceedingly difficult to avoid adopting this dual perspective in which the sociopolitical reality of the war against the contras encroached upon everyday life, and love was redefined as countering the attacks of the aggressor. In a revolutionary context, Belli seems to say, individual love (sexual intercourse) cannot help but involve collective love (the revolution). However, she seems to repress the agonizing human dilemma of taking another's life. Nowhere in this book does Belli address the tragic need for revolutionary activity.

Reproduction is represented as an act of love rooted in biological as well as ethical urges. Motherhood is celebrated and encouraged because it allegedly counteracts the destructiveness of the contras by affirming life. This view, however, tends to equate female patriotism with maternity. In "Seguiremos naciendo" (We will continue to be born) this problematic representation manifests itself clearly. After giving birth, the speaker says:

> Ven y dame la mano,
> esa tu mano joven, militante.
> Ahora que nos unen Revolución y sangre
> enfrentaremos juntas
> este futuro de guerra y de victoria
> y cuando amés a un hombre
> y también brote vida de tu vida,
> naceremos otra vez,
> muchas veces,
> prolongando roja nuestra bandera;
> hija,
> mujer,
> compañera
> Maryam. (111–12)

[Come and give me your hand,
that hand young woman, militant.
Now that Revolution and blood unite us

> we will face this future
> of war and of victory together
> and when you love a man
> and life also blossoms forth from your life,
> we will be born again,
> many times,
> prolonging our red flag;
> daughter,
> woman,
> *compañera*
> Maryam.]

Belli's poetry ultimately reaches an ideological horizon that undercuts the possibility of a realist depiction of experience in a revolutionary situation. I have mentioned a number of thematic features that impede such a materialist development, among them her metaphysical notion of revolutionary and artistic creation. This, it appears, is in keeping with utopian socialism as well as — quite incidentally — with Althusserianism, which, as I noted in the Preface, ends up favoring an unconscious or irrational foundation for revolutionary consciousness. I would further suggest that Belli's highly metaphorical form begins by reifying the revolution, or recreating it in a species of inversion in which the raw material of revolutionary activity — as in the case of Althusser's politics — is metaphorically displaced to the subject. As a result, the text we read appears as a type of refraction of reality that represents sexual oppression firsthand, but experiences the revolution secondhand. Belli's imaginary solutions to real contradictions within revolutionary Nicaragua indicate that her desire for a more harmonious, socialist system is confronted by the historical class struggle in aesthetics and politics that I described in chapter 1. In this respect, Belli's ideological position is representative of the economism or reformism we find in the mainstream of FSLN politics.

Exposing Patriarchal Territories: The Poetry of Daisy Zamora

> *The father, the mother, and the self are at grips with, and directly coupled to, the elements of the political and historical situation — the soldier, the cop, the occupier, the collaborator, the radical, the resister, the boss, the boss' wife — who constantly break all triangulations, and who prevent the entire situation from falling back on the familial complex and becoming internalized in it. In a word, the family is never a microcosm in the sense of an autonomous figure, even when inscribed in a larger circle that it is said to mediate and express.*

> Gilles Deleuze and Félix Guattari, *Anti-Oedipus: Capitalism and Schizophrenia*

To my knowledge, no other book of poetry in Nicaragua addresses as powerfully what Molyneux has called "women's interests" and the manner in which they were or were not put into practice in the revolution as Daisy Zamora's *En limpio se escribe la vida* (Life written on a clean slate, 1988). It is, I would argue, the first poetic and feminist manifesto that undermines patriarchal definitions of the family, reproduction, housework, and the "double day." Zamora's dissection of these traditionally female territories takes place largely on the thematic level, while on the formal level her poetry can be likened to the realism of Ernesto Cardenal.

Zamora's poetic corpus argues for an understanding of the struggle for women's liberation as an actual material and historical representation that is buried in her discourse, that is, it argues that every linguistic sign extracts raw material from reality in order to form itself. *En limpio se escribe la vida* becomes the means for conducting a search for a more comprehensive view of objective reality. This point returns us to the controversial Lukács–Adorno debate: modernism versus realism (see chapter 1). For such a discussion leads us into questions about self-expression, linguistic innovation, and aesthetic commitment on the one hand, and the democratic implications of reaching a broader segment of the population, as well as a belief that objective reality can somehow be tapped, on the other.

Keeping this in mind, let us compare Ana Ilce Gómez's avant-gardist poetry with Zamora's realism. Thematically they argue along similar lines: they expose the exploitation of women in the workplace, and they testify to the sexual objectification of women. Zamora focuses on gender issues within the revolution while Ilce, writing during the prerevolutionary period, obviously does not. Ilce draws much more on women's individual experiences (with men), which act as allegories for their lives in a patriarchal society, yet the most profound sentiment one feels is the anguish of their existence and a sense of distance implicit in her literary form. While individual experience is certainly implicit in Zamora's work, it is not her overriding concern; rather, the actual incidents she describes are caught within a network of social signification. Zamora's poetic corpus makes reference to the division of labor by gender, reproduction, strict gender expectations, and sexism much as women's life in Nicaragua is marked by them, and the poet makes a conscious effort to keep these issues in the foreground and undermine their very logic. In Ilce's poems we see some explicit representation of these issues: many portray the emotional damage inflicted upon women by the church, the state, and traditional gender roles. The most fundamental difference between these two poets lies in their form: Ilce's signifieds prove to be much more elusive than Zamora's; her poetic tour de force is more dependent on metaphorical perspective, which only increases the internal, subjective movement of her verses, whereas Zamora attempts to represent reality in as rich and detailed a manner as possible. Thus, what manifests itself most evidently in Zamora's poetry is the painful sociohistorical plight of women.

Alienation in the Workplace and in the Family

Daisy Zamora assembles the first section of *En limpio se escribe la vida*, "Yo soy las otras mujeres" (I am the other women), so that the speaker linguistically and symbolically identifies herself with the working-class protagonists in each poem. The volume indicates the poet's ethical commitment to uncovering the exploitation of women in revolutionary Nicaragua. Concurrently, she exposes the exorbitant alienation to which they are subjected at the work site, and she does not hesitate to include housework as alienated labor. The subject is distanced from the physical setting and the reader senses the emptiness of the milieu, as well as the impact that material conditions can have on the self. One's empathy for the laborers in these working conditions is heightened by her verses. In "La mesera" (The waitress), for example, the hardship of physical labor and alienation are presented by material elements and concrete language:

> De mesa en mesa
> recoge las botellas vacías de cerveza,
> apila los platos en la bandeja plástica
> y sus gruesos dedos como pinzas
> levantan de una vez
> cinco vasos de vidrio
> que hacen "clic" al juntarse.
>
> Como un cometa gordo recorre su órbita:
> el trajín enciende su rostro
> agita sus brazos y los pequeños pechos
> bajo el vestido celeste con delantal
> que le termina en lazo
> > sobre las ancas. (21)

> [She goes from table to table
> collecting the empty beer bottles,
> she piles the plates on a plastic tray
> and her thick fingers like tweezers
> pick five glasses up
> at once
> and they "click" as they meet.

Like a fat comet she goes around her orbit:
her uniform lightens up her face
her arms shake and her small breasts
under the light-blue dress with an apron
that ends up being tied
    above her buttocks.]

These first two stanzas inundate the reader with the drudgery of a woman's work. She is depicted as someone who has endured repetitive acts that have—we infer—changed her physical appearance: "her thick fingers like tweezers." The emptiness, which will become more prominent metaphorically, is codified in the empty bottles. The second stanza confirms the effects of work on her physical appearance, and the third underscores the alienation that pervades the locale:

Va
   de mesa
   en mesa
hasta que las pláticas se arralan,
se apagan los ruidos de la cocina
y los clientes se dispersan.
Dejan de pasar los buses
y la luna se ve alta
sobre los postes de luz.

[She goes
   from table
   to table
until the conversation dies out,
the noise in the kitchen ceases
and the clients disperse.
The buses stop passing by
and the moon can be seen on high
above the light poles.]

This is an ordinary scene filled with the strains of work, but void of any human contact. All that she is left with, at the end of a day of serving people, is emptiness.

    This poem is the first part of a three-part sequence on oppression. The second poem records more graphic images of alienation. Here the woman is treated like an object: "me tocan las nalgas" (they touch my buttocks). Her partner has left her, and now she is "gorda, cansada y varicosa" (24) (fat, tired and varicose). Working as a waitress in these banal conditions, where she is alienated from her fellow human beings and from her labor, has physically taken its toll on her. Zamora's description of machinelike labor and objectification recalls Foucault's analysis of space and power in *Discipline and Punish: The Birth of the Prison*:

> A "political anatomy," which was also a "mechanics of power," was being born; it defined how one may have a hold over others' bodies, not only so that they may do what one wishes, but so that they may operate as one wishes, with the techniques, the speed and the efficiency that one determines.[22]

Degrading and dehumanizing work sites abound throughout this book of poetry, in which the majority of the workers are women. In a poem somewhat reminiscent of Cardenal's "Marilyn Monroe," Zamora narrates the life of a domestic worker. Like many of the women in this book, she is physically enclosed in patriarchal space: "Animalito doméstico, palomita en jaula" (A pet, a bird in a cage, 32). She has been isolated from her fellow humans, left barefoot and illiterate. She has lived to work for others in solitude:

> Tu camastro recogió soledades, llantos,
> bajo la luz mortecina de la lámpara
> de aquel último cuarto/palomar/alto de tablas.
> Te consolaste amando hijos ajenos
>   rubios, hermosos, exigentes. (32–33)

> [Your run-down bed gathered solitude, tears,
> under the dying light of a lamp
> from that last room/pigeon house/attic
> You consoled yourself by loving alien children
>   blonds, beautiful, demanding.]

For this character, too, there are physical consequences of her painful labor that have given her a half-hearted satisfaction:

> Tu mayor orgullo: los corredores
> que relumbran como vitrales
> con el sol de la tarde.
> Cuerpo de raíz, encorvado y rugoso,
> sobreviviste todas las desgracias.

[You are most proud: the hallways
that light up like store windows
with the afternoon sun.
A hunched, rugged, rootlike body,
you survived all misfortunes.]

Here the family is cast as yet another institution of repression within the society that legislates obedience and work. To be persuaded to perform the most vile forms of labor, the subject needs to be objectified and denigrated, retained in his or her social class (the working class):

Discipline increases the forces of the body (in economic terms of utility)
and diminishes these same forces (in political terms of obedience). In short,
it dissociates power from the body; on the one hand, it turns it into an "aptitude," a "capacity," which it seeks to increase; on the other hand, it
reverses the course of energy, the power that might result from it and turns
it into a relation of strict subjection (Foucault, *Discipline* 138).

Zamora's extreme distaste for familial exploitation, in the relation between husband and wife, for instance, is manifested in "Fiel ama de casa" (Faithful housewife). The housewife literally becomes an object of exchange with a particular use value or labor value for her husband:

Ahora reptas a los pies de tu señor:
Primera en su harén,
tomada o abandonada según capricho.
Madre de los hijos de su apellido
oreando tu abandono
        junto al tendero de pañales
estrujando tu corazón
        hasta despercudirlo en la ropa blanca. (34)

[Now you crawl at the feet of your man:
first in his harem,
taken or abandoned capriciously.
Mother of the children of his last name
airing your abandonment
        next to the clothesline with diapers
squeezing your heart
        until you clean it in the white clothes.]

The power is very clearly on the side of the man, who leaves her with children. While he escapes the responsibility of caring for his offspring, she is overwhelmed with the demands of child care — so much so that her feelings of abandonment are quickly drowned in the chore of washing diapers. Thus, she remains trapped in traditional gender roles, in which domination replaces communication and intimacy:

> Acostumbrada al grito, a la humillación
> de la mano servil ante la dádiva,
> Mujer arrinconada
>   Sombra quejumbrosa
> con jaquecas, várices, diabetes.
>
> Niña guardada en estuche
> que casó con primer novio
> y envejeció escuchando el lejano bullicio
>   de la vida
>   desde su sitial de esposa.

> [Accustomed to yelling, to the humiliation
> of a servile hand before a gift,
> cornered woman
>   whining shadow
> with headaches, varicose veins, diabetes.
>
> Girl kept in a box
> who got married to her first boyfriend
> and aged listening to the far-off noise
>   of life
> from her position as wife.]

One is struck by the speaker's cold depiction of the woman's life and wonders just what alternatives exist in a devoutly Catholic nation like Nicaragua, where abortion is illegal, contraceptives are scarce, and masculinity is socially constructed in such destructive and alienating ways. A community cannot be created, as Nancy Hartsock has poignantly asserted, where feminine and masculine "bodies and their appetites and desires are given no legitimate place" (*Money* 177). By creating a character with whom the reader is unlikely to identify, the poet implies that these traditional gender categories, which mistake domination for love, must change.

If "Fiel ama de casa" attacks patriarchal family relations, the biting criticism in "Fiel al corazón" (Devoted to the heart) makes it clear that these poems are not just Zamora's personal confessions — as José Coronel Urtecho would have it (*En limpio* 17). This poem is clearly Zamora's contemporary rendering of Aeschylus's *Agamemnon*, in which Clytemnestra takes Agamemnon to the sacrificial bath but does not kill him. It is apparent that the speaker in the poem does not bear any likeness to the protagonist of "Fiel ama de casa," except that she could have met a similar fate. While the protagonist of "Fiel ama de casa" devotes all her energies to pleasing her husband, even when he does not reciprocate, the speaker in "Fiel al corazón" refuses to tolerate her mate's promiscuity or to be servile. She asserts her independence to such a degree that her husband reacts against her transgression of assigned territory. Feeling that her love for him is gone, she commits adultery:

> No era yo la esposa que se perfuma para recibir al esposo
>   ausente,
> ni era la mujer que finge y después saca bajo las almohadas
>   los puñales y cuchillos,
> pero lo conduje a la bañera sacrifical,
> yo me lo llevé entonces, viajero que retornaba, a la cama.
>
> Yo era una mujer llorando por ella, por él
> y por el otro hombre que después de tanta desolación
> había hecho retornar el amor a la casa.
>
> Los dos habíamos visto cómo el rostro del Amor se agrietaba,
> cómo el tiempo y los actos arrugaban, arrebataban los
>   encantos al rostro del Amor.
>
> Los dos sabíamos cómo los pilares del tálamo se tambaleaban
> y nuestras cercanías se habían transformado
> en una guerra sin muertos ni sangre, quizá sólo con dos heridos,
> sin derrotados ni triunfadores, sino con dos vencidos.
>
> Balbuceante de culpa, entre lágrimas, logré explicar apenas
>   lo que pasaba.
>
> Pero sordo a mis súplicas, quiso recuperar, resucitar
>   al Amor que yacía a nuestros pies como un hijo muerto
> perdido para siempre y siempre evocado.(42)
>
> [I was not the wife who puts on makeup to await her
>   absent husband,
> nor was I the woman who pretends and later takes
>   from under the pillows
>   daggers and knives,

but I took him to the sacrificial bath,
I took him then, traveler who was returning, to bed.

I was a woman crying for her, for him
and for the other man who after so much desolation
had helped love come back home.

Both of us had seen how the face of Love cracked,
how time and acts wrinkled, stole away
            the spell from the face of Love.

Both of us knew how the pillars of the bride's bed staggered
and our surroundings had been transformed
into a war without casualties or blood, maybe only two injured,
without losers or winners, but rather two who were finished.

Stammering with guilt, among tears, I managed to barely explain
            what was happening.

But deaf to my requests, he wanted to recuperate, to resuscitate
            the love that was lying at our feet like a dead child
lost forever and forever evoked.]

According to the speaker, the husband confuses annoyance with affection, carelessness with intimacy, and domination with love. This alienated male ideology leads to the end of their marriage—much to the chagrin of their families. Because of her actions, she is subsequently shunned by friends and acquaintances, but remains "faithful to her heart" (42–44). Thus, Zamora inverts the traditional meaning of a wife's "devotion" and converts it into a weapon for liberation. Looking at Zamora's poetry as a complete body of work, it is clear that her intention is not merely to present a personal drama but also to comment critically on the construction of gender roles in Nicaragua, and she does so, as my reading indicates, in a much more forceful way than either Ilce or Belli.

Conclusion: The Convergence of Feminine/ Feminist Discourses

The works of Ana Ilce Gómez, Gioconda Belli, and Daisy Zamora intersect with sociopolitical realities of the revolution by presenting the left with the very critical dilemma of the problematic relation between feminism and socialism. Most socialist-feminist theory has been trying to rectify Marx, Engels, and the Frankfurt School and to reexamine the role that patriarchy plays in both capitalism and socialism. One plausible and imperative solution is to make sexual equality one of the main foci of the revolution, not only by affirming that equality rhetorically, but also by enlisting the full support of the political and economic system. Independent feminist organizations in Nicaragua already exist and have been very effective politically. In fact, if AMNLAE did not have 85,000 members and did not actively lobby within the political process, women's gains would not be as significant as they have been. Maxine Molyneux has similarly concluded that:

No se puede resolver la cuestión de los intereses del género y sus medios de representación si no se discute la forma de estado apropiada para la transición hacia el socialismo; por lo tanto, no es sólo una cuestión de qué intereses representa el estado, sino cómo los representa. ("Movilización" 360)

[The question of gender interests and their means of representation cannot be resolved if one does not discuss the type of state that is appropriated for the transition toward socialism; therefore, it is a question not only of what interests the state represents, but also of how it represents them.]

In poetry, we might say that what is needed is a combination of both concerns. These types of material or political interests act upon discourse and provide it with raw material. In Ana Ilce Gómez's poetry we have seen the repressive atmosphere that Catholicism, capitalism, and patriarchy created in prerevolutionary Nicaragua. Her writings focus on gender restrictions, oppression of women in the workplace, and the objectification of women. Yet her traditional Catholic beliefs contribute to her own alienation, which manifests itself so clearly in her verses. Displaced to the subject, the social alienation that encumbers her almost appears as an individual phenomenon. Thus, she casts herself in the role of martyr by blaming herself and life itself for her angst. Nevertheless, there is an undertone of resentment in the speaker's voice for having to act within the gender delineations in her social milieu and for having to put up with a system that treats her like a marginal human being. From the information that Molyneux, Jane Deighton, and AMNLAE provide, it is apparent that there were rhetorical changes in the Sandinista agenda, but the practical, political applications of the revolutionary agenda were very slow in developing. Consequently, it is quite probable that many women were (and are) dealing with issues and conditions similar to those evoked by Ilce.

Similarly, in the case of Gioconda Belli, the contradiction between her liberating affirmation of the female body and her celebration of the highly questionable reproductive role of women in the revolutionary struggle suggests additional ambivalence in contemporary Nicaragua. If Ilce's poetry communicates the active repression of sexuality through a morally legislating discourse, however, Belli's verses openly challenge the canonized definition of female sexuality. Nevertheless, as I have noted, a martyr figure is also invoked in Belli's poetry. In contrast to Ilce, Belli symbolically represents the (male) guerrilla as a heroic defender of the revolution. This image is understandable, given the presence of U.S.-supported contra forces. But Belli's eroticization of this mythic hero engenders a confused picture of the distinction between eros and thanatos. One wonders, in fact, whether this concession to patriarchy might not reflect some of the types of concessions the Sandinista government asked the feminist movement to make. Her construction of gender in poetry — which could also have been viewed with some suspicion in light of the events that transpired during the revolution — cannot be reduced to binary oppositions of passive (female)/active (male), reproduction/production, stationary/dynamic, and so forth. Instead, Belli disperses identity into new representations of women, simultaneously demanding new gender relations and reinforcing traditional relations. On the one hand, centering her poetic discourse on women and their "private" bodily pleasures, thus publicly breaking patriarchal taboos, challenges the male-oriented practice of poetry and the secondary status to which women have been relegated. Women are cast in a leading role as active subjects within the revolution with desires, hopes, and goals. On the other hand, Belli reinforces many of the traditional norms by portraying women as the faithful supporters of male guerrillas. Finally, as I commented earlier, she does not follow and document the intricacies of social relations in the revolution any more than she examines personal relations; the bonding energy that unites individuals is pictured vaguely as something magical.

Belli's poetry differs from Zamora's in its formal approach to feminism. It is not that Belli ever abandoned her practical ties with the revolution, for she was openly committed to it, but her discourse cultivates idealistic portrayals of women in new gender roles and relations. By contrast, Zamora's language is concrete. In a journalistic or testimonial manner, she reports the politics of the actual subjugation of women, emphasizing not the symbolic, but rather the details of everyday life. Alienation in the workplace and in the family become the source of her poetic referentiality. By focusing almost exclusively on these two domains — in this like Wilhelm Reich — Zamora insists that patriarchy's power is predominantly concentrated in the family and in the workplace. Her characters, then, stand in contrast to the depictions of women in male discourse as motherly, passive, comforting, nurturing. In short, her poetry can be seen as an assault on the objectification of women in literature and in patriarchal society.

In the works of Ana Ilce Gómez, Gioconda Belli, and Daisy Zamora we have three unique discursive approaches that question male-centered language. Implicitly, they question the socioeconomic inequalities of Nicaraguan patriarchy. They are united in condemning traditional gender relations, yet each exposes the spatial domains of domination in different ways: Ilce's poetry concentrates on the effect of religion on women's consciousness; Belli's work centers on sexual liberation in the revolution; and Zamora's discourse points to the family, the very heart of society, as an institutional territory binding Nicaraguan women.

In contrast to changes occurring in industrialized countries, sociopolitical change in Nicaragua continues to move in feminist directions. While the lessons of the women's movement in the United States in this postmodern age are being slowly eroded first by Reaganism and now by Bushism, in Nicaragua the momentum of the women's movements has been fueled by the revolution.[23] As the activity of AMNLAE testifies, women are becoming more militant and more organized every day. Furthermore, the success of their resistance to patriarchy makes it much more difficult to suppress and much more likely that "concientization" will lead to a deeper understanding of the political interests of radical feminism.

Given women's participation in and support for the revolution, it is doubtful that Violeta Chamorro's government will be able to impede the further development of women's interests. Because of its broad-based support, the women's movement is likely to continue to be a major political force in Nicaragua and, with or without the support of the Sandinistas, to gain more clout in the years to come. For as the FSLN drifted away from its working class and campesino base, so too in "bourgeois" feminism the demands of working class and campesino women seemed to be delayed in favor of more "urgent" national questions.

CHAPTER 5
POPULAR POETRY: REALISM AS A CULTURAL-POLITICAL AGENT

The proletarian revolution cannot but be a total revolution. It consists in the foundation of new modes of labour, new modes of production and distribution that are peculiar to the working class in its historicial determination in the course of the capitalist process. This revolution also presupposes the formation of a new set of standards, a new psychology, new ways of feeling, thinking and living that must be specific to the working class, that must be created by it, that will become 'dominant' when the working class becomes the dominant class.

Antonio Gramsci, "Questions of Culture"

The concern about the ethical position that the writer takes with regard to his or her art and politics expressed in Sartre's *What Is Literature?* is quite appealing. His essays on engagement are living testimony to the sharp ideological divisions shortly after World War II. According to Sartre, the writer must take an ethical stand in the fight against fascism. Sartre's discussion of the literary economy is displaced to the ideal realm because for him, true commitment and liberation can occur only within a classless society in which the mode of production and reception of art are available to all. This position helps to define changes that need to be effected, but it does not include an aesthetic program for communism's previous development: socialism. Gramsci, too, in "Concept of National–Popular," lambastes writers for losing touch with the "people" and forming their own segregated caste. Like Sartre, he sets forth an ethical call for aesthetic commitment by artists. Given the historical period in which Gramsci and, shortly thereafter, Sartre were writing, it is not entirely surprising that their analyses should focus a great deal of attention on authorial intention. Insofar as their arguments are valid for bourgeois culture, the issue of equal access to the modes of literary production does not receive much attention. In "Questions of Culture," however, Gramsci calls for a working-class culture, thereby transgressing the bourgeois space allotted for aesthetic commitment. Elsewhere he maintains that the superstructure and the infrastructure are sites of struggle between various classes and varying interests within these classes. Therefore, setting up a working-class culture does not completely efface the cultural production of the other classes, but rather places hegemonic control in the hands of the working class. It is assumed that bourgeois and petit bourgeois art will begin to wither away and that the dominant way of perceiving the world will be the proletarian as socialism enters into a stage of maturity so that the working class will face the question of "winning intellectual power."[1]

As I contended in chapter 1, if socialism assumes workers' control of the means of production, the reintegration of mental and manual labor, and the destratification of the bourgeoisie, then it should be equally important to institute a similar process in the cultural realm. Art has been predominantly produced, circulated, and received by the bourgeoisie, yet other social classes have disseminated their own "subordinate" art forms, which have not been recognized as "authentic" art in the aesthetic economy because the criteria used to gauge aesthetic quality are immersed in bourgeois society. In developed countries popular art occupies a marginal status until it is co-opted and marketed by the mainstream. This is among the fruits of liberal pluralism: marginal literature is held up as proof of "heterogeneity" or "democratic selection." In developing countries in Latin America, subaltern groups have even less access to mainstream cultural production.

Like other ideologies (and economies), art is the site of struggle not only between social classes, but also within each social class. Legitimizing the discourse of the subaltern groups and of the working class should be one of socialism's major goals in the aesthetic sphere. Just as once-marginalized social groups contributed economic and political energy that gave rise to socialism in the first place, they should similarly be expected to help theoretically formulate and practically implement an aesthetic model based on their real class, race, and gender relations.

Several poststructuralist critics today have begun to steer their research away from mainstream canonical works, intent on investigating the heretofore occulted blindspots of literary criticism (i.e., "marginal" literature). Thus, studies on and by "third world" critics and artists are now being accorded more recognition in the United States and in Europe. (I am thinking of Gayatri Spivak, Edward Said, and Jean Franco, for instance.) As imperialism has covered the globe and as the United States and Europe have become a home for exiles from developing countries, the vital information about the "colonies" has become more abundant. As I maintained in chapter 1, among leftists in the United States and Europe in particular, "marginal" literature — as a heterogeneous body of "subcultures" — has gained more attention than the "old" types of proletarian art. In effect, marginal literature has become the new literary avant-garde, on the cutting edge of revolutionary *studies*, but not necessarily of revolutionary *action*. The result is that for advocates of marginal sectors of the population in the United States or of "third world" cultures in general, it is "revolutionary" for a subculture or a movement to lay claim to the discursive territory from which it is excluded — especially when the appropriation of this once-denied space occurs within the capitalist system itself. Hence, rather than envisioning these movements as so many potential allies in the revolutionary struggle with and within the working class, they are treated instead as radical regardless of their class affiliation. In her insightful essay on Julia Kristeva, Toril Moi recognizes the political limits of this current within postmodernist thought:

> [Kristeva] conveniently chooses to overlook the differences between the 'dissident' groups she enumerates: the rebel (who attacks political power), the psychoanalyst, the *avant-garde* writer and women. Elsewhere, as we have seen, she equates the struggle of women with that of the working class. But in Marxist terms these groups are fundamentally disparate because of their different location in relation to the mode of production. The working class is potentially revolutionary because it is indispensable to the capitalist economy, not because it is marginal to it. In the same way women are central—not marginal—to the process of reproduction. It is precisely because the ruling order cannot maintain the *status quo* without the continued exploitation and oppression of these groups that it seeks to mask their central economic role by marginalizing them on the cultural, ideological and political levels. The paradox of the position of women and the working class is that they are at one and the same time central and marginal(ized).[2]

From a Marxist/feminist perspective, then, one could argue forcefully in favor of canonical studies because they are the most hailed products of bourgeois culture and thus accumulate the values of the dominant class and the contradictions between classes in a way that "marginal" literature does not. On the other hand, to a greater or lesser degree, the left would still be valorizing and reproducing canonical works and their modes of production. But the whole issue at hand is at least as complex as Moi has described it: the working class is central to the mode of production, and the accumulation of surplus value is dependent upon this relation between capital and labor while, at the same time, its rendering of itself (working-class culture) is marginalized. As Moi clearly notes, with women the matter is analogous: women are central to reproduction—that is, the system cannot function without them—but they are marginalized in other facets of society, including cultural production.

Studies of the marginal or even working-class culture—to say nothing of bourgeois artistic works—I would argue, risk acting as though "pure theory" or cultural studies, in and of themselves, involved physical political work. In other words, what can this array of sophisticated literary analyses tell us about the utter absence of viable left-wing political parties in the United States? As Terry Eagleton has poignantly posited in his discussion of criticism and the left, the question ultimately is: "How is a Marxist-structuralist analysis of a minor novel of Balzac to help shake the foundations of capitalism?"[3] Taking this a step further, we might ask instead: How is any analysis of any major or minor work going to shake the foundations of capitalism? It is here that praxis should step in as the modus operandi. For it is evident that a materialist evaluation of cultural production consists of critically examining the artistic mode of production and working to create a socialist aesthetic practice that is bound to socialist revolutionary struggle, and that a new culture will not fully come into being until revolutionary change has taken place.

But within bourgeois culture, the North American and European New Left has perhaps taken up the banner of marginality because of a long-held belief that the proletariat ends up as a disappointing revolutionary agent, that it is somehow incapable of carrying out the profound task that history has assigned it. It should be enough, the reasoning goes, to do molecular politics, literary or countercultural studies of specific "subcultures," which are revolutionary not because of their class origin, but because they are marginal. The notion of revolution as an actual political motor of history has somehow been glossed over with the small victories *within the system*.

But the popular Nicaraguan poetry that I analyze in this chapter should not be classified as marginal literature. It is, rather, *central* to the revolutionary period, because it was the working class and the campesinos who led the heroic and tragic struggle, and it was they who kept the economy going when the Somoza regime had been demolished and a new revolutionary government (the FSLN) was in power. Once these radical changes had taken hold of the nation, the democratization of culture became a real possibility and not just an experimental communal model in capitalism. This poetry embodies a new, developing consciousness as the working class and campesinos begin to have more control over the means of production.

Popular Poetry and Political Consciousness

In Latin America, popular poetry was an outgrowth of the collective political organizing that proved so effective during the 1960s. Christian base communities and popular educational centers were formed during these years, in order to develop political consciousness. Paulo Freire, Camilo Torres, and Ivan Illich worked in Brazil, Colombia, and Mexico, respectively, to educate the illiterate. These thinkers came to the conclusion that instituting social change necessarily involved the working class and the campesinos. Unlike previous social theorists, who sought to "modernize" Latin America, they felt that the region's economic woes were due to class antagonism in developing countries.

Undoubtedly, this great political and ideological shift in the 1960s was heavily influenced by the Cuban revolution and changes in the Catholic Church. Cuba's popular revolution in 1959 was a startling reminder of the possibility of social change occurring under the guidance of the working class. Equally important during this period was the reversal of Catholic policy regarding social involvement after Vatican II. Indeed, the bishops' meeting in Medellín in 1968 led to a rift in Rome's hegemony and to a questioning of its ostensibly nonideological stance. From this date forward, liberation theology has flourished on the periphery of the Catholic Church, retaining the basic religious structure while incorporating socialist concepts.

This historical background explains the growth of the Christian base community in Solentiname, Nicaragua, under the leadership of Ernesto Cardenal. At first, the members of the community scrutinized the Bible to find its contemporary relevance to the poor in Nicaragua in the late twentieth century. Their studies focused on the sociohistorical circumstances that made the working classes poor, illiterate, and powerless, and on what could be done to alter this situation. In 1976, in consultation with Cardenal—then the minister of culture (1979–88)—Mayra Jiménez created poetry workshops throughout the country. After 1979, the workshops were sponsored by the Ministry of Culture, until it was integrated into the Ministry of Education in October 1988, ostensibly due to economic hardship. The number of workshops decreased from as many as fifty-three in 1985 to twenty-one in 1988.

As I mentioned in chapter 1, much debate surrounds the collapse of the Ministry of Culture, indicating that finance was perhaps not the only issue at stake. Much of the controversy related to the leadership of Mayra Jiménez (a Costa Rican poet who joined Cardenal in Solentiname). Cardenal was also implicated in the charge that they neglected different poetic styles. One senses the divisiveness of their position in this passage from Jiménez's *Poesía campesina de Solentiname*:

> Sus poemas, como todos los que escribieron los demás compañeros que irían al combate, están llenos de pueblo, de elementos naturales que conforman su mundo, sin artificios, sin imágenes metafísicas, sin babosadas literarias. Esta poesía campesina será un ejemplo para las clases proletarias del mundo. Esta poesía es una excelente muestra de cuál es la función del verdadero arte y su acercamiento a los intereses del pueblo.[4]

> [Their poems, as is the case with all those written by the rest of the *compañeros* who went to combat, are filled with people, with natural elements that are a part of their world, without artifices, without metaphysical metaphors, without literary nonsense. This peasant poetry will be an example for the proletarian classes of the world. This poetry is an excellent show of what the function of true art is and its approach to the interests of the people.]

To be sure, there is little room for difference in this aesthetic theory — it posits popular poetry as the only "true" or "real" art. Cardenal also became rather inflexible in his stance on art in the revolution. When I interviewed him in November 1988, however, he denied advocating one aesthetic model alone. Yet in *Envío* he is quoted as not only denying the relevance of art for art's sake, but also virtually implying that it does not abide by Christian doctrine: "Pero el auténtico cristianismo enseña que Dios es el amor al hombre; entonces tenemos que decir que todo tiene que estar subordinado al amor al hombre; y no cabe el arte por el arte, el arte tiene que estar subordinado al hombre: esto es la Revolución como todo lo demás" (But authentic Christianity teaches that God is the love of man; so we have to say that everything has to be subordinate to the love of man: this is the Revolution as with everything else).[5] Cardenal and Jiménez's descriptions of revolutionary aesthetics seemed to create a binary opposition between "art for art's sake" and "committed art." It is not surprising that many artists, critics, and government officials objected to the suggestion that concrete poetry was the only possible revolutionary medium. Upon closer examination, however, the formal properties of the workshop poetry are not as homogeneous as critics maintained. One wonders finally if there is not something more to these objections to the democratization program, if they do not in fact show a certain reticence on the part of critics to the whole principle of the primacy of working-class and campesino art.

This literary/political debate raged on until Comandante Bayardo Arce redirected the issue to the question of quality, maintaining that after nine years of cultural development, the Ministry of Culture and the ASTC had not met the qualitative goals set in 1980. In an interesting twist, the renowned singer Enrique Mejía Godoy insisted on a dialectical consideration of quantity and quality, proposing that an excess in quantity is helpful because it increases the involvement of the masses in artistic production, which, in turn, boosts qualitative production. On the surface there appeared to be little opposition to the theory of democratization of culture. It was ostensibly its implementation that angered artists, critics, and officials, because it was felt that workshop participants were being encouraged to use only "concrete" language and not to delve into non-"realist" language. As we will see shortly, however, the poetic form was not as uniform as many critics contended.

For Cardenal the aim of the workshops was raising consciousness. In an interview with Steven White he stated that "later, other poets, other *compañeros*, began to participate in the discussion until the poetry became a collective and social phenomenon where the campesino poets themselves discussed different lines, rejected them, changed them, transformed them."[6] According to Cardenal, the objective of democratization was to protect the right of the oppressed to produce, distribute, and receive art. Thus, culture became a means of empowerment for those who were "unarmed" artistically.

Given the events that have transpired since the election in 1990, it is worth asking whether bourgeois culture was so entrenched in Nicaragua that uprooting it in favor of a long-lasting proletarian culture was beyond the ideological horizons of the Sandinistas, many of whom—including Rosario Murillo—had little difficulty publishing their work during the revolutionary period. As in so many other areas of the revolution, culture may be yet another sphere of contestation that the bourgeoisie and the petite bourgeoisie were not totally willing to give up. In essence, the class interests of many Sandinistas may have had a far more deeply ingrained effect on their political decisions than they had imagined as revolutionaries, and it was only in the course of history that these aporias cropped up. These Sandinistas, however, would be those who were recognized as members of the intelligentsia—in spite of their political persuasions—even before the revolutionary years, those who came from petit bourgeois and bourgeois families. So the creation of a proletarian culture, as in the case of the social revolution itself, may not only go against the grain, but also cut deeper into the heart of the class struggle. If for some years in their lives they stepped out of their class regalia and into the revolutionary forces and, in so doing, undermined the basic values of their class as they went, they would have had to wipe out almost every semblance of their background had they fully embarked on a proletarian cultural project—if, that is, we accept the idea that the aesthetic tries to encompass emotional life. If that is so, then at a certain moment they reached the proverbial point of no return, the core of their conscious identity, and they refused to institute the necessary transformations in the aesthetic realm. All of this, however, developed as they retreated from Marxist-Leninist political and economic positions to some of the bourgeois ideas that were so much a part of their background.

In a sense, then, when we penetrate the sedimented layers of ideology (*sandinismo*, in this study) and arrive at its emotional core—the aesthetic—the class positions seem to be even more entrenched than the previous layers, even more solidified. In the other layers of *sandinismo* we found an amalgam of populism, nationalism, anti-imperialism, liberalism, Marxism, and Christianity. But the most "sacred" underpinnings of bourgeois ideology, its most subtle yet strongest accumulation in consciousness, would appear to be aesthetic. It is here that the reform-minded bourgeoisie stops dead in its tracks. It is here that the full, subjective justification for bourgeois life resides. This explains why the socialization of art in Nicaragua was such a tremendously vital point of contention among the different social classes. It was not just another sphere of influence within the society, but rather the emotional nucleus of a bourgeois way of life.

Revolutionary History and the Workshops

In large part, the poetry that came out of the workshops was thematically consistent during the revolution. It was, first and foremost, a testimonial poetry that recorded revolutionary history: the workshop poets' participation in the armed struggle, their loss of loved ones, their learning and becoming literate, their own sensibilities. As long as the United States kept funding the contras with military aid, the war remained a central issue in most citizens' lives.

This military challenge to the revolution was disrupting commerce; destroying clinics, schools, and government buildings; killing and wounding campesinos. As a result, the Sandinistas needed to allocate approximately 60 percent of their budget for the military. This, in turn, hampered Nicaragua's development in other areas of vital interest, such as the construction of schools, clinics, libraries, and other public facilities. By the time of the elections in 1990, the economic situation in Nicaragua, despite well-intentioned aid from other, predominantly European, countries, was bleak. In spite of the disconcerting economic forecast, Nicaraguans relentlessly persisted in forming their society, even as they steadfastly worked at promoting democratic culture. As John Beverley has suggested, this project conceived of poetry as "a generalized discursive-ideological space engaging directly or indirectly very broad sectors of the population, including those elements which constitute, potentially or in fact, the revolutionary vanguard."[7] It is the neo-Gramscian concept of hegemony that best explains the existence of contesting forces in the FSLN and the desire to extend that pluralism to the cultural realm. In that sense Nicaragua clearly broke with Cuba, where the single party line (the vanguard) continues to exercise exclusive power. As I contended in chapter 1, it is this class and ideological diversity in Nicaragua that allowed the opposition to organize itself against the revolution or, at least, to create great ideological disparity among different factions within the FSLN, which ultimately led to the party's search for political and economic solutions that did not lie in their best interests, and that inaugurated their political defeat.

Nonetheless, Nicaragua's situation is similar to Cuba's insofar as the majority of the population belongs to the peasantry or the working class.[8] Until the revolution of 1979, cultural activities in Nicaragua were minimal and pertained only to the bourgeoisie. Those who were educated tended to come from affluent families who benefited from the Somoza oligarchy. As the economic and political circumstances became more intolerable and damaging to all classes except the elite, the educated bourgeoisie and petite bourgeoisie aligned themselves with the opposition and organized to depose Tacho Somoza. This, in fact, had been the political strategy of the Insurrectionalists within the FSLN leadership: from the beginning they encouraged immediate armed conflict by the workers while they cultivated a broad alliance with the bourgeoisie.[9]

The decisive ongoing participation of the campesinos and the working class in the armed struggle had given them—initially—a place of increasing prominence in Nicaragua. Because of their major involvement in the revolution, the other political parties joining under the umbrella of *sandinismo* were obliged to consider the crucial role of the working class in the new Nicaragua. The successful appeal to the petite bourgeoisie and the intermediate sectors was due largely to the FSLN's downplaying of the Marxist-Leninist influence within the party so that—even though the working class was spearheading the revolutionary struggle—the FSLN aimed at building a multiclass anti-*somocista* movement.

In the last moments of the revolutionary struggle, and once the insurrection had taken place, the FSLN began to reconsider the definition and configuration of culture as a unified space of public creativity. For the Sandinista government, culture became an ideological locus for combating imperialism. As early as the First Conference of Cultural Workers in 1980, Comandante Bayardo Arce insisted on this aesthetic goal: "Whenever the artist sets out to paint, to write a poem, to publish a book, to compose a song, we want him to consider the extent to which his work will be understood by the people, the extent to which it will help the people to transform themselves" (*Intellectual Foundations* 259). The canonical rearticulation of poetry, then, as part of a broad-based culture, included aesthetic and ideological contributions that had challenged the hegemonic conception of culture in Latin America. However, the Sandinistas were divided on this question from the very inception of the new cultural projects. While Ernesto Cardenal's version undertook a reevaluation of the cultural mode of production in socialism, Bayardo Arce's perspective seemed to fall in line with the Sartrean notion of the committed artist—where literary representation exists much as it does in bourgeois art. Hence, although popular poetry sprang forth as a natural response to the sociohistorical conditions, from the very beginning it was struggling against semitraditional forms of representation *found in the Sandinista ideological framework*. So, even as the popular workshops were being formed and even as the Ministry of Culture was promoting cultural activities particularly in working-class and campesino neighborhoods and towns, a discrepancy arose among Sandinista artists and politicians as to the nature of democratization itself: was it to entail a total reworking of the literary economy or was it designed to give the working class and the *campesinado* access to cultural production? It was in this matter, as I have argued throughout this study, that the radical divisions that once separated the Insurrectionalists, the Guerra Popular Prolongada, and the Tendencia Proletaria came to the surface once again and prefigured, in many ways, the political difficulties of approximately, 1988 to 1990.[10] Judging from the economic and political data available to us, one could surmise that the Insurrectionalist tendency—which finally gained a majority in the FSLN directorate—may have adopted an anti-imperialist stance, but it rarely moved beyond a nationalist or petit bourgeois political position. This conclusion, as I intimated earlier, can be verified by the Sandinistas' stance vis-à-vis the aesthetic—that final bourgeois terrain that harbors a class's self-consciousness.

Indeed, what is most disturbing to the bourgeoisie is the end of surplus value as they have known it and taken advantage of it. This is why, in times of crisis, and *only* in times of *extreme* crisis, they will resort to reformism (they will increase the total wage bill for workers) in order not to relinquish the stranglehold that they exert over workers; they will rob the workers a mite less. Rather than sacrifice their fortune, they are checkmated into negotiating against their will in order to maintain their economic power. A similar process is carried out in cultural production. The dominant mode of production is, and for the moment continues to be, bourgeois. The most scandalous scene of all for the bourgeoisie is to imagine that the proletariat might wrest control of the cultural means of production away from them. It is then that the deeply seated vestiges of all that is bourgeois will come to the foreground and there will be talk of "democratization" and "pluralism." Suddenly the bourgeoisie will feel the need to cling to multifarious representations—even though that only became a concern *when their very existence was threatened*. Suddenly, "fair play" and the "virtues" of bourgeois democracy will take center stage. And when the proletariat moves to seize those productive means, the bourgeoisie will cry out, it will—as Marx comments in the *Eighteenth Brumaire*—become indignant. But the appropriation of the cultural means of production by the proletariat *is* in fact the ultimate goal of communism. This is the historical and class tradition that preceded the rule of the Insurrectionalists in Nicaragua and that applied very well to their own case.

Historically, then, the Sandinistas wanted to transcend the limitations of a literature—from the fiction of the independence period to the "Boom"—that, in Latin America, was created by and for an educated elite. Testimonial or documentary narrative in Latin America, which began with Miguel Barnet's pseudo biography and testimony of the Cuban ex-slave Esteban Montejo, represented a step beyond the liberalism of the Boom and a way of reaching a broader audience. However, the political divisions among the Sandinistas themselves were only exacerbated when it came to working out a revolutionary aesthetic program because the same class differences surfaced once again. Some, as I have noted, sided with liberal bourgeois art (the Boom), others insisted on "concrete" or socialist realist literature, and still others advocated a variety of aesthetic projects. Their positions react to a historical development of the arts and of politics in Latin America from the 1960s to the present, which I will examine in this chapter.

Testimonial Literature and the Boom in Latin America

As the political climate has encroached upon everyday life in Latin America, making it virtually impossible to ignore the atrocities committed by the state (in Argentina, Uruguay, Chile, Brazil, Guatemala, and El Salvador, for example), many writers have responded by directly depicting these crimes. Literature situates itself in the forefront, challenging the official story of the dictatorial regime that veils its own institutional violence. Literature finds itself at this crossroads, as Jean Franco has keenly observed, when the state violates the heretofore sacred institutions in the society: the family and the church.[11] Once the conventional delineation between private and public space has been swept aside by capital and the military as its right arm, once, in other words, dehumanization reaches such extreme limits that it threatens to extinguish anything that gets in its way, then the aesthetic takes on a very different mission within the political forces that unite against the dehumanization of neofascism: it becomes a medium to realistically portray and vehemently denounce these atrocities.

New realism's antecedent, the "Boom" (or the beginning of the postmodern age in Latin America), is characterized and defined by a number of sociocultural factors.[12] It comes about as rapid demographic changes, intense industrialization, and the United States' ideological penetration via the mass media (rampant since the late 1940s, but hitting with greatest force beginning in the 1960s). In March 1961, the Kennedy administration devised a plan to avoid more social revolutions in the Americas. It encouraged U.S. investment in Latin America and it attempted to provide economic and civil stability to the region by allocating millions of dollars to the military. Once secure American markets were established in several Latin American nations, President Kennedy reasoned, then the institutions in these societies would prosper. In that manner an educated middle class would come into being and would form a solid professional sector. This, in turn, would give this middle class the economic power to be able to consume American goods. Initially the aid being shipped to the region was supposed to be destined for Latin American businesses that would grow economically and thus stimulate production. However, most of the funds went to paying off the national debts, revitalizing the military, and bolstering the status of multinationals in the region. Furthermore, in the end, the Alliance for Progress did not produce the economic results it had promised. Clearly, the Alliance for Progress, the Peace Corps, and, finally, *The Rockefeller Report on the Americas* were designed to shore up these "dependent" economies and thereby prevent a major conflict between social classes; ultimately, however, they failed in their objective of holding off more social upheaval. The Cuban revolution had challenged U.S. hegemony in the hemisphere (much as other revolts had: Sandino in Nicaragua, Arbenz in Guatemala, etc.), particularly since Cuba not only severed ties with the United States, but also allied itself with the Soviet Union, a move that assured its economic stability. In short, Kennedy's "peaceful revolution" seemed to reinforce the idea that military force was the only option for U.S. policy in Latin America.[13]

Publishing houses and mass media promotion helped to provide a cultural base for the middle classes, resulting in the Boom. Just as the new and technologically innovative were being encouraged in the economic sphere, a spirit of modernization arrested the consciousness of artists, publishers, literary critics, and the reading public.[14] In what other way could we explain the fact that a select group of novelists (Mario Vargas Llosa, Carlos Fuentes, Julio Cortázar, and Gabriel García Márquez) suddenly burst onto the literary scene? The Boom did not emerge — as John Brushwood claims — as a long-awaited "maturation" of fiction, but rather as a formal response to socio-historical factors that invaded both form and content.[15] Similarly, since the Boom's demise, fiction has responded to similar and new historical, political, and social circumstances. Clearly, the political climate bears some resemblance to the 1960s, but the military is much more organized in its repressive tactics. The way reality is depicted has also changed in fiction. While Carlos Fuentes, Gabriel García Márquez, and Mario Vargas Llosa continue to write today, they represent but one current within contemporary Latin American literature. There is no question that the *novísimos* follow in their footsteps in some ways, but they also distinguish themselves from the Boom novelists by not indulging in formal innovations the way their predecessors did, and by highlighting political content.

By 1972, according to Angel Rama, the impact of the Boom began to decline ("Tecnificación" 85). During this same period, U.S. strategy for Latin America went in another direction. The plan to bolster Latin American economies and establish a middle class did provide a larger market for U.S. consumer products. Nevertheless, since Latin American labor costs went up, this plan paradoxically worked against U.S. interests, as it prevented the multinationals from reaping the profits that they had previously enjoyed. Ostensibly, this period had given entrepreneurs some breathing space and allowed them to export and import much more freely. According to Latin American military officials, however, it led to higher inflation, unemployment, and debts. Furthermore, guerrilla groups sprang up during the 1960s and 1970s in Peru, Argentina, Uruguay, Bolivia, Nicaragua, and El Salvador. The solution posed by the national bourgeoisie and the military to these political and economic crises were austerity measures and authoritarianism. Thus, neo-fascist dictatorships gained backing, from both local middle classes and the

U.S. government, because it was thought that they would enhance economic efficiency at home and guarantee that U.S. interests would not be threatened.[16]

Neorealism and so-called testimonial fiction emerged out of this political moment. If the Boom novels could be described as deemphasizing the historical referent, exalting the unconscious ego, insisting on the autonomy of art, promoting all that is "modern," breaking with traditional chronology and point of view, and implementing linguistic innovations, this newer fiction, on the other hand, recuperates realism, history, and popular characters and speaks in colloquial language.[17] In the testimonial novel, for example, the speaker becomes the synecdochic representative of the collective, the lower class, or an oppressed racial or ethnic group. There are instances in which the working class or the campesinos are not representing themselves, in which their narrative is filtered through a compiler or an editor. And in the cases of Miguel Barnet's *Biografía de un cimarrón* (Autobiography of a Runaway Slave) and Rigoberta Menchú's *Me llamo Rigoberta Menchú y así me nació la conciencia* (I, Rigoberta Menchú, transcribed and edited by Elizabeth Burgos-Debray), the subject communicates with us through Barnet and Burgos-Debray. By contrast, the popular poetry I will be analyzing in this chapter, as well as other testimonials, sets itself apart because the working class and the campesinos narrate and publish their work themselves.

At this point, it is worth summarizing the formal and thematic tensions between testimonial literature and the canon. Testimonial literature is not fictional in the traditional sense of the word: although any interpretation represents its own particular troping, documentary literature deals with the author's firsthand experience in historical transformation. In addition, the protagonist is normally a "real" person who narrates "real-life" moments and does not consciously inject his or her desire for an imagined "reality" into the narration (as an intentionally created fictional world). Thus, she or he is simultaneously protagonist, narrator, and author, although, technically, none of these because the poetry written in the workshops is always cross-examined, dissected, filled with the suggestions of fellow writers, and then regrouped into the literature we read. Naturally, as John Beverley has pointed out, no interpretation of reality can forgo unique and selective textualization pertaining to the subject's interpellation with a plethora of social forces ("Anatomía" 11). We are always already dialectically relating ourselves to the world that surrounds us and is in us. As Marx and Engels put it in a memorable passage of *The German Ideology*, "circumstances make men as much as men make circumstances."[18] And these poets do not have the free time to contemplate the world, as the middle classes might, but rather see reality as process, as *living praxis*. In his monumental *History and Class Consciousness* Georg Lukács convincingly maintains that:

The place in society and hence the viewpoint of the proletariat goes further than the example just cited [the representation of social upheavals in Shakespeare and Aeschylus] in one vital qualitative way. The uniqueness of capitalism is to be seen precisely in its abolition of all 'natural barriers' and its transformation of all relations between human beings into purely social relations. Bourgeois thought, however, remains enmeshed in fetishistic categories and in consequence the products of human relations become ossified, with the result that such thought trails behind objective developments. The abstract, rational categories of reflection which constitute the objectively immediate expression of this—the first—socialisation of the whole of human society, appear in the eyes of the bourgeoisie as something ultimate and indestructible. (For this reason bourgeois thought remains always in an unmediated relation to such categories.) The proletariat, however, stands at the focal point of this socialising process. On the one hand, this transformation of labour into a commodity removes every 'human' element from the immediate existence of the proletariat, on the other hand the same development progressively eliminates everything 'organic', every direct link with nature from the forms of society so that socialised man can stand revealed in an objectivity remote from or even opposed to humanity.[19]

It would be easy—and incorrect—to read the worker's engagement with the world, his praxis, as something that draws on intuition alone, or on the spontaneous collection of sense data. It is rather a more central and conscious form of praxis that allows those who are most exploited a perceptive and acute perspective of the inner workings of history. The workshop poetry, then, is embedded in life struggles, as well as filled with liberating aspirations.

Like the "New Song" movement in Latin America, this poetry has acquired widespread support within Nicaragua as a means of communication, and it runs counter to the culture industry that is bolstered by U.S. multinational corporations. This alone places it on the fringes of mainstream international culture. According to Fernando Reyes Matta, both poetry and the New Song are "inserted into the popular culture precisely at those points where we find the forms and language of a folklore excluded from the 'culture industry' controlled by the trans-national capitalist system."[20] At the same time, popular culture forms part of revolutionary movements. The most important aspect of this poetry is that, as cultural praxis, it comes from below and not from above: it is poetry written by members of the working class who have seized the means for representing themselves.

The Epic Present

The workshop poetry collected in *Poesía libre* (Free poetry), *Poesía campesina de Solentiname* (Peasant poetry from Solentiname), and *Fogata en la oscurana*

(Bonfire in the darkness) serves as a kind of archive, now that workshops have diminished in number or are lying dormant.[21] Yet the level of political consciousness still persists today, living, as it were, amid the hardships of political and economic reality and radiating the hope and expectation that things will change. Mediation in these poems is reduced to the relation between the immediate observer and actor and the struggle in which he or she is involved. Since the audience has already discussed these poems collectively and since they are destined for those who are helping to build a community (socialism on a larger scale), the notion of authorship is replaced by a more nebulous notion of origin that focuses on the social nature of human beings.

"Son las tres y media, poeta" (It's three-thirty, poet) illustrates the type of political "witness" that characterizes much of this poetry:

> Son las cuatro de la mañana
> > Roque Dalton
> el muro enemigo ha sido derribado
> y se izan
> por todas partes
> nuestras banderas rojas. (*Poesía libre*, vol. 14)

> [It's four in the morning
> > Roque Dalton
> the enemy wall has been toppled
> and all over
> our red flags
> are being lifted.]

> Manuel Noguera
> Poetry Workshop of the
> Ministry of the Interior

The end of the poem disseminates a message from the battlefield to El Salvador's mythic poet/revolutionary, Roque Dalton. In so doing, the poem, which deals with the immediate political need to defeat the contras in battle, opens up lines of communication with another popular revolutionary cause—that of the FMLN (the Faribundo Martí National Liberation Front) in El Salvador. The poem therefore transcends a narrow nationalism in its affirmation of collective revolutionary activity in two Central American contexts. What is just as pertinent is the equivalence between the writer and the protagonist, since it nullifies the traditional conception of authorship. In addition, the poem appears to the reader to be a current report from the battlefields and, thus, is directly tied to sociohistorical circumstances.

While a great number of the poems in these volumes are openly vocal regarding the armed struggle against the U.S. military presence, others address personal questions in this context. Often, the poets are more inclined to consciously employ metaphors:

Sólo queda el sabor de tus labios como una huella imperecedora
Me queda la suavidad y tibieza de tu cuerpo,
    como una ilusoria imaginación.
Tu cuerpo desnudo, envuelto en una toalla blanca
y yo poco a poco desprendiéndote de esa escasa vestidura.

(Poesía libre, vol. 14, 41–42)

[All that is left is the flavor of your lips like an imperishable print
I am left with the softness and warmth of your body,
    like an illusory imagination.
Your naked body, wrapped in a white towel
and I slowly but surely loosen that scanty clothing.]

Second Lieutenant
Justo Pastor Salgado
Poetry Workshop from Estelí

This love poem is characteristic of popular poetry in that the subject is absent or disappearing. All that is left of the speaker's lover are the tactile impressions that have marked his memory. While there is a sense in which this reconstruction of his lover is "illusory," the poet's sensations also derive from physical contact. A sense of the *warmth* and *softness* of her skin and the *flavor* of her lips permeates the poem, and the reader cannot help but imagine that the speaker has her before him.

In these lines, the poet tries to recover the materiality of bodily sensations yet is condemned to remaining at a temporal distance. The poet is able to remember her so clearly because his memory of her is based on sense data, which serve as the material foundation for his recollection. As we read later in Pastor's poem, they are separated—"me pedís que te olvide y que no te pregunte nada" (you ask that I forget you and that I not ask you anything)—yet his senses have engraved this vital information in his memory.

The theme of personal loss or mourning encroaches on the political sphere as another form of poetic expression. The realism of a wartime commitment that endangers one's life overshadows such poetry. The poet may mourn the loss of the loved one and pay homage to him or her, or the deceased may become immortalized as an epic hero (much as we observed in Cardenal's poetry). "José Luis Chevez Savogal" is paradigmatic of the former:

Siempre trabajaste con tu pseudónimo Carlos.
Desapareciste.
El 30 de mayo de 1978 te capturó la guardia.
Hoy, libres, te busco
en las cuadrillas de los carpinteros
que reconstruyen Nicaragua.
Y no te encuentro. (*Poesía libre,* vol. 8, 32)

[You always worked with your pseudonym Carlos.
You disappeared.
On May 30, 1978, the National Guard captured you.
Today, we are free, I look for you
among the groups of carpenters
who reconstruct Nicaragua.
And I can't find you.]

Karla Chávez
Poetry Workshop of State Security

Everyday human experience ("el 30 de mayo") is written explicitly in verse. The speaker longs to bring her husband back to life in the revolution. Murdered by the death squads, he is left out of the collective project for which he fought and is not resurrected as a martyr by the poet. Like Cardenal in his documentary poetry, the poet gives a date and name, thus recalling the life of a real human being and not that of a fictional character. In fact, I would suggest that fiction, as we traditionally conceive of it, loses all its impact and relevance since everything appears to be a textualization of sense data. Indeed, the popular testimonial poet intentionally does a portrayal in the text of her everyday life, and thus negates the irrational notion of fiction (in the abstract) as exterior to empirical life. In short, she is not depicting a *deliberately* imagined or desired world, but rather a lived experience. The poet feels impelled to "save" the life of the deceased, to resurrect him from his tragic death. And it is significant that she looks for him among the carpenters who now "reconstruct Nicaragua" because she envisions him as acting upon material reality and as working toward a new future.

"Despedida de Elbis" (Elbis's farewell), written by Irene Agudelo Builes, a child, represents the theme of a guerrilla's death giving life to the community:

cuando te fuiste para la comuna a entretenerte
fue la última vez que te vi.

Alejandro y vos se subieron al bote
y fueron desapareciendo

Y nos decíamos todos adiós
mucho tiempo después pregunté por vos

me dijeron que estabas muerto

Y el día que llevaron tus huesos a la plaza
estabas en nuestros corazones. (*Poesía libre*, vol. 3, back cover)

[When you went to the camp to train
it was the last time I saw you.

Alejandro and you got in the boat
and disappeared little by little

And we all bade farewell
Much later I asked about you

They said you were dead

The day they took your remains to the plaza
you were in our hearts.]

Dealing with the drama of the death of the speaker's brother, this poem embodies the anguish and despair of a child. It addresses the subjective fabric of Nicaraguan life ("you were in our hearts") and the degree of cultural democracy that existed there during the revolution. The last two lines of the poem speak symbolically to the relation between individual and collective consciousness: Elbis's bones are taken to the plaza—the center of activity of the town and of the community—where the people commemorate him. He thus spiritually enrichens the town as a (physical) sacrificial example. Once again, an absent member of the community is resurrected in it.

What is of interest in this poem is that it was written by a child of the community who captures the essence of its collective life and that a child's testimony is taken seriously enough to be published in the Ministry of Culture's journal of popular poetry. Children played an increasingly important role in the revolution, in large part because they represented hope for a more stable and prosperous national future.

As in Cardenal's poetry, it is not uncommon for the poet to address the deceased as though she or he were alive and living out the revolution with the community. Similarly, in "Carmen" the speaker continues the dialogue on the anniversary of her death:

Te traje flores Carmen,
Hoy cumplís un aniversario más
igual que todos los asesinados en septiembre.
No te quedés callada Carmen
decime algo.
Vieras qué rojas las flores de malinche este año.
La Felipa
    tu mamá
ya sabe leer.
Tu hijo Oscar va alegre a la escuela
donde estudian los hijos de Enrique
        (el mondonguero)
que te denunció a la guardia.
Ya no hay operaciones limpieza,
sólo Brigadas de Salud para terminar la malaria y el dengue.
Y yo en los talleres de poesía de Bluefields
escribiendo poemas para la Revolución. (*Fogata* 47)

[I brought you flowers Carmen.
Today is another of your anniversaries
the same as all those who were assassinated in September.
Don't stay there in silence Carmen
say something.
You should see how red the *malinche* flowers are this year.
Felipa
    your mother
now knows how to read.
Your son Oscar goes to school happily
with the children of Enrique
    (the gutless one)
who reported you to the National Guard.
There are no longer any cleanup operations,
there are only Health Brigades who work at eliminating
    malaria and fever.
And I'm in the poetry workshops in Bluefields
writing poems for the Revolution.]

Pleading for Carmen to come to life, the speaker invokes the achievements of revolutionary Nicaragua and tells of the impact that they have had on her family. Her death has provided a seed for social change and the collective has benefited thanks to her sacrifice. What is almost implied is that the materiality of these social changes is a part of her, that is, that she is embodied in the community and, consequently, has allowed it to grow (like the roses themselves). Taking on a dialogic form ("don't keep your mouth shut Carmen"), the poem exceeds traditional poetic codes because the poet carries on a conversation with the deceased. In this case, the form has a significant impact on the content: the poet rearticulates Carmen's death as life by structuring the poem within a radical Christian ideology (i.e., Carmen cannot be fully deceased because the act of dying heroically gives life to the living). The reader is caught, as it were, in the flow of action (the growing incarnated in the flowers), which the poet communicates by contrasting Carmen's static state with the motion of the revolution—represented in the acts the poet enumerates and in the verb forms (the present participle "writing" is emblematic of this changing situation).

In a similar poem about the hardships of wartime and homesickness, Rudy García "relives" from afar his life with his daughter through a photo:

> Veo tu mirada.
> Está hacia el vacío de aquella habitación
> con luces por todos lados
> que se llena de perfumes
> > diario
> que te llena de interrogantes. (*Fogata* 41)

> [I see your look.
> It is directed toward the emptiness of that room
> with lights on all over
> which are filled with perfume
> > daily
> which fill you with questions.]

The speaker later imagines the child in his presence: "Tus ojos los veo con lágrimas" (I see tears in your eyes), and further on: "Casi siento el latido de tu corazón / que cada vez se hace más rápido" (I almost feel your heartbeat / which with each beat becomes more rapid). The speaker tries to negate the pain of her absence by awakening his senses: he smells the scent of her perfume and hears the beating of her heart, which only sharpens his vision, allowing him to relive momentarily the material reality of his home while he is away from home. By the end of the poem, the reader almost forgets that father and daughter are not physically together. As in "Carmen," the most salient aspect of these lyrics is the poet's perceptive capacity to retain and later recall physical actions and features.

"Un niño, un gato y una paloma" (A child, a cat and a dove) by Juan Urbina Osegueda is neither neorealist nor conversational, lending itself instead to an allegorical reading:

> Un niño
> sentado de cuclillas
> con una taza roja en la mano
> le da agua a una paloma blanca.
> Ella se aproxima
> y le picotea los pañales
> cuando él la quiere agarrar.
> La paloma se le esquiva dando vueltas.
> Alza vuelo y se pierde la paloma.
> Desde un rincón de la cocina
> un gato negro agazapado
> mira al niño que está llorando. (*Fogata* 39)

> [A child
> crouching
> with a red cup in hand
> gives a white dove water to drink.
> She comes closer
> and pecks at his diapers
> when he tries to grab her.
> The dove escapes his grasp by circling around him.
> The dove flies off and loses itself.
> From a corner of the kitchen
> a crouching black cat
> looks at the child who is crying.]

The white dove symbolically represents peace; the child stands for the young, revolutionary Nicaragua; and the black cat metaphorically refers to the revolutionary forces. Thus, no matter how much Nicaragua might try to lure peace into its grasp, it seems to escape. The image of the red cup collaborates with the blackness of the cat to show the colors of the FSLN flag. The destiny of the two is meaningfully interrelated by association of the squatting child with the hunched cat. An intertextual interpretation of the referent for the black cat can be observed in Urbina Osegueda's following poem, "El gato cumuluco" (The cumuluslike cat), in which the cat moves from mountain to mountain, checking on every detail as it goes (39). If we analyze its metaphorical role in both poems, the cat seems to represent the FSLN. Both readings attest to the tragic decade (1979 to 1990) in Nicaragua when the war consumed a major part of the country's political and economic energy.

In many of the popular workshop poems, the agent of history herself reports the making of history to her *compañeros*, commonly in a dialogic manner. The information we receive has not been selectively sorted out by any mediator beyond the poet herself, the person who empirically engages herself in the revolution. With all of the poets we have examined in *Aesthetics and Revolution*, the reader runs up against the limitations of reported speech — filtered through the lens of a reporter/poet who did not witness the narrated incidents first hand. Here, however, we hear the voice of those who confront class struggle face to face as participants in the revolution. Poetry is thus removed from its distant, elevated status and placed in the interstices of what Ernesto Cardenal calls "concrete" life:

> Decías que para vos la muerte era
> como un bello poema
> y cuando caíste tu sangre regó las mazorcas de maíz
> que llevabas en los bolsillos del uniforme
> y sobre tu cuerpo puyoniaron los granos
> y crecieron grandes y fuertes espigas. (*Poesía campesina* 63)

> [You said that death for you was
> like a beautiful poem
> and when you fell your blood watered the corn ears
> that you carried in the pockets of your uniform
> and on your body the grains were buried
> and they became strong and big ears of corn.]

The speaker in this poem first recalls an intimate thought that Chicha (Tony) had shared with Bosco Centeno (the author) and then describes how this desire was fulfilled as he — the author — was able to witness it. Chicha's death in revolutionary battle is consequently seen as giving life, as part of a natural cycle. The poem allows at least two complementary readings: one literal (a precise description of his death) and the other metaphorical (by implication Chicha's death is accompanied by the birth of a generation of followers, a new generation of revolutionaries). Here we see a close — and not altogether contradictory — collaboration between liberation theology (the content) and materialism (the form, concrete poetry).

In the tradition of Ernesto Cardenal's concrete poetry, the poet frequently mentions the most specific details so that the report or poem will live up to the accuracy that is expected of it. In "Desde una colina en el frente sur Benjamín Zeledón" (From a hill on the Benjamín Zeledón southern front) the poet, Iván Guevara, records the details of a prerevolutionary battle in Nicaragua and the raw material for his ideological framework:

Y estoy aquí en mi trinchera
camuflado con zacate recién cortado.
Los veinte compañeros que tengo yo en la colina
todos están en sus trincheras
apostados vigilando atentos.
El "chupi-sopla" pasa veloz,
más atrás un avión de reconocimiento un D43.
Y se oyen morteros de 120 y 82.
Los aviones dejan ir ráfagas de ametralladoras calibre 50.
El "push-and-pull" zigzagueando en picada
ametrallando las colinas
roqueteando a Peñas Blancas y Sapoá,
el helicóptero que se para allá arriba
y deja caer bombas de 500 libras,
bombas que suministraba el gobierno de Norte América
para matar la población . . . (*Poesía campesina* 83)

[And I am here in my trench
camouflauged with recently cut *zacate*.
The twenty *compañeros* I have on the hill
are all in the trenches
at their posts watching out attentively.
The "inhale and blow" passes by quickly,
behind it a plane that looks like a D-43.
And mortars are heard all over
canon blasts and 120 and 82 mortars.
The planes spit flames from their 50-caliber machine guns.
The "push-and-pull" zigzags in downward flight
machine gunning the hills
launching rockets at Peñas Blancas and Sapoá,
the helicopter that hovers above
and drops 500-pound bombs,
bombs that the government of North America provides
to kill the population . . .]

Why this inordinate interest in detail? What does the reader gain from this specific depiction? First, Iván Guevara portrays his own position as a guerrilla in the hills and the environment around him—which is described in an almost scientific fashion. Based on this information, the reader understands that this poet is an experienced guerrilla who is fully aware of military operations. But the specificity of his description also says that this poem is not just a poem, it is a live report from a source that will most likely challenge the hegemonic power (the Somozan government). The more detailed and carefully crafted his rendering of reality, the more credible is his report. Thus, the guerrilla is not idly passing his time in the jungle, but rather has a sense of calling that tells him that he should record this experience for collective memory. Neither is he jotting down facts that might interest the military observer. No, the act of naming precisely is embedded in his ideological belief that the bombing is a provocation caused by U.S. aid to the Somozan military. This indictment of imperialism is significantly reinforced by the use of English military vocabulary, which also invades the Spanish language so that some things can be named only by applying the English word ("push-and-pull"), while others indicate the degree to which English affects the structure of Spanish (the newly created verb "roquetear" is a prime example). The poem is written for a reading public that is taking part in the revolutionary struggle against the dictatorship, hence, it serves as praxis: it is the moment in which he reflects about this military attack while he is in the midst of the action. As readers, I would suggest, we capture this testimony just prior to that qualitative leap in the dialectic that marks a confrontation between the concrete reality and the poet's acute observations about that reality.

This concern to depict reality in the most vivid way possible is also found in the postrevolutionary "Un poema de dos poetas" (A poem about two poets):

> Marcelino, te miro
> en la acera de la casa cural en Masaya.
> Allí dormís
> sentís frío
> y peleás cuando te quitan el lugar.
> Con tus 60 años
> todavía sos útil a la Revolución.
> Toda tu vida ha sido de calles,
> de harapos, y desprecio.
> Ahora nosotros los de la Central Sandinista de Trabajadores
> hemos platicado con vos
> queremos que nadie duerma en las calles
> no más gente harapienta
> no más mendigos
> no a los lisiados pidiendo.
> Queremos que todos vayamos a cortar café
>   algodón
>   yuca,
> Todos a hacer vigilancia revolucionaria.

Algún día te miraré
alfabetizando en la Revolución.
Y vos dirás lo mismo
que digo en este poema.
Marcelino
soy tu hermano y poeta
por eso te digo
que la Revolución es de todos. (*Fogata* 111)

[Marcelino, I look at you
on the sidewalk of the priest's home in Masaya.
There you sleep
you feel cold
and you fight when they take your place.
With your 60 years
you are still useful for the Revolution.
All your life you have spent in the streets,
in rags, and in disgrace.
Now those of us of the Sandinista Workers' Center
have talked with you
we don't want anyone to sleep in the streets
no more people in rags
no more beggars
no more handicapped asking for money.
We want everybody to go cut coffee
                cotton
                yucca,
All of us should do revolutionary guard.
Some day I'll see you
teaching literacy to people like you
and leading them in the Revolution.
And you will say the same thing
I am saying in this poem.
Marcelino
I am your brother and a poet
that's why I tell you
that the Revolution is for everybody.]

This homeless man, Marcelino, is compared with others cast aside by the Somozan dictatorship: the beggars, the handicapped, and the poor. In the revolution lies the hope of those who were marginalized; now they can join in labor and protect the revolution for which they fought. A variation of sorts, perhaps, on Bendetto Croce's "everyone is a philosopher," the title of the poem recalls the common saying in Nicaragua that "everyone is a poet." Indeed, in this poem Marcelino rises from a position of servitude or destitution to that of co-master of his circumstances; from isolated individual to the community.

In reference to Solentiname we should keep in mind that the poets who were members of this utopian community considered it a foreshadowing of revolutionary transformation, and their active participation in the FSLN-inspired attack on the National Guard garrison in San Carlos in 1977 was living testimony to their commitment to something beyond the Solentiname commune itself: socialism. They were not content with living in virtual isolation in their community, but rather believed in a political and theological calling to engage in armed struggle in order to smash the brutal dictatorship that continued to oppress the great majority in the name of the small minority. In Solentiname the members of the community had the opportunity to live a life less alienating than life under the dictatorship: they carried out collective labor, they reflected on their life in a conscious, collective manner, and they heightened their relationship with nature on the island. So it is that—given the capacities of the community—they were able to lay the groundwork for a socialist consciousness of society and anticipate the material transformations that were to take place.[22]

One type of popular poetry during the revolutionary struggle and during the revolution itself is based on an oral tradition, subsequently written down in what is almost diary form. Particularly between 1975 and 1980, the revolutionary cadres carried on an illegal dialogue with the citizens. Poetry was thus converted into one of many practical discourses that engaged in the struggle to record and denounce the barbarity of Somoza's National Guard and to encourage the people to rise up against the dictator.

Poetry in Struggle:
Graffiti and Primitivist Painting

> Cállense todos
> y síganme oyendo
> en las catacumbas
> ya en la tarde
> cuando hay poco trabajo
> pinto en las paredes
> de las catacumbas
> las imágenes de los santos
> de los santos que han muerto matando el hambre
> y en la mañana imito a los santos.

> [Quiet all
> and keep listening to me
> in the catacombs
> already well into the afternoon
> when there is little work
> I paint images of saints
> of the saints who have died killing hunger
> on the walls
> of the catacombs
> and in the morning I imitate the saints.]
>
> Leonel Rugama

Art infused into the revolutionary process did not confine itself to the traditional private milieu, but rather openly engaged with the public sphere. Acting in the intersubjective arena of political activity in the revolution, the presence of the working class and *campesinado* in culture revealed art in action, as well as the theoretical complexity of increasing political consciousness. Graffiti played a major role in the insurrection, documenting the events of the day, pointing to a new future, and allowing people to communicate clandestinely with one another. In a very organized way, painting that before the revolution was called "primitivist" or "naive" depicted the ideological nexus between Marxism and Christianity. As members of a Christian base community, these painters grappled with the reality of armed struggle in the face of the violence provoked by the Somozan state. In Solentiname, people also expressed themselves through sculpture, pottery, and poetry while creating a community similar to the early church as it is described in the Bible. It was on this island that Ernesto Cardenal, with Mayra Jiménez, began to develop poetry workshops that would serve as a model for the revolutionary workshops he would later organize as minister of culture. Much as Paulo Freire assembled clusters that affirmed the political nature of education as they relied upon the material reality of the students' surroundings, the poetry workshops encouraged political consciousness raising.

Writing poetry became a means of empowerment and of "conscientization" (Freire's term for raising political consciousness) of the have nots, the campesinos. There are many parallels, therefore, among the graffiti, painting, and poetry: their testimonial character, their collective point of view, and their reflection upon reality. In the graffiti there is an obvious abandonment of the notion of authorship, since it is quite commonly anonymous. Moreover, unlike the poets, the authors of graffiti express their own desires and hopes as well as those of political groups (the author acts as a microcosm of the community). While this is not entirely uncommon with poetry, it is the norm with graffiti, as we shall see.

The Locus of Subjectivity

Most of the graffiti written during the revolutionary struggle was lyrics either cited or written anonymously on the walls of cities and towns in Nicaragua. Political slogans, often written to rhyme, became a type of poetry accessible to all. This can be seen in different ways in two slogans: "Sandino vive, la lucha sigue" (Sandino lives, the struggle goes on) and "Reacción es tu última canción" (Reaction is your last song).[23] The second appears to be more metaphorical than the first because there are at least three possible meanings for "canción": the primary definition is "song," but we also can read it as "poetry" and as "battle cry." To extend the interpretation further, "reacción" is also a metaphor, for it is referring to reaction as physical force, as taking up armed struggle. The phrase attains meaning when we situate it in its prerevolutionary context and associate "reacción" with "canción." "Reaction" thus metamorphoses into armed struggle and "last song" into death (martyrdom). The spray-painted phrase communicates the development of political consciousness in the midst of the revolution. In the first slogan, Sandino is upheld as a mythic hero who inspires the guerrillas to keep fighting.

The writer's identification with the collective is tangible and is linked to enactment of the ideas of the FSLN. In essence, the graffiti artist's work itself becomes a praxis; it unites contemplation with action. By writing on the walls of private homes, restaurants, statues, and public buildings, these artists transgressed the boundaries between public and private property and denied the traditional division between writing and politics. During the revolution, walls in Managua, León, and almost every other city in Nicaragua became symbols of resistance, means of combating censorship and repression.

Beyond politico-poetic graffiti, one finds the canon transposed from books onto walls—verses by poets Rigoberto López Pérez and Leonel Rugama, for instance. Rugama's famous verse "que se rinda tu madre" (let your mother surrender) could be seen on billboards and heard on the streets all over Nicaragua. Poetic discourse in this Central American nation continued to engage the politics of everyday life in revolutionary subjectivity. At the same time, one must recognize that a sexist slogan like Rugama's also magnifies the problematic relation between machismo and militarism, reinforcing homogeneous gender definitions that glorify male participation in war and perpetuating rhetorical violence against women.

It is significant that graffiti, unlike "high culture," pays no homage to property rights or authorial origin. Readers do not know the author's identity and therefore cannot identify the author's social status within society and culture: "author" is a social construct that includes an array of social relations to sustain it. Thus, as Michel Foucault has noted: "An anonymous text posted on a wall probably has a writer but not an author. The author's function is therefore characteristic of the mode of existence, circulation, and functioning of certain discourses within a society."[24] A series of discourses, I might add, that are buried political and economic agents. Although the graffiti writer, as an illegal violator of private property, does not have the same social function as an author, graffiti is not necessarily any less rich in content and in form than poetry (and perhaps is even more important in given sociohistorical contexts). In fact, while the graffiti writer can loosely adhere to anarchist ideology, he or she can also be the spokesperson for a conscious, revolutionary vanguard. In a sense, then, graffiti writers can mark the first step away from bourgeois art (and bourgeois artists) because they do not operate within the traditional literary, economic, and political institutions.

Cultural Democracy and Popular Poetry

The experiment in popular poetry was a step forward in making the literary mode of production available to the working class. This phenomenon is integrated into the formerly dominant ideology of *sandinismo*, which intended initially to empower the working class with land, political rights, arms, and the word. Poetry appropriately became a means of defense against the once-dominant bourgeois ideology and attempts to preserve its economic and political power, as well as a vehicle for working-class access to culture. Whether the professional inclination of the ASTC is any indication of art in Nicaragua in the future remains to be seen. Literary critic Jorge Eduardo Arellano, when I interviewed him in 1988, was skeptical about any new national cultural program and saw none being prepared. Ernesto Cardenal felt (idealistically, perhaps) that, in spite of the Ministry of Culture's withdrawl of support for the workshops, they would be able to carry on without institutional backing. Against that point of view, I would argue that the existing inequalities in the cultural domain were still pervasive and that the institutional support that the ministry provided was essential in order to augment the participation of the working class. But these last comments merit further exegesis in the realm of political representation, which I will take up in my conclusion. In brief, I might state that the status of the working class in constructing its own art in Nicaragua is sewn into a larger fabric that consists of the nature of the relation between the working class as vanguard and the state. It is paramount in this domain — as in the realm of culture itself — that the working class play a determining role; that it, in effect, represent itself. While the poetry from the workshops heads in that direction, it represents an embryonic artistic development that needed to go through a process of maturation in order to be able to depict the depth and the complexity of the campesinos' lives.

CONCLUSION
THE NICARAGUAN REVOLUTION AND THE DEMISE OF THE CULTURAL AND POLITICAL DEMOCRATIZATION PROGRAM

> *In its mystified form, the dialectic became the fashion in Germany, because it seemed to transfigure and glorify what exists. In its rational form it is a scandal and an abomination to the bourgeoisie and its doctrinaire spokesmen, because it includes in its positive understanding of what exists a simultaneous recognition of its negation, its inevitable destruction; because it regards every historically developed form as being in a fluid state, in motion, and therefore grasps its transient aspect as well; and because it does not let itself be impressed by anything, being in its very essence critical and revolutionary.*

> Karl Marx, Postface to the second edition of *Capital*

In the process of outlining the different aesthetic (and political) tendencies within Nicaraguan poetry during the revolutionary period, I have tried to highlight the most significant aspects of a materialist way of analyzing literature. Before beginning this section, I would like to sum up a few of the philosophical tenets that I have followed throughout this study and that will become more evident in this concluding analysis of Nicaraguan aesthetics.

First, objective reality exists as something that is both external and internal to the artist and that can be at least partly apprehended by him or her. This is the premise as it is developed first by Marx and Engels, then by Lenin, and, finally, by Lukács. *Aesthetics and Revolution* examines artistic, social, and political relations in a postcapitalist or quasi-capitalist society; Lukács could be seen as a dialectical partner:

The Platonic "ideas" occasionally inflated and attenuated in the idealism of the period of bourgeois ascendancy, though artificially isolated from social reality, were reflections of decisive social problems and thus for all their idealistic distortion were full of content and were not without relevance; but with the decline of the class they more and more lose content. The social isolation of the personally dedicated artist in a declining society is mirrored in this mystical, subjective inflation of the principle of form divorced from any connection with life.[1]

187

My approach differs in that we are dealing with a country that faced imperialism on a constant basis from 1979 to 1990 and that attempted to change *somocismo*, the political and economic framework of its strictly dependant situation. Within this context, then, we see the ascendancy of a "new" class or at least a resurgence of a particular social class—a faction of the bourgeoisie in the FSLN, as I will later argue—during the revolutionary years. (Let us bypass the specific details of the Nicaraguan revolution until the theoretical foundation has been laid.)

The poet, intentionally or not, reacts to this objective reality in varying degrees of abstraction. On one end of the spectrum, for instance, the artist may consider art to be an autonomous realm and solely a medium of individual expression. In choosing this path the poet will have reduced his or her grasp of objective reality. At the other extreme, the artist may choose to maximize his or her knowledge of objective reality and communicate this concrete reality in as faithful a form as possible. In this case, according to Lukács—who follows Lenin's philosophical argument in *Materialism and Empirio-Criticism*—the artist pursues the inexhaustibility of reality with all of the formal and thematic devices in hand. So, depending on the artist one selects and how his or her work expresses objective reality, the reader will encounter a series of gradations—or abstractions, as Bertell Ollman has demonstrated in his study of Marx's dialectical thinking—of the social, economic, and political circumstances.[2] The artistic product is also dependent on the class, race, and gender of the artist. One of the things I have attempted to do in this study is to locate gender and class interests and the role they play in this poetry.

A second principle that can be found throughout this study is the Marxist notion of ideology as inversion. I am referring here to Marx and Engels's conception of all mental processes as deriving from or interacting dialectically with material life. In capitalism, the bourgeoisie lives under the illusion that in fact the inverse is true, that is, that mental activity somehow determines the outcome of material life. As Marx and Engels put it in *The German Ideology*:

> In direct contrast to German philosophy which descends from heaven to earth, here we ascend from earth to heaven. That is to say, we do not set out from what men say, imagine, conceive, nor from men as narrated, thought of, imagined, conceived, in order to arrive at men in the flesh. We set out from the real, active men, and on the basis of their real life-process we demonstrate the development of the ideological reflexes and echoes of this life-process.[3]

In that sense too, these different poetic tendencies mark distinct representations of ideology. Some poets' class and gender demarcations and their failure to break with them lead to inversions or severely limited perspectives of the class struggle in Nicaragua. For others who are more inclined to explore the inexhaustibility of reality, the distortions are much less apparent and, hence, the representations much more complex. For Marx and Engels this conception of ideology is grounded in material life: it is not consciousness that determines life, they assert in *The German Ideology*, but life that determines consciousness (47). In contrast to the Althusserian approach, ideology is not produced independently from the social relations of production, but rather is immersed in that very material milieu.

In a materialist vein, this study maintains that form and content are subject to dialectics as well. In the Lukácsian (and Marxian) tradition, there is an objectivity of artistic form and content that is presupposed in this analysis. Their concreteness can be ascertained by analyzing the social, political, and economic features that make each cultural work unique. Without this understanding of the dialectic between formal and thematic characteristics, literary criticism abandons any sense of scientific method and, consequently, is in danger of positing the irrational — feeling or pleasure as the modus operandi of cultural criticism — in its place.

In addition, little attention has been paid by either Latin American or U.S. literary critics to the "aesthetic economy" itself. I have argued in *Aesthetics and Revolution* that there must be a correlation between the economic, political, and aesthetic spheres and a properly materialist analysis of literature. In the economic realm I follow Marx's work in its contention that the proletariat is central to the mode of production because the clash between labor and capital is the most intense expression of class struggle. This conclusion, of course, is based on Marx's scientific study of the labor theory of value, whereby the proletariat creates value while capitalists usurp the surplus value created and use it for their own benefit.

The political stage could be seen as deeply intertwined with the economic. The proletariat is potentially more conscious of the class struggle than any other group in society, and the development of a politically conscious vanguard is a natural social product of this economic condition. In fact, without this revolutionary vanguard, the possibility of changing the system through revolutionary means becomes implausible (this is Lenin's and Lukács's formulation).

Finally, the seizure of state power and of the means of production should also include the usurpation of the aesthetic means of production. Aesthetics is precisely one of the areas of society where the dominant ideology is most effectively reproduced. It follows that, because of its centrality in the productive process and in the revolutionary vanguard, the proletariat should appropriate the "aesthetic means of production." This is what happened to a certain degree with the workshop poets, the Ministry of Culture, and the FSLN in Nicaragua, although, as I have contended, this democratization process never fully consolidated in art any more than it did in the economic and political realms.

Having briefly summarized the main theoretical points in the argument fowarded in this book, I would like to examine the effects that political pluralism, the mixed economy, and nationalism had on Nicaraguan poetry from 1979 to 1990.

Aesthetics and Politics in Nicaragua

In an article written in 1985, Carlos Vilas holds that nationalism, while it is potentially an instrument of the bourgeoisie, nonetheless can also be a weapon against imperialism for the masses in Latin America. [4] Vilas claims that, caught between U.S. imperialism on the one hand and the local oligarchy on the other, nationalism takes on a more radical role in the superstructure. In essence, then, class struggle is momentarily displaced in favor of national liberation (26). This national struggle for identity, he contends, is made up of a "plurality of classes" who are not central to the relations of production. Furthermore, this struggle for national liberation is not a contradiction between classes because this movement encompasses myriad anti-imperialist forces or "groups." These different groups and classes are potential vital forces for the new society that will be constructed after national liberation. It is not suprising that Vilas then turns to pluralism and nationalism in Nicaragua.

One of the problems Vilas faces right away is this: if *sandinismo* is only a national struggle against imperialism, then how does the Nicaraguan revolution differ from bourgeois revolutions? While a class struggle of sorts can be identified internationally, it is nowhere in sight domestically. Imperialism is the enemy, it is true, but what of the internal enemies? As his study of the FSLN suggests, the political and economic pluralism in Nicaragua is not a weakness, but rather a strength. The Sandinistas tried to reach—as Donald Hodges has demonstrated as well—the "elementos patrióticos y honestos de las clases medias, incluso a algunos elementos de la burguesía opuestos a la dictadura" (31) (patriotic and honest elements of the middle classes, even some elements from the bourgeoisie opposed to the dictatorship). But the idea of the proletariat being the "grave diggers" of capitalism never is written into Vilas's analysis, nor is there an indication that this model—a mixed economy and political pluralism—may just be liberalism or reformism. From other sources we know that Vilas's article does indeed register many of the principal beliefs of the Sandinistas; it is just that he analyzes the political and economic situation in Nicaragua with little critical distance.

Is it true that the FSLN was a nationalist movement and not necessarily a Marxist-Leninist organization? Let us turn to two insightful studies:

Donald Hodges's *The Intellectual Foundations of the Nicaraguan Revolution* and Richard Stahler-Sholk's "Stabilization, Destabilization, and the Popular Classes in Nicaragua, 1979–1988." Hodges's well-documented work provides a clear account of the origin, development, and evolution of the FSLN and is perhaps the most appropriate place to begin in evaluating the political platform of the party. The Sandinistas initially consisted of three different ideological branches: the Guerra Popular Prolongada (People's Prolonged War), the Insurrectionalists, and the Tendencia Proletaria (Proletarian Tendency). The GPP and the Insurrectionalists were particularly influenced by Sandino's nationalist and moral (not scientific) movement.

The Proletarian Tendency (PT), by contrast, did not veer from its Marxist-Leninist belief in scientific socialism. Rather than urging a spontaneous insurrection, the PT favored organizing a revolutionary proletarian party and a long-term strategy that "aimed at preparing the workers for a nationwide political strike supported by local uprisings and armed actions" (235). Moreover, unlike the Insurrectionalists, the PT made it clear that they would dictate the terms to petit bourgeois sectors and not vice versa.

In 1976 and 1977 there was a crisis in the leadership of the FSLN because Carlos Fonseca had died, Henry Ruiz was participating in guerrilla warfare, and Tomás Borge was imprisoned. Two of the remaining members of the National Directorate, Insurrectionalists Humberto and Daniel Ortega, convinced Víctor Tirado of the viability of their cause, thus shifting the balance in their favor. Meanwhile, the PT stepped up its criticism of the Insurrectionalists, accusing them of staging spontaneous and unorganized uprisings. This accusation, as it turned out, was not unfounded. The insurrections launched in 1977 and 1978 proved—at least to the PT and the GPP—that the Insurrectionalists had acted prematurely in the first case and had little knowledge of popular uprisings in Monimbó and Matagalpa in the second instance. Both the PT and the GPP argued that the Insurrectionalists acted without having met any of the requirements that would have guaranteed military victory.

By 1979, however, the FSLN party had come together with the objective of putting an end to *somocismo*. Once the revolutionary forces had triumphed, there was an attempt to establish a balance of powers among the different factions within the FSLN. Since at least February 1979, the FSLN had begun including in its ranks—following the desires of the Insurrectionalists—liberals, social democrats, and social Christians. By then, the general ideological physiognomy had been tempered and, in fact, the FSLN at times took on anticommunist stances. This was the example of Bayardo Arce, who responded in the heat of debate that

> if you find a political project such as ours where 70 percent of the economy is in private hands, where you have 12 legally existing political parties,

where all religion is freely operating, where you have radios and
newspapers that freely operate pro and con . . . , that is Sandinismo, and
that type of project certainly does not attract communists!"[5]

This political stance and similar denials of their Marxist-Leninist roots indicate which tendency within the FSLN won out in the end. The revolutionary
years confirm the unpreparedness of this amorphous body, as Richard
Stahler-Sholk poignantly notes: "The rapid growth of mass organizations after 1979 was not always matched by policies that reinforced the real material
base of these constituencies or by a corresponding development of consciousness."[6] It is apparent that the more conservative elements and the Insurrectionalist group of the FSLN were the ones who gained hold of the most
powerful positions in the new government—Daniel Ortega, for example,
was the figurehead of the National Directorate and was elected president in
1984, while his brother, Humberto, was head of the Sandinista army.

As the crises grew worse in the late 1980s, the Sandinistas kept searching
for right-wing solutions. In an excellent postelection article, Carlos Vilas
commented that as the "economic crisis worsened, subsidies to middle-class
and wealthy entrepreneurs were increasingly financed by cutting back the
consumption, income, and living conditions of the revolution's natural base
of support, the workers and peasants."[7] Among the most outspoken leaders
of the revolution, there does not appear to be (at least publicly) any open debate on the mistakes that were committed during the revolution. A case in
point is Tomás Borge, who, in an address on May 24, 1990, seemed to be
heading in two directions simultaneously: one a type of Marxist understanding of these historic changes, and the other a type of Christian or Guevarist
influence in which he declares that *sandinismo* must undergo a "moral renova-
tion."[8] In addition, the nationalist flavor in his ideology, as well as in that of
other Sandinistas, indicates that the party is still fighting on Sandino's terrain.
Throughout Borge's speech, one finds constant references to, for instance,
the "National Police," to defending "national sovereignty" while avoiding
"total confrontation" within Nicaragua (46). At any rate, a more objective
reevaluation of the tactical mistakes made by the FSLN during the revolutionary years has not taken place in the way that it should, much less from
a materialist perspective.

Now the divisions, which are, in my estimation, a series of class and gender struggles in Nicaragua even among the Sandinistas themselves, are also
present in the aesthetic realm.[9] The democratization program spearheaded by
the Ministry of Culture, like the Sandinista political and economic platform
set up after the revolution, is absolutely key in gauging the goals of the revolution in all of those domains. For if the FSLN as vanguard did not demand
working-class and campesino control of the actual means of production,

how could they be expected to advocate the seizure of the "cultural means of production"? If, in other words, the Proletarian Tendency's radical socialist plan was never factored into the total social equation, then how can we help but find anything other than reformist policies in the cultural realm?

But the theoretical and practical implementation of the democratization project cannot be dismissed so easily because the minister of culture and architect of the popular cultural experiments — such as the poetry workshops — was the liberation theologian Ernesto Cardenal. For Cardenal, the democratization initiative did entail some sort of workers' control of their own means of ideological reproduction:

> Our culture is not elitist, but democratic — a culture by and for the people. But this does not mean that we denigrate the writer, painter or musician who, because of his excellence, necessarily belongs to the elite! Nor does it mean that we believe culture and the arts must be adapted or simplified so that they will be accessible to the masses. What we strive for is a culture of excellence that will be at the same time a culture of the people. (8)

On closer inspection, in fact, it is evident that Cardenal sees the Ministry of Culture as an instrument of the vanguard (the FSLN) that must fulfill a dialectical relation in the democratization process both as a promoter of popular or worker and campesino art and as a means by which the proletariat can begin to appropriate the modes of self-knowledge in the society. While Cardenal is not alone in this, the conceptualization of the cultural sphere in the revolution never *fully* became a goal of the vanguard. To be sure, the subjective intentions of some FSLN cadres pointed to the necessary tie between the democratization of culture and socialism. During an open debate on culture in 1988, Tomás Borge echoed that position: "La democratización de la cultura, en última instancia, es la verdadera democratización de la sociedad"[10] (The democratization of culture, in the last instance, is the true democratization of society). Even within this position, however, there is a contradictory (bourgeois) tendency to assume that this democratization process will somehow grow spontaneously and not through the politically conscious and concerted effort of the vanguard. Once again, Borge's remarks encapsulate the general feeling of the comandantes:

> Tal vez haya sido mejor que no hayamos creado políticas culturales, encasilladas en un documento institucional. Desde luego que nuestra visión cultural rebasa las fronteras de la institución, y si señalo lo institucional es para recordar la importancia que le hemos dado a la materia. El nuestro es un Estado revolucionario que se interesa por acariciar sus raíces, por encabezar

el deleite de su razón de ser, por buscar y reafirmar sus áreas diferenciadas, por aceptarse como es y multiplicar el placer de su ser. (89)

[Maybe it was better for us not to have created political culture, boxed in an institutional document. Of course our new cultural view surpasses the borders of institutions, and if I point this out it is to remember the importance which we have given to this subject. Ours is a revolutionary State that is interested in cherishing its roots, in fortifying the delight of its reason for being, in looking for and reaffirming its differentiated areas, in accepting itself as is and in multiplying the pleasure of being.]

The sense of rational planning that is entailed in any democratization program is here abandoned in one fell swoop. In its place Borge places a cultural laissez-faire that, he should definitely recognize, will only allow those who have held cultural power to gain full control over the means of artistic production once again. It is not too farfetched, I would argue, to suggest that this cavalier attitude reflects the position of the FSLN vis-à-vis the political economy. In this cultural-political position we can identify the essence of pluralism: a mixed economy—where the capitalists are allowed to coexist with the revolutionaries—a multifaceted vanguard party, and an equally "heterogeneous" cultural life.[11] However, what fueled the whole political and cultural debate, which began shortly after the revolution and then ignited in 1985 and 1988, was a formal issue that, of course, had thematic repercussions.

This debate can be described as a conflict between a Leninist or at least a quasi-Leninist philosophy (Cardenal) and a quasi-bourgeois or pluralist position (exemplified, for instance, in Borge's ideas). In contrast to Borge's stance and that of a majority of the Sandinistas, Cardenal has been one of Latin America's most renowned advocates of "concrete poetry," which is, as he explains to Kent Johnson, "poetry of concrete realities, realist and communicative, lends itself to transmit a political or social theme much more naturally than a poetry which is abstract, introspective and instead of communicative, hermetic" (14). Cardenal goes on to define the differences between hermetic and concrete poetry more completely: metaphorical poetry is "that which purposely dissociates itself from the objective world, and in so doing, distances itself from political and social reality" (16). In a historical materialist tradition, Cardenal rejects poetry that refuses to engage in a process of—in Bertell Ollman's terms—abstracting reality and thus succumbs to a collapsing of objective reality, which for Marxists exists outside of consciousness, into subjective intention. By contrast, for Cardenal, poetry is an ongoing process of investigating reality in a meticulous and tireless way, of dialectically relating consciousness and reality. It was this political and aesthetic stance that led to the debates that came to a boiling point in 1988 and that reflected the internal political and artistic differences among the Sandinistas as well as the entire role that the party had assumed during the revolution.

The results of these debates make it quite clear, as I have maintained throughout *Aesthetics and Revolution*, that socialism was never an explicit part of the FSLN's main agenda—contrary to the desires of the GPP and PT—neither in the political and economic spheres nor in the cultural realm. Consequently, the whole notion of democratizing culture became an ill-conceived project that was almost doomed to fail because of the internal political and ideological discrepancies between the FSLN leadership and its membership.

NOTES

PREFACE

1. Gregory A. Dawes, "Contemporary Nicaraguan Poetry: Aesthetic Commitment in an Age of Postmodernism," Ph.D. diss., University of Washington, 1990.

2. John Beverley and Marc Zimmerman, *Literature and Politics in the Central American Revolutions* (Austin: University of Texas Press, 1990). Hereafter cited in text.

3. Beverley articulated this theoretical stance in his seminal article, "Ideología/deseo/literatura," *Revista de crítica literaria latinoamericana* (1st semester 1988): 7–24.

4. See especially, "Anatomía del testimonio," *Revista de crítica literaria latinoamericana* (1st semester 1987): 7–16.

5. Georg Lukács, *Essays in Realism*, trans. David Fernbach, ed. Rodney Livingstone (Cambridge, Mass.: MIT Press, 1981), 23–32.

6. Terry Lovell, "The Social Relations of Cultural Production: Absent Centre of a New Discourse," in Simon Clarke et al., *One-Dimensional Marxism: Althusser and the Politics of Culture* (London and New York: Allison and Busby, 1980), 245. Hereafter cited in text. To verify Althusser's position on this matter consult his *Lenin and Philosophy and Other Essays* (New York: Monthly Review Press, 1971), 170–71.

7. Althusser, *Lenin and Philosophy and Other Essays*, 160–61.

8. See Jacques Lacan, *Ecrits: A Selection* (New York: Norton, 1977), 1–7.

9. The question here is: how far does Beverley and Zimmerman's Althusserian theory take us from the type of dualism that Volosinov describes so precisely in his critique of Freudianism?: "Inner experience [for Freud], extracted by means of introspection, cannot in fact be directly linked with the data of objective, external apprehension. To maintain a thorough consistency only the one or the other point of view can be pursued. Freud has ultimately favored the consistent pursuit of the inner, subjective point of view; all external reality is for him, in the final analyis, merely the 'reality principle,' a principle that he places *on the same level* with the 'pleasure principle'" (emphasis in the original). V. N. Volosinov, *Freudianism: A Marxist Critique* (New York: Academic Press, 1976), 72.

10. Carlos Vilas, "What Went Wrong," *NACLA: Report on the Americas*, vol. 24, no. 1 (June 1990): 10–18.

11. Here I am following the brilliant work of Bertell Ollman in his article "Putting Dialectics to Work: The Process of Abstraction in Marx's Method," *Rethinking Marxism*, vol. 3, no. 1 (Spring 1990), 26–74; as well as Georg Lukács's pathbreaking thoughts in *History and Class Consciousness*, ed. Rodney Livingstone (Cambridge, Mass.: MIT Press, 1988).

12. Georg Lukács, " 'Tendency' or Partisanship?" in *Essays on Realism*, trans. David Fernbach, ed. Rodney Livingstone (Cambridge, Mass.: MIT Press, 1981), 40–41.

13. See Nancy Hartsock, "The Feminist Standpoint: Toward a Specifically Feminist Historical Materialism," in her *Money, Sex, and Power: Toward a Feminist Historical Materialism* (Boston:

Northeastern University Press, 1985), 231–51; Catherine A. MacKinnon, *Toward a Feminist Theory of the State* (Cambridge, Mass.: Harvard University Press, 1989), 1–59.

14. Karl Marx and Frederick Engels, *The German Ideology* (New York: International Publishers, 1977). See their critique of Feuerbach, 39–96.

15. Marta Harnecker, "The Question of the Vanguard and the Present Crisis in Latin America," *Rethinking Marxism*, vol. 3, no. 2 (Summer 1990): 39.

16. Richard Stahler-Sholk, "Stabilization, Destabilization, and the Popular Classes in Nicaragua, 1979–1988," *Latin American Research Review*, vol. 25, no. 3 (1990): 55–88.

CHAPTER 1. SANDINISMO AND POSTMODERNISM

1. Some of the analyses that see in Nicaragua a promising new socialist economy are collected in José Luis Coraggio and Carmen Diana Deere, eds., *La transición difícil: la autodeterminación de los pequeños países periféricos* (Managua: Editorial Vanguardia, 1987) and Orlando Núñez and Roger Burbach, *Democracia y revolución en las Américas* (Managua: Editorial Vanguardia, 1986).

2. See Andrew Ross, ed., *Universal Abandon? The Politics of Postmodernism* (Minneapolis: University of Minnesota Press, 1988).

3. I should state at the outset that the argument presented in chapter 1 is in fact more of a retrospective reworking of and battle with my doctoral thesis.

4. Peter Dews, *The Logics of Disintegration* (London: Verso, 1987), 33–34. Hereafter cited in text.

5. Ernesto Laclau and Chantal Mouffe, *Hegemony and Socialist Strategy: Towards a Radical Democratic Politics* (London: Verso, 1985), 2. Hereafter cited in text.

6. See Adolfo Sánchez Vásquez, "El Marxismo en la América Latina," *Casa de las Américas* 172–73 (1990): 3–14.

7. For an excellent analysis of the types of political negotiations that took place with the military and allowed them to seize power of the state see James Petras, *Estado y régimen en Latinoamérica* (Madrid: Editorial Revolución, 1987), 67–93.

8. Petras, *Estado y régimen*, 80.

9. Petras, "Sobre la transición al socialismo en Latinoamérica," *Estado y régimen*, 95–121.

10. See Jean-François Lyotard's *The Postmodern Condition* (Minneapolis: University of Minnesota Press, 1985), and Toni Negri's unpublished manuscript, "The Class Situation Today" (1989). Hereafter cited in text.

11. See Lyotard's statistics corresponding to the years 1950–71 in *The Postmodern Condition*, 87. For more recent data and a very persuasive argument against the disappearance of manual labor, consult Alex Callinicos's *Against Postmodernism* (New York: St. Martin's Press, 1990), 132–44, as well as David Harvey's major study in this area, *The Condition of Postmodernity: An Enquiry into the Origins of Cultural Change* (Oxford: Basil Blackwell, 1989), 157.

12. Ross, *Universal Abandon?*, xiv.

13. Neil Larsen, "Postmodernism and Imperialism: Theory and Politics in Latin America," *Postmodern Culture* (Fall 1990).

14. José Coma, "La Crisis económica conmociona a la sociedad chilena," *El País*, October 18, 1990.

15. Georg Lukács, *Realism in Our Time*, trans. John and Necke Mander (New York: Harper & Row, 1964), 20.

16. Georg Lukács, "Marx and the Problem of Ideological Decay," in *Essays on Realism*, trans. David Fernbach, ed. Rodney Livingstone (Cambridge, Mass.: MIT Press, 1981). Hereafter cited in text.

17. Neil Larsen, *Modernism and Hegemony: A Materialist Critique of Aesthetic Agencies* (Minneapolis: University of Minnesota Press, 1990), xxxiv. Hereafter cited in text.

18. Theodor W. Adorno, "Reconciliation under Duress," in *Aesthetics and Politics*, ed. and trans. Ronald Taylor (London: Verso, 1977), 159. Hereafter cited in text.

19. Theodor Adorno, "Commitment," in *Aesthetics and Politics*, 194.

20. See Georg Lukács, "Art and Objective Truth," in *Writer and Critic and Other Essays* (New York: Universal Library, 1971), 61–88.

21. Terry Eagleton, *The Ideology of the Aesthetic* (Oxford: Basil Blackwell, 1990), 350–51. Hereafter cited in text.

22. See Dews, *Logics of Disintegration*.

23. Fredric Jameson, in the foreward to *The Postmodern Condition*, xix.

24. Toni Negri, "The Class Situation Today," unpublished manuscript, 5. Hereafter cited in text.

25. Consult "The Class Situation Today," 11. Another controversial intervention on Negri's part is *Communists Like Us: New Spaces of Liberty, New Lines of Alliance*, tr. Michael Ryan (New York: Semiotext[e], 1990), written with Félix Guattari. Generally following in the tracks of the discourse of the marginal and the social movements, Negri and Guattari's essay is both idealistic and provocative. Its strains of idealism can be found in their assertion that the post-1968 economic conditions have changed in such a way as to affect the composition of the labor force and, thus, to shift the weight of revolutionary subjectivity from the working class to marginal sectors of the population. *Communists Like Us* was apparently written in a pamphlet or essay form, because nowhere does it attempt to substantiate its grandiose claims. I would reiterate the argument that I have stood by so far in this chapter, namely, that there is no question that developed and developing countries have been hit by the redistribution of labor spaces, but the figures do not warrant any reformulation of Marxist theory in that respect. For instance, according to labor force statistics, in 1960, for the Organization for Economic Cooperation and Development, 35.3 percent of the work force was employed in the industrial sector. By 1981, this figure had decreased to 33.7 percent. Meanwhile, the service sector grew from 43.0 percent in 1960 to 56.3 percent in 1981, while agriculture dropped from 21.7 percent to 10.0 percent (see David Harvey, *The Condition of Postmodernity* [Oxford: Basil Blackwell, 1990], 157). As one can plainly see, there is a definite tendency in that general direction, but where did this vanishing industrial sector disappear to? Negri and Guattari do address the question of the industrialization of "third world" countries but, once again, the information they offer on this matter is very thin. They do recognize that the extreme forms of exploitation are now being moved to the industrial sector of developing nations, but they do not seem able to derive any significant conclusions from this. It is as though the working class in the developing nations does not carry the weight of the working class in the developed countries, or that no telling international proletarian ties can be drawn. In place of this analysis we get a supplementation: the working class is no longer central to the means of production in capitalism. In its place we find — in a postmodernist vein — "new subjectivities" who are part of the marginal sections of society and who summarily rise above the old, tired bodies of the proletariat (38, 42). So, on the economic horizon, we can expect these once ancillary forms of the productive relations to take hold of the reins of modern capitalist production.

Accompanying this economic appraisal is an equally idealistic political analysis of the state of revolution in these days of postmodernism. Here Negri and Guattari generally — they contradict themselves (92, 97) — espouse a Rosa Luxemburg spontaneist solution to revolutionary organization over against the apparently failed model of Leninism. There is an attractiveness to this spontaneity. For what the authors are attempting to execute is some sort of negotiation between spontaneity — their version of workers' control — and democratic centralism. This is interesting and illuminating precisely because it is quite possible that, as Negri and Guattari argue, we might need to pass on historically from capitalism to communism and not take the intervening route through socialism, which only seems to return to point A. The provocative segment of their thesis is exactly that. What we need to work toward now, then, is the abolition of the state and of wage labor and the inauguration of workers' control. If the authors would agree with the first two points, however, their economic study does not allow them to conceive of what used to be known as geniune workers' control. And it turns out that not only is the proletariat not central to the means of production today, but it is also responsible for the defeats that took place in the 1960s and 1970s (103) (curiously, there is no deep examination of the internal dynamics of the conflicts that afflicted the social movements or of exactly what led to their eventual cooptation). Thus, the authors conclude: "It is clear that the discourses on workers' centrality and hegemony are thoroughly defunct and that they cannot serve as a basis for the organization of new political and productive alliances, or even simply as a point of reference" (122–23). But there is much more to this realignment of the relations of production and to revolutionary subjectivity, as they remark later: "The traditional working classes should resign themselves to this. But what could the meaning of their revolt be if they do not understand that they no longer represent a social majority — either numerically, nor as an ideal value, not even as a produced economic value? They are obliged, if they want to legitimate their rebellion, to socially recompose themselves, in alliance with the immense mass of exploited people, of marginalized people, which includes the large majority of young, women, immigrants, the sub-proletariats of the Third World and minorities of every kind" (127–28). It is hard not to respond sarcastically to this condescension and lack of knowledge on the part of the intelligentsia. But let us add these charges together: (1) the proletariat is today marginalized with respect to the means of production, (2) it is responsible for the political defeats presumably from the 1920s and 1930s to the present, and, finally, (3) it is so marginalized that it had better get its act together and realize that times have changed (*dixit* the intelligentsia). All these half-hearted conclusions point clearly at the core of what today is the New New Left or the vestiges of the New Left: their politics never was based on any scientific grounding — because of their great distrust of the sciences. Instead it has been anchored on the floating sphere of ethics. Consequently, while analyses like these might stir some intriguing ideas as to why the Eastern Bloc collapsed and why the Popular Front failed in its ultimate objectives, they have nothing or little to offer in their place (see p. 104). Rather, Negri and Guattari suggest — in a curious reversion to Popular Front politics — that the only "revolutionary" road is the peaceful road to communism (139–47). It would be difficult, if not impossible, to come up with such a strategy given what we should have learned about the Paris Commune, the struggle against fascism, the lessons of the Chinese Revolution, the 1960s, and more. However, since Guattari and Negri never examine these historical, political, and economic matters meticulously, I would contend they lose the grounding they need to sustain their hypothesis. Hence, as is the case of many postmodernist theories of marginality, the authors end up carrying out a heavily tainted theoretical enterprise, and praxis gets left behind somewhere.

26. Néstor García Canclini, "El debate posmoderno en Iberoamérica," *Cuadernos hispano-americanos* 463 (January 1989): 80. Hereafter cited in text.

27. I am indebted to Neil Larsen's insights in "Postmodernism and Imperialism."

28. See the following articles by George Yúdice: "Marginality and the Ethics of Survival," in Ross, *Universal Abandon?*, 214–36; "¿Puede hablarse de postmodernidad en América Latina?," *Revista de crítica literaria latinoamericana* 29 (1989): 105–28; and "Postmodernity and Transnational Capitalism in Latin America" (unpublished).

29. Yúdice, "Marginality," 214.

30. See, for example, Karl Marx, "Machinery and Large-Scale Industry," *Capital*, vol. 1 (New York: Vintage, 1977), 492–636.

31. Yúdice, "Marginality," 227.

32. I refer the reader to Neil Larsen's very cogent critique of Dussel in *Modernism and Hegemony*, xxvi–xxxii.

33. Laura Kipnis, "Feminism: The Political Conscience of Postmodernism?," in Ross, *Universal Abandon?*, 153–54. Hereafter cited in text.

34. See, for example, Stanley Aronowitz, "Postmodernism and Politics," in Ross, *Universal Abandon?* " 'Socialism,' then, is not being brought to the workers of the semiperiphery from the outside, by intellectuals. In many instances, it is the name given to economic democracy, not to the centralization of ownership and control by the state. Even in revolutionary societies like Nicaragua, such policies are no longer proposed, much less implemented. Nicaragua has adopted, instead, a model of the garrison state under the weight of the United States intervention, while its economy remains in private hands" (60). Here we see the inherent contradiction between Aronowitz's heralding of economic democracy and the results: a mixed economy. *What is "economic democracy" if not workers' control of the means of production?*

35. I refer the reader to a very brief bibliography: *La transición difícil: La autodeterminación de los pequeños países periféricos*, ed. José Luis Coraggio and Carmen Diana Deere (Managua: Editorial Vanguardia, 1987); the June 1990 issue of *NACLA: Report on the Americas* devoted to Nicaragua; David MacMichael, "Nicaraguan Elections: The U.S. Plays the *Contra* Card," *The Nation*, February 5, 1990; Richard Fagen, *Forging Peace: The Challenge of Central America* (New York: Basil Blackwell, 1987); Thomas W. Walker, *Nicaragua: The Land of Sandino* (Boulder, Colo.: Westview, 1991).

36. Donald Hodges, *The Intellectual Foundations of the Nicaraguan Revolution* (Austin: University of Texas Press, 1988), 245; hereafter cited in text. See also George R. Vickers, "A Spider's Web," *NACLA: Report on the Americas*, vol. 24, no. 1 (June 1990): 19–27.

37. Orlando Núñez and Roger Burbach, *Democracia y revolución en las Américas* (Managua: Editorial Vanguardia, 1986).

38. On the question of negotiation of power, see Petras *Estado y régimen*, 95–121.

39. Carlos Vilas, "What Went Wrong," *NACLA: Report on the Americas*, vol. 24, no. 1 (1990): 11. Hereafter cited in text.

40. V. I. Lenin, *State and Revolution* (Peking: Foreign Language Press, 1973), 14. Hereafter cited in text.

41. Fagen, *Forging Peace*, 64.

42. Ross, *Universal Abandon?*, xiv.

43. "Zizagueos de la cultura," *Envío*, September–October 1988, 30–47. Hereafter cited in text.

CHAPTER 2. IDEOLOGICAL FLUCTUATIONS AND DESIRE IN THE POETRY OF PABLO ANTONIO CUADRA

1. For a very complete overview of the Nicaraguan *vanguardia*, consult Jorge Eduardo Arellano, "El movimiento nicaragüense de vanguardia," *Cuadernos hispanoamericanos* 468 (June 1989): 7–44.

2. I am using the term *postmodernist* to refer to Fredric Jameson's periodization of cultural practices from the 1960s to the present, or as a more advanced stage of imperialism. See Jameson's "Postmodernism; or, the Cultural Logic of Late Capitalism," *New Left Review* 146 (1984): 53–92. In my opinion, however, David Harvey's *The Condition of Postmodernity* (Oxford: Basil Blackwell, 1990) is a much more complete and consistent Marxist analysis of postmodernism.

3. Nelson Osorio, "Para una caracterización histórica del vanguardismo literario hispanoamericano," *Revista iberoamericana* 47 (1981): 227–54.

4. Manlio Tirado, "Conversando con José Coronel Urtecho," *Nicaráhuac* 9 (1983): 94. Hereafter cited in text.

5. Walter LaFeber, *Inevitable Revolutions: The United States in Central America* (New York: Norton, 1984), 64–68.

6. Francisco de Asís Fernández, ed., *Poesía política nicaragüense* (Managua: Ministerio de Cultura, 1986), 17. Hereafter cited in text.

7. Steven White, *Culture and Politics in Nicaragua: Testimonies of Poets and Writers* (New York: Lumen, 1986), 19. Hereafter cited in text.

8. Pablo Antonio Cuadra, *Torres de Dios* (Managua: Ediciones El Pez y la Serpiente, 1985), 158–59. Hereafter cited in text.

9. Sergio Ramírez, *Balcanes y volcanes* (Managua: Editorial Nueva Nicaragua, 1985), 76.

10. See Ernesto Cardenal's introduction to *Poemas de un joven*, cited in note 11.

11. Joaquín Pasos, *Poemas de un joven*, ed. Ernesto Cardenal (Managua: Editorial Nueva Nicaragua, 1986), 144.

12. Renato Poggioli, *Theory of the Avant-Garde* (Cambridge, Mass.: Harvard University Press, 1968), 131–47.

13. Jorge Eduardo Arellano, "El corpus poético completo de Pablo Antonio Cuadra," *Cuadernos hispanoamericanos* 442 (1987): 48–51.

14. Carlos Monsiváis, "De las relaciones entre la 'alta' cultura y la cultura popular," *Texto crítico* 33 (1985): 48–52.

15. Angel Rama, in the introduction to *Rubén Darío y el modernismo*, Angel Rama, ed. (Caracas: Universidad Central de Venezuela, 1970), xx.

16. Pablo Antonio Cuadra, *Obra poética completa* (San José: Libro Libre, 1983–1988).

17. On the ideological elasticity of populism and its role vis-à-vis literature see Doris Sommer, *One Master for Another: Populism as Patriarchal Rhetoric in Dominican Novels* (Lanham, Md.: University Press of America, 1983).

18. See "El tío Invierno" (Uncle Winter), 123–25:

"Luego, en la noche, encerrar nuestra nostalgia
—la melancolía recostada dulcemente en tu recuerdo—
secos ya bajo las rojas chamarras
escuchando los salivazos del tío Invierno
arrojados contra la tierra que se estremece
con un rumor de lejanas batallas" (125)

[Later, at night, enclose our nostalgia
—melancholy leaning sweetly on your memory—
dry now neath red blankets
listening to Uncle Winter's spitting
on the ground which shakes
with a rumor of distant battles]

19. See chapter 3 for a more detailed analysis of Leonel Rugama's importance to Nicaraguan letters and revolutionary politics, or consult John Beverley and Marc Zimmerman, *Literature and Politics in the Central American Revolutions* (Austin: University of Texas Press, 1990), 75–78.

20. Pablo Antonio Cuadra, *Tun—la ronda del año* (San José: Libro Libre, 1988), 19. Hereafter cited in text.

21. Steven White, "Modern Poetry in Nicaragua: The French and American Influence," diss., University of Oregon, 1987, 71–125. Hereafter cited in text.

22. Steven White, "An Interview with Pablo Antonio Cuadra," in *Culture and Politics in Nicaragua*, 23.

23. Steven White, "Poetry and the Temptations of Power," in *Lives on the Line: The Testimonies of Latin American Authors*, ed. Doris Meyer (Berkeley: University of California Press, 1988), 284. Hereafter cited in text.

24. George Black, *Triumph of the People: The Sandinista Revolution in Nicaragua* (London: Zed Press, 1981), 219. See Thomas W. Walker's latest analysis in *Nicaragua: The Land of Sandino* (Boulder, Colo.: Westview, 1991), 54–62.

CHAPTER 3. POETRY AND "SPIRITUAL MATERIALISM": ERNESTO CARDENAL

1. Steven White, *Culture and Politics in Nicaragua: Testimonies of Poets and Writers* (New York: Lumen, 1986), 62–63.

2. The introduction by Marc Zimmerman to Ernesto Cardenal's *Flights of Victory*, trans. and ed. Marc Zimmerman (New York: Orbis, 1985); Jorge H.Valdés, "Cardenal's Poetic Style: Cinematic Parallels," *Revista canadiense de Estudios Hispánicos* 11.1 (1986): 119–29; and Robert Pring-Mill, "Acciones paralelas y montaje acelerado en el segundo episodio de Hora O," *Revista iberoamericana* 118–19 (1982): 217–40.

3. A fascinating study of the history of the epigram and its confluence with Cardenal's is Claire Pailler, "Ernesto Cardenal, épigrammes romaines, épigrammes nicaraguayennes: fragments d'une autobiographie poétique," *Cahiers du monde Hispanique et Luso-Brésilien* 36 (1981): 99–118.

4. Consult Steven White's "Entrevista con Carlos Martínez Rivas," *Cuadernos hispanoamericanos* 469–70 (1989): 93–104.

5. Carlos Martínez Rivas, *La insurrección solitaria* (Managua: Editorial Nueva Nicaragua, 1986).

6. Ernesto Mejía Sánchez, *Recolección a mediodía* (Managua: Editorial Nueva Nicaragua, 1985).

7. Ernesto Cardenal, *Epigramas* (Mexico City: C. Lohlé, 1962). Hereafter cited in text.

8. In his interview with Margaret Randall, published in *Risking a Somersault in the Air* (San Francisco: Solidarity Publications, 1984), Cardenal summarizes the events that led to his writing political poetry after the April Conspiracy of 1954: "Later mutual friends of Báez Bone's and mine said why didn't I dedicate that poem about the guerrilla's tomb to him instead of to Sandino. Sandino was a well-known figure, they said, while Báez Bone was relatively unknown. And no one knew where he had died, either, nor where he was buried. He was an unknown hero and martyr; no one knew where his body was. I gave the poem a new name, 'Epitaph for Adolfo Báez Bone's Tomb.' And I began to feel I had found a way of writing political poetry. So I kept on writing epigrams, along with the epigrams that were love poems" (99).

9. John Beverley and Marc Zimmerman, *Literature and Politics in the Central American Revolutions* (Austin: University of Texas Press, 1990), 68.

10. See, for instance, Ernesto Cardenal, *Canto a un país que nace* (Puebla: Editorial de la Universidad Autónoma de Puebla, 1978), 23–24.

11. See Ernesto Cardenal, *Nueva antología poética* (Mexico City: Siglo veintiuno editores, 1978), 59, 61.

12. Ernesto Cardenal, *Antología* (Managua: Editorial Nueva Nicaragua, 1983), 194–95.

13. See "Oráculo sobre Managua," in Cardenal, *Antología*, 215.

14. See Coronel Urtecho's preface to Leonel Rugama, *La tierra es un satélite de la luna* (Managua: Editorial Nueva Nicaragua, 1983), 11–18.

15. Beverley and Zimmerman, *Literature and Politics*, 76–77.

16. See José Porfirio Miranda, *Marx and the Bible* (New York: Orbis, 1974), 1–33.

17. Ernesto Cardenal, *Vuelos de victoria* (Managua: Editorial Nueva Nicaragua, 1985). Hereafter cited in text.

18. Terry Eagleton, *The Ideology of the Aesthetic* (London: Basil Blackwell, 1990), 214–15.

19. See Robert Pring-Mill, "El saber callar a tiempo: En Ernesto Cardenal y en la poesía

campesina (Solentiname)," in *Separada de la Revista Insular de Filología* (Palma de Mallorca: Caligrama, 1987): 17–41.

20. Consult Jane Deighton et al., *Sweet Ramparts: Women in Revolutionary Nicaragua* (London: Third World Publications, 1983).

21. Gustavo Gutiérrez, *A Theology of Liberation: History, Politics and Salvation* (New York: Orbis, 1973), 159.

22. Ernesto Cardenal, *Canto a un país que nace* (Puebla: Editorial de la Universidad de Puebla, 1978), 64. Hereafter cited in text.

23. Quoted in Terry Eagleton, "The Marxist Sublime," in *Ideology of the Aesthetic*, 196–233.

24. See Pring-Mill, "Acciones paralelas," and Paul W. Borgeson, Jr., "Textos y texturas: Los recursos visuales de Ernesto Cardenal," *Explicación de textos literarios* 9 (1981): 159–68.

25. Walter J. Ong, *Orality and Literacy: The Technologizing of the Word* (London: Methuen, 1982), 21.

26. Jean-Michel Rabaté, *Language, Sexuality and Ideology in Ezra Pound's* Cantos (London: Macmillan, 1986), 82.

CHAPTER 4. FEMINIST AND FEMALE SELF-REPRESENTATION IN REVOLUTION

1. See Margaret Randall's interview with Sergio Ramírez in *Risking a Somersault in the Air: Conversations with Nicaraguan Writers* (San Francisco: Solidarity Publications, 1984), 27. Hereafter cited in text.

2. George Black, *Triumph of the People: The Sandinista Revolution in Nicaragua* (London: Zed Press, 1981), 84–86.

3. John Beverley and Marc Zimmerman, *Literature and Politics in the Central American Revolutions* (Austin: University of Texas Press, 1990), 88.

4. The radical difference between the women's movements in Nicaragua and the United States reflects the vastly different political and economic circumstances in the two nations. In the United States, the women's liberation movement reached maturity during a period of general unrest and dissatisfaction with U.S. foreign and domestic policy. Yet the mainstream portion of the movement assimilated itself into society. Once certain concessions had been granted by the political system, the core of the movement quickly forgot the anti-establishment stance that marked its origins (such as the enactment of antidiscrimination laws). In the 1960s, however, middle-class feminism was concerned with confronting specific issues that institutions within the United States should address, rather than with questioning the underlying socioeconomic structure that gave rise to sexual inequalities at the most elementary level. Since the 1960s, ideologically conscious organizations have multiplied, many of them investigating the relations between gender, class, and ethnicity, as developed in the postmodern age of capitalism. Nevertheless, these radical movements are in the minority compared with mainstream organizations like the National Organization of Women (NOW).

5. Maxine D. Molyneux, "¿Movilización sin emancipación? Intereses de la mujer, el estado y la revolución: el caso de Nicaragua," in *La transición difícil: La autodeterminación de los pequeños países periféricos* (Managua: Editorial Vanguardia, 1987), 357. Hereafter cited in text.

6. Stephens says that the FSLN banked on the premise that "revolutionary transformation of the social and economic order is a necessary prerequisite to the liberation of women." *Monthly Review* 40 (September 1988): 3 (hereafter cited in text). While this is true, what impact would the *lack* of socialist social and economic measures have on women's liberation? For if, as I have argued, the socialist transformation was never fully implanted, then how could we expect great strides in gender equality? What occurs instead is a reformism that does, in effect, change gen-

der relations—much as the women's movement did in the United States in the 1960s—but only within the framework of capitalist social relations or nationalist politics.

7. Her latest work, *Ars combinatoria* (Managua: Editorial Nueva Nicaragua, 1988), is a very experimental, heterogenous poetic text that combines fables with short narrative and prose.

8. See "La mujer nicaragüense en la literatura" *Plural*, September 1981, 19; Jane Deighton et al., *Sweet Ramparts: Women in Revolutionary Nicaragua* (London: Third World Publications, 1983), 50–52, hereafter cited in text; Molyneux, "Movilización," 348.

9. These are unpublished personal interviews that I conducted between October and December 1988 with Ernesto Cardenal, Jorge Eduardo Arellano, Ana Ilce Gómez, Gioconda Belli, Daisy Zamora, Alvaro Urtecho, and Juan Chow.

10. Preface to *En limpio se escribe la vida* (Managua: Editorial Nueva Nicaragua, 1988), 19.

11. Jorge Eduardo Arellano, "Daisy Zamora y la plenitud de su poesía" *Ventana*, December 14, 1988, 3.

12. Gilles Deleuze and Félix Guattari, *Anti-Oedipus: Capitalism and Schizophrenia* (Minneapolis: University of Minnesota Press, 1977), 51–137.

13. Ana Ilce Gómez, *Ceremonias de silencio* (Managua: Ediciones El Pez y la Serpiente, 1974), 15. Hereafter cited in text.

14. An implicit reading suggests that the speaker who "does not leave an imprint of herself" except her voice may be engaged in abstract labor. That is, the product of her daily work may not be recognized in society; it may be housework.

15. Nancy Hartsock, *Money, Sex, and Power: Toward a Feminist Historical Materialism* (Boston: Northeastern University Press, 1985), 176. Hereafter cited in text.

16. Gayatri Spivak, *In Other Worlds: Essays in Cultural Politics* (New York: Routledge, 1988), 82.

17. See V. N. Volosinov, *Freudianism: A Marxist Critique* (New York: Academic Press, 1976).

18. Hélène Cixous and Catherine Clément, *The Newly Born Woman* (Minneapolis: University of Minnesota Press, 1986), 96.

19. Gioconda Belli, *De la costilla de Eva* (Managua: Editorial Nueva Nicaragua, 1987), 17. Hereafter cited in text.

20. Bertell Ollman, *Alienation: Marx's Concept of Man in Capitalist Society* (Boston: Cambridge University Press, 1978), 83.

21. I am referring here to Marx's concept of the dialectic as negation of the negation, quantitative changes that lead to qualitative changes (and vice versa) and the interpenetration of opposites.

22. Michel Foucault, *Discipline and Punish: The Birth of the Prison* (New York: Vintage, 1979), 138.

23. For a relatively recent example of the relation between feminism and *sandinismo*, see Beth Stephens, "Women and Nicaragua," *Monthly Review* 40 (September 1988): 1–18.

CHAPTER 5. POPULAR POETRY: REALISM AS A CULTURAL-POLITICAL AGENT

1. Antonio Gramsci, *An Antonio Gramsci Reader: Selected Writings 1916-1935* (New York: Schocken, 1988), 70.

2. Toril Moi, *Sexual/Textual Politics: Feminist Literary Theory* (London and New York: Routledge, 1989), 171.

3. Terry Eagleton, *Against the Grain* (London: Verso, 1986), 59.

4. Mayra Jiménez, ed. *Poesía campesina de Solentiname* (Managua: Ministerio de Cultura, 1985), 8.

5. "Zizagueos de la cultura," *Envío* 87 (1988): 34.

6. Steven White, *Culture and Politics in Nicaragua: Testimonies of Poets and Writers* (New York: Lumen, 1986), 108.

7. John Beverley, "Poetry and Revolution in Central America," in *The Year Left: An American Socialist Yearbook*, ed. Peter Davis, Fred Pfeil, and Michael Sprinker (London: Verso, 1985), 155.

8. By 1972, according to Jaime Wheelock — in *Imperialismo y dictadura: crisis de una formación social*, 5th ed. (Mexico City: Siglo XXI, 1980) — the working class had surpassed the campesinos numerically as the largest sector of the work force.

9. Donald C. Hodges, *The Intellectual Foundations of the Nicaraguan Revolution* (Austin: University of Texas Press, 1986), 240. Hereafter cited in text.

10. Many of the political and economic divisions that I have outlined were perceptively identified by Richard Fagen as early as 1981. See his "Revolution and Transition in Nicaragua," *Socialist Review* 11:5 (September–October 1981).

11. Jean Franco, "Beyond Ethnocentrism: Gender and Power and the Third World Intelligentsia," in *Marxism and the Interpretation of Culture* (Bloomington: Indiana University Press, 1988), 505.

12. Here I am following Fredric Jameson's periodization of postmodernism (see his now classic article, "Postmodernism; or, the Cultural Logic of Late Capitalism," *New Left Review* 146 [1984]: 53–92). I, however, take only his historical marker as the *coupure* with previous capitalist development. The major difference between this stage of capitalism and its antecedent is, to my mind, the fact that imperialism has been further intensified and not — as the Social Text collective would argue — dispensed with altogether.

13. E. Bradford Burns, *Latin America: A Concise Interpretation* (Englewood Cliffs, N.J.: Prentice-Hall, 1977), 242–51; Jean Franco, "Del milenio efímero a la vanguardia que fue," *Nexos* 9 (1979): 16; Walter LaFaber, *Inevitable Revolutions: The United States in Central America* (New York: Norton, 1984), 145–60.

14. Angel Rama, "La tecnificación narrativa," *Hispamérica* 30 (1981): 29–82. Herafter cited in text.

15. John S. Brushwood, *The Spanish-American Novel: A Twentieth Century Survey* (Austin: University of Texas Press, 1975), 211.

16. Alan Angell, "The Soldier as Politician," in *Latin America*, ed. Eduardo P. Archetti (New York: Monthly Review Press, 1985), 277–94.

17. See John Beverley, "Anatomía del testimonio," *Revista de crítica literaria latinoamericana* 25 (1987), hereafter cited in text; and Jean Franco, "Beyond Ethnocentrism."

18. Karl Marx and Frederick Engels, *The German Ideology* (New York: International Publishers, 1977), 59.

19. Georg Lukács, *History and Class Consciousness*, trans. Rodney Livingstone (Cambridge, Mass.: MIT Press, 1988), 176.

20. Fernando Reyes Matta, "The 'New Song' and its Confrontation in Latin America," in *Marxism and the Interpretation of Culture*, ed. Cary Nelson and Lawrence Grossberg (Bloomington: Indiana University Press, 1986), 447.

21. *Poesía libre*, 13 vols. (Managua: Ministerio de Cultura, 1980–1987); Mayra Jiménez, ed., *Poesía campesina de Solentiname* (Managua: Ministerio de Cultura, 1985); Mayra Jiménez, selection and prologue, *Fogata en la oscurana: Los talleres de poesía en la alfabetización* (Managua: Ministerio de Cultura, 1985). Hereafter cited in text.

22. In Felipe Peña's "Plagas" this socialist consciousness is most evident:

> Las plagas pueden ser naturales o artificiales.
> En Solentiname las plagas son
> los loros, guatuzas, los zanates, ratones;
> zompopos, también hay polillas,

como también hay comerciantes que devoran las cosechas
de los campesinos,
como también patrones que devoran el trabajo de los peones,
igual que los loros, guatuzas, zanates,
ratones, zompopos, devoran el maíz, el arroz, los frijoles.
También las plagas humanas constituyen un sistema de plagas.
Aquí en Solentiname la Compañía ha hecho desaparecer los loros,
los ratones, las guatuzas,
que son parte de las plagas que joden al campesino
y creo que la compañía hará desaparecer
la plaga humana, claro que no la Compañía del Tránsito
sino la del proletariado. (*Poesía* 19)

[Plagues can be natural or artificial.
In Solentiname the plagues are
parrots, *guatuzas*, the *zanates*, mice;
zompopos, there are also moths,
as there are also merchants who devour the campesino's
crops,
as there are also bosses who devour the laborer's work,
as the parrots, *guatuzas, zanates*,
mice, *zompopos*, devour corn, rice, beans.
Human plagues also constitute a system of plagues.
Here in Solentiname the Company has gotten rid of the parrots,
the mice, the *guatuzas*,
which are some of the plagues that screw the campesino
and I think the company will get rid of
the human plague, not the Transit Company of course,
but rather the proletariat.]

23. Omar Cabezas and Dora María Tellez, *La insurrección de las paredes* (Managua: Editorial Nueva Nicaragua, 1984), 59, 70.

24. Michel Foucault, *The Foucault Reader*, ed. Paul Rabinow (New York: Pantheon, 1985), 108.

CONCLUSION: THE NICARAGUAN REVOLUTION AND THE DEMISE OF THE CULTURAL AND POLITICAL DEMOCRATIZATION PROGRAM

1. Georg Lukács, *Writer and Critic and Other Essays* (New York: Universal Library, 1971), 41–42.

2. Bertell Ollman, "Putting Dialectics to Work: The Process of Abstraction in Marx's Method," *Rethinking Marxism*, vol. 3, no. 1 (Spring 1990): 27–74.

3. Karl Marx and Frederick Engels, *The German Ideology* (New York: International Publishers, 1977), 47. Hereafter cited in text.

4. Carlos Vilas, "La nación como atributo del pueblo," *Casa de las Américas*, no. 151 (July–August 1985): 23–33.

5. Quoted in Donald Hodges, *The Intellectual Foundations of the Nicaraguan Revolution* (Austin: University of Texas Press, 1988), 194.

6. Richard Stahler-Sholk, "Stabilization, Destabilization, and the Popular Classes in Nicaragua, 1979–1988," *Latin American Research Review*, vol. 25, no. 3 (1990): 67.

7. Carlos Vilas, "What Went Wrong?" *NACLA: Report on the Americas*, vol. 24, no. 1 (June 1990): 12.

8. Tomás Borge, "Revolution and Democracy" *Envío*, vol. 9, no. 107 (June 1990): 44.

9. Cardenal himself has acknowledged this link: "For us, culture and revolution cannot be separated. Everything that belongs to the sphere of culture we consider to be in the sphere of the revolution . . . and vice versa." See Kent Johnson, ed., "Interview: Ernesto Cardenal," in *A Nation of Poets: Writings from the Poetry Workshops of Nicaragua* (Los Angeles: West End Press, 1985), 7–8. Hereafter cited in text.

10. Tomás Borge, "Lo bueno, lo malo, lo feo: Anotaciones culturales," *Casa de las Américas* 172–73 (1989): 89. Hereafter cited in text.

11. See Richard Stahler-Sholk's "Stabilization, Destabilization," 81.

INDEX

Adorno, Theodor, 65; and modernism, avant-garde, realism, 9–15. *See also* aesthetic debates; Lukács, Georg

Aeschylus: *Agamemnon,* 153

aesthetic debates: in Theodor Adorno and Georg Lukács, 10–15; in Nicaragua, xiii, xviii, 28–32, 162–67, 187–95. *See also* avant-garde; FSLN; modernism; realism

Agudelo Builes, Irene, 174–75

alienation: in Gioconda Belli, 135; in capitalism, 20, 45, 72, 98, 101, 105; in Ana Ilce Gómez, 118–27, 155. *See also* Marx, Karl; Ollman, Bertell

alliance: class, 26, 47; multiclass, xv, 35, 166; political, 6, 23

Althusser, Louis, viii–xv, 146; concept of ideology, viii–xv; ideological effects, x, xiii. *See also* ideology

AMNLAE (Luisa Espinosa Association of Nicaraguan Women), 110, 129, 155, 157

anarchism, 14, 20, 26, 186

April Conspiracy, 75, 203 n. 8. *See also* Cardenal, Ernesto; Somoza García, Anastacio

Arce, Bayardo, 163, 166, 191. *See also* aesthetic debates; FSLN

Arellano, Jorge Eduardo, 33, 44, 186; on aesthetic debates, 28–29; on Daisy Zamora, 117–18

Aronowitz, Stanley, 201 n. 34

Asís Fernández, Francisco de, 36

ASTC (Sandinista Association of Cultural Workers), viii, 31, 33, 186. *See also* Murillo, Rosario; professionalists

autonomy: aesthetic, 61; generation, 109

avant-garde: European, 33–34, 51; and the generation of 1940, 66; literary, 8–31, 47; as "revolutionary body," 1–3; and techniques, 104. *See also Vanguardia*

Baéz Bone, Adolfo, 75, 203 n. 8

Barricada, 51. *See also* FSLN; Ventana

Belli, Gioconda, xviii, 3, 28, 107, 110, 127–40, 154, 156–57; and armed struggle, 135–40, 144–46, 155–56; and Casa de las Américas prize, 129; and Julio Cortázar, 130–31; and *De la costilla de Eva,* 130–42; and depiction of social relations, 138–39; and erotic poetry, 130; and gender, objectification of, 130–31; and idealism, 130, 142; and *Línea de fuego,* 130, 141–42; and militarization, 144–46; and naming the body, 142–44; and nexus between language and passion, 133–35; and poetry, mysteriousness of, 133–35; and reproduction, notion of, 137, 145–46, 155–56; and sexual liberation, 140–46, 157; and *Sobre la grana,* 129; and utopian socialism, 137, 146. *See also* feminism; FSLN; gender

Berger, John, 87

Betrayed Generation, xix, 109

Beverley, John, 165, 170; *Literature and Politics in the Central American Revolutions,* viii–xv, xviii, 80; and Marc Zimmerman, viii–xv, xviii. *See also* Louis Althusser; testimonio; Zimmerman, Marc

Bloch, Ernst, 83

Greg Dawes is assistant professor of Latin American literature and culture at North Carolina State University. He has published articles on postmodern culture, contemporary critical theory, and Latin American literature. He is currently working on a critical study of the voices of the Old Left in Latin America.